DEVELOPING THE SOCIALLY USEFUL ECONOMY

DEVELOPING THE SOCIALLY USEFUL ECONOMY

Stephen Bodington, Mike George and John Michaelson

MACMILLAN

First published 1986

Published by
THE MACMILLAN PRESS LTD
Houndmills, Basingstoke, Hampshire RG21 2XS
and London
Companies and representatives
throughout the world

Photoset in Times by
CAS Typesetters Southampton
Using LINOTRONIC 100/APPLE II SYSTEM.

Printed in Great Britain by
Camelot Press Ltd, Southampton.

British Library Cataloguing in Publication Data
Developing the socially useful economy.
1. Great Britain—Economic conditions—1945–
2. Great Britain—Politics and government—1979–
I. Bodington, Stephen   II. George, Mike
III. Michaelson, John
306'.3   HC256.6
ISBN 0–333–39428–3
ISBN 0–333–39632–4 Pbk

This book is dedicated to the memory of Danny Conroy, who tragically died in spring 1985. He was a key figure in the Lucas Aerospace Combine Shop Stewards Committee, whose efforts to replace redundancy and unemployment with socially useful work has had a profound influence on all who seek to create an economy 'as if people mattered'.* Danny himself had a quite ferocious commitment to social justice, yet seldom sought public recognition. To the end he stayed at 'the base', believing that activity with 'ordinary' working people was the best way of achieving a more democratic, just and satisfying society.

* This phrase is the subtitle of E. F. Schumacher's book *Small Is Beautiful*.

Contents

Preface

In 1984 a series of seminars were organised, aimed at examining a range of new and relatively new approaches to the conduct of economic affairs in Britain. The three authors of this book were intimately involved with the preparation and running of this seminar series – which was called 'Developing the Socially Useful Economy'. Such was the quality of the papers presented at these workshops, and of the discussions that took place within them that it was decided to prepare a book – which includes and reflects a very interesting and important six-months' investigation.

The seminars were organised by CAITS (Centre for Alternative Industrial and Technological Systems),* and Middlesex Polytechnic staff, particularly those concerned with the Polytechnic's innovative degree course 'Society and Technology'. We drew upon the expertise of a range of academic, trade union, and local authority sources, some of whom prepared papers, some addressed the seminars, some wrote 'discussant' papers. In all some eighty people were involved in the seminars, and this book would not have been possible without the input of all; every seminar was tape recorded, and this material has been used in this book, as well as the papers. While inclusion of parts of the participants' papers has been cleared with them, the authors remain responsible for the end product, and any errors or omissions.

We would like to thank Gina Jennings who helped with the typing in a very efficient and supportive way, staff at CAITS and Middlesex Poly, and of course all those who turned up to make the seminar series so rich and fruitful; it is regretful that we cannot include all the names of the participants, and we hope they will accept this omission.

* See Appendix.

Introduction

As Britain approaches the era of a painful downturn in North Sea Oil revenues with rising unemployment, cuts in social welfare provision, mass dislocation in the labour market already in full evidence, many people are casting around for an economic philosophy and practice which may help us avoid becoming ever more underdeveloped as a nation, and not only economically.

Voices opposing a decade of so-called Monetarist doctrines are growing in number and stridency. The great 'experiment' in applying narrowly-based financial criteria to the mass of rich traditions and practices which go to make up our society, is being seen increasingly as a failure. Unemployment has tripled, firms have increased profitability in recent years – but at most people's expense, public sector provisioning is increasingly in tatters. Furthermore the *political* use of Monetarism (which in many ways has been more in evidence than its economics) has installed an authoritarian power in the land. People have been 'put in their place' – or rather the place that those in power (Government, corporations, etc.) have chosen for them; that is, on the margins, outside the bodies which wield power. We are witnessing a more thorough-going anti-democratic political and economic programme than has been seen for many years.

Yet we must be careful not to simply revert to the *status quo ante*, that is, a bit more public expenditure and the removal of some of the harsher legislation and policies, for instance in the area of control over trade unions. We have been down that road, and few will honestly say that the 1960s and much of the 1970s was marked by any important, deep or lasting reorientation of Britain's political economy towards the interests of so-called ordinary people; that Monetarism could be so easily introduced during a Labour administration is just one piece of evidence attesting to this.

But what, the reader may ask, are we seeking, when we counterpose what we have called a Socially Useful Economy, against both Monetarism and the 'welfare capitalism' which preceded it? First, we face a host of economic problems when our cushion of oil revenues deflates –

1

already the value of imported goods and materials outstrips exports. Unemployment is set to rise even higher, real wages, including the social wage (i.e. health and social security benefits) are set to drop – especially for those already on low wages. Our productive base, which is not just made up of manufacturing, is set to shrink yet further.

These and all their associated social problems seem set to increase, that is, unless we put new life in our economy in ways which are more fundamental than anything seen since the Second World War; 'more of the same', or 'less of the same' simply will not do. The ideas contained within the approach we follow aim for a clear break with post-War history – *as an economic necessity*.

Second, and of equal importance, our economy must be *subservient* to the needs of the people as a whole – not, as at present – an economy which is like a 'god', to which we are expected to offer up sacrifices. For to discuss the *political economy* of a country inevitably makes overt the values that a society holds, whereas in more recent years the unhealthy separation of 'economics' from societal values has hidden this basic connection. Our starting point therefore is to place prime value on meeting the needs and aspirations of all sections of the community. This is not as banal as it may sound. Consider the values of a society – or rather the values of the dominant elites – in which little is done to help 4 million unemployed people, where in fact social security benefits for unemployed people are under attack. Consider the values of a society that puts almost nil resources into research to help Britain's growing elderly population, yet which spends perhaps £12 billion on a single military programme, i.e. Trident. Consider the values of a society in which employees who question the investment strategies of their firm are sacked – as happened in Lucas Aerospace in the late 1970s and early 1980s.

The values which predominate in a capitalist form of political economy are 'exchange values' – basically money values. But to properly meet the needs and aspirations of people requires these sorts of values to be replaced with 'use values' – that is, the *actual* utilities produced by goods and services. These are only very indirectly expressed through 'the market', and those who don't have the money, i.e. the 'money-power' to control or even fully use 'the market' are legion.

At this point the reader may well suspect that we are pointing ourselves towards a socialist political economy, she/he would be quite right. We are considering democratic forces, the issues of power, of secrecy, non-accountability within political economy. But as socialism encompasses a wide range of intersecting strands of thought, policy and organisation of activity it is always necessary to try and define what one means. For instance we do not regard socialism as 'the Gas Board writ large' or 'Big Brother', nor are we wedded to the command economies of the Eastern Bloc. By going back to basics, to the fundamental values in political economy, namely use values, we hope to shed light on the ideas and practices of a truly liberating socialist political economy.

What lies at the root of much that follows is a recognition of and faith in the abilities of so-called ordinary people to forge ways and means that more fully satisfy their needs – both material and otherwise. The reader will not find many 'blueprints' in this book, it is an exploration of constraints and possibilities, based on what we have called the Socially Useful Economy.

We have started, as we must, in Part I with some detailed examination of the capitalist framework under which we labour. Chapter 1 *may* look 'difficult', but we urge you to read it, for it lays out our fundamental analysis from which much else proceeds. The 'lazy' reader (of course, none of you will be that, however . . .) may care to read Chapter 2 first, which summarises the *effects* and *issues* arising from capitalist political economy.

We then move on in Part II (Understanding what Cripples Us), to a more detailed examination of 3 key aspects of the problems that confront us. First, the political use and power of conventional economic orthodoxy. Second, the political usage and power of technology in our society. Lastly, the 'structures of authority' which organisationally hold us back.

Part III (How We Can Reconstruct) lays foundations for the Socially Useful Economy. It contains four aspects of reconstruction, some of the key concepts required, ways and means of 'negotiating' our way towards SUE (Socially Useful Economy), what organisational forms and procedures we could put in place, and how we see SUE being financed. Part III also contains most of the important elements of what we mean by a Socially Useful Economy.

We have then interspersed two case studies (Part IV), which throw extra light on the differences between SUE and OPE (Orthodox Political Economy). And finally, we conclude with 3 chapters, in Part V which is called 'Building the New from the Old', which suggest various ways in which we can *now* start to create our Socially Useful Economy.

We include as an appendix a list of seminars, the topics, the papers and the speakers from which the ideas and proposals in this book have sprung. We trust you will enjoy this exploration into political economy, though we offer few 'neat' solutions – we characterised the seminar series of the same name as 'jumping into a muddy pool from hopeful-looking angles', enjoy the process!

Part I
Defining the Problem

Why has 'the economy' become a sort of god-like entity in society, to which 'we', people, have to make sacrifices? Why has this crucial aspect of human life become abstracted, so that few of us feel we have any real understanding of the workings of economics and relate to it as 'an external force' over which we have no control? Chapter 1 tries to put this into context, by showing, in brief, how the main motors of capitalist economics work in the world.

'Sound finance' is a dominating principle in the current organisation of people, plant, equipment, public sector provision, even invention. We show how this principle is applied in practice, and point to some of the crucial consequences of its acceptance. Obviously we take this principle and all that flows from it to be a major problem for us who live in Britain, and to other 'ordinary' people elsewhere.

What happens 'now' is of course of critical importance for all who seek to improve the ways that we use resources in society. This first chapter sketches some essentials of the situation under which we now labour and live.

Chapter 2 opens up our thinking about what we mean by a Socially Useful Economy, and deals with the motivations that underlie our endeavours. We counterpose human need to the workings of markets and what we refer to as money-power, we examine the problem of mass unemployment, of environmental degradation, resource wastage, the crisis of the Welfare State, of human rights and freedoms. Here we lay out the principal reasons why we urge a fundamental re-think of ideas and criteria that guide economic analysis and practice.

1 Britain in the World Economy

With their money they bought ignorance
and killed the dreamer
Alice Walker

INTRODUCTION

In June 1984 a striking Durham miner interviewed on television asked a simple question: 'Why pay me £60 a week to do nothing if I'm unemployed, when, with this or less to help cut the cost, I could be usefully mining coal?'. At much the same time another simple question was being asked: 'If food surpluses are piling up unused here and elsewhere people are starving, why is not the food sent where the need is?'. To store EEC surplus grain for four years costs £200 a tonne; to transport it to where the need is costs £25 a tonne (*Observer*, 28 October 1984). Why are not resources moved to needs, saving people and money?

With unemployment running at 4 million and with at least 8 million people living in or on the margins of poverty in Britain, Government Ministers are saying this is indeed 'a tragedy' – but not of their making. 'We are all the victims of a world recession' – and they point to the 14 million unemployed in the European Community. We should pause to think about the full meaning of such statements: they declare we are part of an economy that is much more than Britain, indeed part of a world economy, *and* they are also saying we are part of an economy *that we cannot control*. The question we have very seriously to put to ourselves is *whether this must be so*. How can we as sensitive, caring human beings fatalistically accept the inevitability of social disaster? Do we not owe it to our own humanity to think carefully about Britain's relationship to the economy of the world as a whole and to seek out what can be done to change things?

First, it is necessary to look with open eyes at some of the broad contours of this world of which we are part. Huge companies and State corporations, pushed by some inner logic, have expanded and continue to still further expand operations that span the whole globe. We see too military establishments adding billions to billions of socially useless expenditure in order to perfect applied sciences of destruction. We see too millions upon millions of people standing by in hunger and despair unable to get access to resources and to use their own energies to make livings for themselves. We see a world sleepwalking to disaster. It is there readily to see, but we cease to look; for, we say to ourselves, what can we do about it? We go back to whatever routines of daily existence we have. The giants of industry and finance also are guided by their inherited routines of 'successful business'. The military re-enact age-old traditions of organised force, heads down and blind to the destination of their steps. But reality does not cease to exist because we do not look at it: signals of social disaster continue to multiply – not only present death and starvation, also the despair of unemployed youth, extraordinary psychological disturbance, derangement, violence, crime, innumerable crises of unannounced suffering everywhere. Forty years ago a United Nations Charter declared that human beings had a right to work: to make such promises and so signally to fail to deliver on them is conduct which, since nowhere else arraigned, declares its own verdict in the malaise everywhere in evidence. We need the courage to look again at reality and seek again answers to the problems we see.

Individuals on their own can do little. So how can we combine to change things at the level of macroeconomics, and how can we initiate alternative processes that are viable in face of economic forces at national and world levels?

THE DOCTRINE OF TINA (THERE IS NO ALTERNATIVE)

Accepted wisdom 'regrets' the plight of the wretched of the earth, the unemployed debarred from working and the food that does not reach the starving, but, firmly announces that there is no alternative. It argues along some such lines as the following. We must get our national finances straight, take corrective measures against inflation and generally adopt and be seen to be adopting sound financial policies such as the International Monetary Fund would endorse as satisfactory and such as would ensure our ability to attract funds with which to redevelop our economy on a sound basis. Given a sound basis great prospects lie ahead of us; we live in an age of unprecedented technological advance and, once we have a healthy economy, the whole community will reap the great benefits that modern science and technology have to offer. The present is indeed uncomfortable; we are simultaneously facing two vast social upheavals – and perhaps it is unlucky that they coincide. Anyhow we have (i) to cut from our economy dead wood that has become diseased and is sapping our vitality and (ii) to cope with the inevitable dislocations that accompany – and in the past have always accompanied – profound technological change. Steam power caused great social upheavals at the beginning of the 19th Century, electrical power, new materials and mass production caused great social upheavals at the end of the 19th Century and beginning of the 20th Century, now inevitably the microchip, robotisation and the 'information revolution' cause social disturbance as new industries advance and old industries decline.

This line of reasoning then goes on to 'diagnose the sickness in the British economy'; this, accepted wisdom says, is largely due to ill-considered public spending and its cure obviously requires that public spending be brought again under proper control. In public spending, they say, there is a twofold poison: the macroeconomic poison of inflation that is destructive of social and economic relations in society as a whole, and the microeconomic poison that afflicts individual businesses when, feather-bedded by public funds and not braced by the disciplines of competition and profit-and-loss, they lose all momentum and fall victim to wasteful, bureaucratic management.

Words such as these fall on a good many receptive ears in a society in which there has indeed been heavy inflation, where there is already unemployment, where people complain about taxes and rates and where frustrating bureaucracy is much in evidence. Also there are many people who would like to hope that a free market economy, in which everyone is able to make good money and enterprise is generously rewarded, would be possible if only the bureaucrats and scroungers of public funds, big and little, were pushed out of the way. As for technology, they think, is it not obvious that 'science can do anything these days'? So should we not hasten to get through the painful years of re-adjustment and put ourselves in a position to enjoy the benefits of advanced technology? After all it is well known, this line of thought continues, that Britain has been in the forefront of technological invention, but vested interests, restrictive practices, stick-in-the-mud organisation have prevented us from harvesting economic advantage from our great technological potentials. Hence the argument moves to the conclusion that we need to free our economy, to run it on financially

sound principles so that our potential economic strength may become
real, that is, strength that wins success in the real world and proves itself
in what after all, they claim, can be the only real test – competition. If the
Japanese can succeed, then surely we too will succeed once we have had
the courage and resoluteness of purpose to see through the difficult
(and, admittedly, in the short-term painful) process of, 'financial
purification', and, 'technological adaption to the future'. The social
costs of Japan's competitive success have been very heavy; but against
this they would say that it is self-defeating to allow social expenditure to
cripple competitive strength.

THE TRANSNATIONAL WORLD: RECENT AND RADICAL CHANGES OF STRUCTURE

That broadly speaking is the answer that accepted wisdom is giving to
the Durham miner when he asks why is it 'good economics' to pay people
to be unemployed, when they want instead, as he does, to be part of the
community, working for it even at such a dangerous and arduous job as
mining coal. The seminars on whose discussions this book is based
pointed overwhelmingly to the conclusion that, for today, the wisdom of
the Durham miner had more intellectual and moral substance behind it
than the 'accepted wisdom' of the financial world. The accepted wisdom
gains credence from two myths, mirages made to appear real by the
political and ideological atmosphere through which they are viewed.
The two mirages, the two mirrors of deception with which it is all done,
are 'finance' and 'technology'. One quite easily discovers that these are
empty mirages if a realistic survey is made of the economic terrain on
which Britain now finds itself – that of transnational capital. What does
such a survey of Britain show? It shows an economic scene dominated by
financial – industrial giants. The living space of these giants is the world
and their concern is to use their capital successfully anywhere in this
international arena, that is to say to reproduce their capital on an
enlarged scale and to command more territories in which they can
engage in profitable business. This is the logic of the commodity-
exchange structure, of which they are part, of the market system by
which their economic activity is motivated. *No economic logic and no
economic discipline equates their achievement to use of British resources.*
Organised labour and democratic political pressure at a national level
no longer have their former leverage over the policies of capital that now
has so many alternatives to choose from internationally. 'Principles of

sound finance' and the disciplines of money and the market under such circumstances do not make for the ending of unemployment in Britain. What is prosperity for transnational firms does not carry within it the logical implication that Britain's economic potential will be brought into use for the well-being of the British people. Nor indeed does transnational capital act for this nation or South America, India, Africa or Asia; its logic is simple – its own expansion and reproduction. We sketch below the circumstances that have brought us to this situation; but if we accept that the logic of transnational capital by-passes the well-being of peoples, it suggests (does it not?) that new ways of using resources, new criteria and new motivations, are essential to cultivate the waste-lands neglected by capital even when capital itself successfully achieves the objectives that come naturally to *it*. To discuss development of a socially useful economy is to discuss how well different ways of using economic resources serve human needs and what new ways have to be brought into play.

Britain in the last century was the centre of the most successful capitalism. But other centres, in Germany and the USA in particular, developed powerful industries able to compete against firms based in Britain. Wherever capital became powerful it looked for markets and investments overseas and alongside this trade there developed powerful financial institutions. British banks and finance houses established strong bases all over the world. Capitalism became a world system. With expansion there was more and more concentration and centralisation of capital. This was a 'logical' consequence of competition: the bigger the agglomeration of capital functioning as one unit, the greater, generally speaking, its competitive strength. Big concerns could afford more effective marketing organisations, could spend more on research and experimentation, could offset losses in one place by profits in another, could survive while waiting for new techniques to be tested and matured by experience, had sufficient resources to weather periods of slump and indeed in such periods could cheaply buy up smaller firms when they ran into difficulties. They were also well placed to attract investments – 'to him that hath shall it be given'. Small shareholders directly or through pension funds and insurance policies looked first to big concerns for 'safe investments'. (Today perhaps as much as half the capital of the biggest companies comes from pension and insurance funds.) The end result of the tendency of competition within the market system to generate larger and larger units is that a few hundred very large transnational companies, originating from Britain and other European countries, from America and from Japan, together with associated financial giants, now dominate the world capitalist economy.

Within the last two or three decades the structure of the world capitalist economy has developed a distinctly new form – that of 'transnational capital'. To say that capital is 'transnational' implies that it is something more than just 'international'.

For a century and more, successful capital has traded in many countries and invested overseas; in the more recent transnational phase, coordinated production spreads across many national boundaries. Bits of production are allocated to different plants in various countries. Plans as to where to produce or where to sell are continuously adjusted to fit changing tariffs, taxation, prices, labour conditions, political conditions and so forth so as to maximise returns and enlarge or tighten control over fruitful fields of operation. The most technically advanced and pre-eminent groupings of British capital have in the last few decades become transnationalised in this sense, the country to country linkages being both industrial and financial. Big transnational capital probably controls more than half of the British manufacturing and most of the rest of industry and, hence, practically the whole of the economy here depends upon an economic climate created by the movement of transnational capital. But its influence over Britain is much greater than Britain's influence over it: British capital as it becomes transnational capital is no longer tied exclusively or even closely to British subcontractors, or to British labour, or to the infrastructure of the British economy. The logic of big capital is the same as that of all capital – that is, to make profitable use of the opportunities open to it. Transnationalisation means ability to pick and choose internationally where to locate productive activities, from whom to order components and materials, where to sell and so forth.

It is moreover the needs of the very big companies that determine the main direction of technological development. Very logically (by the logic of capitalist competition) they look for techniques that reduce dependence on special skills located in a few industrial centres. Insofar as skills can be put into the machines, operatives require little more than literacy and work discipline, and the potential labour force on which capital can draw is enlarged by hundreds of millions in all parts of the world. Labour instead of an awkward 'factor of production' in a position to drive a good bargain with capital, becomes a homogenous, malleable, controllable factor of production. Technique for capital means making managerial control more effective. This control makes it possible to adopt whatever methods most increase takings relatively to costs. Also the whole shape of production is moulded by 'produceability' from the managerial point of view. Productive choices are guided not only by consumer wants but also by convenience and commercial advantage to the producing capital. Once a project for production has been settled, a marketing exercise is undertaken to prepare sales outlets. Production may even be designed to frustrate consumer needs, as when replacement of whole units, instead of only the defective parts, is imposed. In such ways not only are home and local repairs made impossible, but the technology of the product is made unnecessarily strange and alien to the consumer. Social usefulness evidently is not the target of new techniques; at best it is only a by-product in that society may be able to benefit from the smaller input of social productive time that may result from new profit-inspired methods of economic organisation.

Another important aspect of transnationalisation of capital is what one might call the 'generalisation' or 'financialisation' of capital. In the early days of industrial capital the typical producer was a manufacturer in a particular line of business that he understood well, for example, textiles or chain-making, say. As dominant groupings of capital grew larger and larger, producing units were linked to one another 'horizontally' and 'vertically' as Unilever, for example, took interests at all levels of food production from basic agricultural materials such as oilseeds through to packaging and sale across the counter and also spread 'sideways' to associated commodities such as soap, margarine, candles and other goods sold by grocers. With the emergence of transnational companies, groupings still concern themselves with broad product areas whose politics and technology they have been especially associated with, as IBM was strong in calculators and then computers and Exxon in oil and other products used in the automotive industries; but at the same time they move towards greater diversification. Their main concern becomes more simply to be able to make profitable use of financial resources, indeed to become a magnet for financial resources. Their strength goes far beyond 'their own capital' and depends upon ability to make profitable use of whatever financial resources are put at their disposal. In this way huge 'financial' undertakings mesh in very closely with 'productive' undertakings. There is in fact extensive overlapping and interchange of personnel, and the objectives and motivations of productive, commercial and financial management are complementary.

Productive management organises the production of commodities which, on sale, bring exchange-values back to prime the continuing turnover of the capital. At the same time these exchange-values realised from sales must exceed values expended as costs so that capital 'lives' yielding interest and profit and an accumulation, from which to enlarge and strengthen the enterprise. Financial management has the double function of gathering money to be used as capital and maintaining – in all parts of the world – social, economic and political frameworks in which processes of capital turnover may continue to bring adequate returns on loans of financial resources. Capital as money assumes its most abstract and generalised form; it is exchange-value that may become active in one of many thousands of different possible forms. Financiers – and merchant bankers in particular – study and control managerial personnel in specific spheres and use the financial pressures at their disposal to see that managerial policy follows underlying principles that best advance continuing profitable turnover for capital. The way in which transnational companies engaged in production view their capital is not much different from that of those engaged in finance. Production is guided by the aim of sustaining the turnover of capital (which requires the making of profits and paying of interest). Financial and productive capital so merged *are moved by a dynamic of their own and this dictates to world economic processes a logic that is quite unrelated to the material needs of suffering humanity*.

How different all this is from the rhetoric that politicians use about market economics! And, what is far more serious, behind this rhetoric lies an ideology that dominates social attitudes and also huge academic disciplines making theoretical presentations and mathematical analyses of models in which all who offer services, and all who as consumers have preferences, are supposed to exert continuous interactive forces which govern the course of economic developments. The economic reality is utterly different from this ideology and from these models to which students are asked to address themselves. However this rhetoric and these models evoke an image of enterprising individuals flexibly directing their energies to the needs of those about them. The hopes these models inspire are empty mirages; the actual world market system is dominated by agglomerations of billions of pounds of capital. Local exchanges, small people buying and selling all live under the shadow of the giants; it is transactions between the giants, financially as well as commercially, that determine the climate of the markets in which lesser folk operate. There may be haggling and ups and downs of prices in street markets and corner shops – but what people have to spend there, and the quantities and prices offered by sellers, are governed ultimately by market conditions in the big-time league of financial and market relations between the giant organisations. Yet this economic gigantism that oppresses the world today derives 'logically', 'naturally' from the market relations that coordinate and motivate the economic system on which we all depend for provision of means of existence. Capital competes with capital to grow bigger, and by growing bigger is more strong to compete.

THE MARKET ECONOMY AS A MODEL OF SOCIAL LIFE-FORM

The smoothly democratic mechanisms portrayed by the ideologists of the market and monetarism are a million miles wide of reality; but it is crucial to recognise that market forces themselves are not empty mirages but potent facts of life. They are forces *that determine the social life-form of the world we live in*, that fix the practicalities of our day-by-day economic behaviour and galvanise, for better or for worse, the destiny of nations. The same logic that leads toward macroeconomic structural changes also dictates microeconomic structures of social activity. It is a useful analogy to think of the world market system as if it were a biological organism whose 'cells' are of various sizes – individual people, small companies, medium-sized companies and huge institutions organising tens of thousands of people or linking some hundreds of diversely located companies or other component units. The market system in the real world does not exist 'in pure form' but is mixed up with other economic modes of exerting social effort – households making direct provision for their own needs, economic activities directly organised by States, structures surviving as relics of older systems, customary practices and much else that is not governed by 'the logic of the market'. But the market system *predominates* today – materially and ideologically. Understanding how it reacts to other structures and how other structures react to it is of great importance but one cannot move towards such understanding without first seeing what the essential characteristics of the market system are in isolation conceptually, what its essential life process is, one might say. What, one needs to know, determines the living interactions between the 'cells' of the whole organism? The smallest cell is the individual who himself or herself either produces something for sale (as a carpenter produces a kitchen unit, say, or a cleaner the service of cleaning) or sells his or her capacities to an employer who organises a work-unit (as a furniture company employs carpenters or a company managing offices employs cleaners). The individual needs money so as to buy from others the means of living and this money the individuals get either by direct sale of their products or by sale of their capacities for a wage or salary. The purchaser of labour is 'the company' that organises cooperation of diverse capabilities, reaping the advantage of greater output per work-hour that this makes possible. Accumulated funds, 'capital', make this possible and the use of funds this way is motivated by the possibility of selling the products of the cooperating team for more than the costs of setting it to work (material, tools and plant, wages).

One needs to call to mind these very obvious facts about the economy in which we live to see that 'the logic of the market system' so far from being 'just an abstract idea', is an idea that describes the 'life-principle' of our society. It lives, it moves, it develops because people engage constantly and continuously in a series of commodity exchanges (labour-capacity for money, money for goods, capital funds for materials, semi-finished products for money and so on). These exchanges are motivated by money and 'disciplined' by money: producers produce what they can sell at a profit and, if they let the costs run too high, they fail to make profits and must go out of business – that is, they are 'disciplined' by money; if individuals buy too many things or at too high prices, they have no money left and have to stop buying – they too are 'disciplined' by money; competition between producers causes them to be 'disciplined' by this trial of strength which favours the bigger units and hastens concentration and centralisation, this necessary pursuit of money 'disciplining' the whole trend of development that the system follows.

The 'hidden hand' that long ago guided allocation of work between cobbler, carpenter or farmer, now 'guides' the motivation of trans-national giants – and the essence of today's problem is that human wisdom and 'morality' have no control over 'the hidden hand'. Huge concentrations of social power are blindly subservient to the market possibilities within which finance and production are imprisoned.

OTHER THAN MARKET ECONOMICS?

We have been emphasising that 'we live in a market economy', 'that our destiny is ruled by market forces', 'that economic change means taking into conscious social control what the market now runs blindly and automatically'; but one only has to glance at Britain and other countries today to see that market forces, directly at least, have little to do with the running of many economic activities. We have mentioned households and the military establishment and there are many other 'extra-market' activities of which State management of the social infrastructure is among the most important. What then does it mean to say 'we live in a market economy'? Essentially it means that the market economy dominates, that money-power so prevails that, when political decisions are taken, they always tend to give priority to the market structure on which the unhampered operations of capital essentially depend. It means also that the ideology of the market predominates, justifying inequalities of income in pursuit of wealth and measurement of efficiency in money terms, and competition as economically health-promoting and much else by which day-to-day standards of social morality are determined. However once it is seen that the hegemony of capital and money-power is a social reality and that it needs first to be conceptually isolated in order to grasp well its major characteristics, it is important then to build back into one's picture of Britain's economic anatomy the numerous economic structures that exist alongside the market. This is important because the search for alternatives must make good provision for these parts of the social whole and also because it may be that, in what one might call the 'non-market zones', it will be possible to build strong bases for social power to counterpose to money-power and market forces. It is important to discover how far economic structures motivated by different economic logics may prevail against the logic of the market. Economic change in practice must mean pitting new economic systems and methods against what now prevails. What now *prevails* is commodity exchange; but the model of the commodity exchange system is not a formula to explain all aspects of British economic life; it is an abstraction that picks out one aspect only – albeit the most important as things now are – of a many-sided complex totality. The commodity system shapes our daily economic practice, it shapes broad trends of economic development, it gives to social power what is at present its characteristic form – that is 'money-power'. Other economic formations are important not just because they are there – albeit subordinately – but also because they need to be assessed as possible footholds for change.

In particular, special attention has to be given to one form of economic organisation where market motivations appear not to rule and which is often presented as *the* alternative to the market system, namely, centralised planning of state-owned resources. Centralised planning constitutes the predominant system in the so called 'existing socialist countries' such as the Soviet Union, China or Hungary, but it exists also, alongside and in subordination to the market system, in

Britain and other market economies, for example in nationalised industries such as coal or gas.

Centralised planning as a predominant system as in the Soviet Union or as a subordinate system as in nationalised industries, is violently attacked by the ideologists of the market, who at the same time present it as the only possible alternative to the market system. It is, they argue, bureaucratic, authoritarian and anti-democratic since control over resources is in the hands of the bureaucratic elite who choose what to produce either to suit their own ends or, if mindful of others, arbitrarily and paternalistically choosing what they think is good for them. It must be admitted that nationalised industries and 'existing socialist countries' have plentifully provided empirical evidence in support of such charges. Furthermore centralised planning is defective in so far as producers produce only according to instructions issued by central planners. (It is a great defect of the Webbs and other Fabian economic thinkers that they, in common with Stalinist planners, believed that producers must be instructed from above and themselves have minimal autonomy.) 'Instructions from above' will often necessarily be insufficient, taking scant account of local circumstances and unchanging or slow to change when circumstances change. People themselves know best how to use their resources and planning from outside throws this potential away. Central planners, coping with some of these inadequacies have tried, rather unsuccessfully, to move back towards market mechanisms. Indeed, central planners and market economists both seem to make the (false) assumption that the only meaningful possibilities for change are either from central planning towards market control, or from market control towards central planning. This suits the defenders of market economics very well since, by attacking lack of democratic choice in centralised planning structures, they draw fire away from the lack of choice that most people suffer in an economy dominated by money-power. When money incomes are inadequate there is not much freedom about choosing how to spend them; moreover variety of social choice is narrowed by the single-mindedness with which money-power is compelled to focus on profitability in choice of investments. Both systems in fact block democratic choice. What both structures have in common – and it is a common defect – is that control over resources is in the hands of a few people at the centre of things: on one side an elite of money-power, on the other of bureaucratic power.

In Britain money-power coexists with state-power; but despite the important differences between 'state-owned' and 'privately-owned' as regards economic dynamic, there are extraordinary organisational similarities in that both typically are undemocratically run by top managements with relatively authoritarian powers of decision.

The question of democratic control is important. 'Central planning' in the sense of central administration of services such as sewage and roads, and in the sense of coordination between interdependent economic activities is indispensible in a modern society. But does the necessity for coordination and for central services necessarily imply centralisation of power and surrender of democratic possibilities which differ both from the centralised planning of Stalin, the Fabians and nationalised industries on the one hand and centralisation through the agency of money-power on the other? The gains of decentralisation need to be combined with the advantages of centralisation by making central administrations accountable to those on whose behalf they act. Indeed, democratic power to control decision-making either directly, or through the accountability of representatives, is probably the only way ultimately to give socially positive meaning to such expressions as 'efficiency' and 'social advantage', since who knows what is best for people but people themselves?

'MONEY-POWER'

If organisations of people linked to one another through the exchange of commodities may be compared to the cells that make up a living body, then analogous to the blood circulating in the body is money circulating through the economic system. Finance gives life to the system. The secrets of the market are all shrouded in the 'mystery of finance'. An aura of holiness seems to inhibit a straightforward look at the ends that financial policies serve. When the Durham miner asks 'Why pay me to do nothing, why not instead pay to enable me to do useful work?' his straightforward question is met by reference to mysterious 'principles of sound finance' which are said to preclude this. His simplicity flies in the face of forces that give life to the commodity exchange system. That is what the true believer in the system feels. It is the attitude towards economics that the dominance of commodity exchange generates and causes to become a sort of common sense that it is improper to query. Discussion of the 'socially useful economy' is in fact an attempt to analyse and query the mystified orthodoxies that underlie current economic practice and theory. Must 'principles of good finance' dominate all economic desisions? What indeed are 'the principles of good finance'? How did they come to command such respect? What good purpose or whose interests do they further?

In the mythology of 'sound finance' it is assumed that market economics and the discipline of money ensure the best possible distribution and use of resources. The market system starting some three thousand years ago as an organiser mainly of *trade* between peoples, only became predominant as organiser of industrial and agricultural *production* a few centuries ago. It developed into its modern form of industrial capitalism in Britain at the end of the 18th Century and, in the course of the 19th Century, raced ahead in Europe and America. Industrial capital rapidly pushed commodities into world markets and by the beginning of the present century was well established as the dominant world economic system. But can it be said that as a world system it has used and distributed resources well? Throughout this century the world has toiled under the affliction of widely spread poverty and unemployment, and things get worse. As 'efficient' market economics penetrates to new territories evidence suggests that it by no means necessarily brings prosperity with it; only too often successful modern enterprises have brought employment and good incomes to a few at the cost of unemployment and separation from earlier means of living for the many. Changes brought by the development of the capitalist methods that expanding markets have fostered, too often included forced sales of land, collapse of craft industries, destruction of older occupations in ways that cut off access to material resources. In 'industrially developed countries' a fair number of people may have prospered with the advance of market economics, but on a world scale the empirical evidence that market economics is 'the best mechanism for efficient use and distribution of economic resources' is meagre in the extreme. Its defenders may argue that the 'perfectly free' market so far has always been interfered with by states, by monopolies, by unions bargaining collectively for the sale of labour. Such champions of market economics overlook that the tendency for big capital units always to grow bigger still is inherent in market competition giving inordinate strength to the biggest concentrations of money-power. Against this, democratic organisation and pressure for countervailing legislation becomes essential. Certainly academic models of a theoretically pure market economy were *not* the motive force behind the vast historical changes that, over three centuries, brought market economics to its present practical and ideological ascendancy.

Market economics – as organiser of industrial and agricultural production and distribution – became established and dominant over other socioeconomic formations because it gave economic strength to a new class and commanded wide social support. *In relation to older social orders* it was liberatory. A great number of people whose freedom of action, movement and speech were heavily restricted within feudal or absolutist–monarchist regimes, gained freedom with the developing market system. Money liberated those who had it, the new men who developed new machines made possible a greater production of material goods for a smaller input of labour time. That there was appalling poverty alongside the new wealth is well known; but the new wealth and the new economic system that produced it, challenged and broke the elitism of birth that had dominated social life. It is undoubtedly a fact that the new social order based on market economics (well enough termed 'industrial capitalism') released new human potentialities and raised high libertarian hopes (well expressed in the writings of Adam Smith himself and later by such men as John Stuart Mill). Capitalism was also liberatory in a technical sense; a new mastery over material forces created a feeling that human progress could take giant strides forward, a feeling that released enthusiasm to try out new ideas and be technically adventurous, a belief almost in the infallibility of science – indeed the uncritical impetus of this belief carries over even into the present for us and others, influencing cultural attitudes in the Soviet Union no less than in the USA.

So market economics won social support and historical viability. But from the truth of such facts of history no empirical evidence at all can be drawn for the belief that the market system is 'the most efficient', 'most rational', 'only possible' mechanism for organising the use and allocation of economic resources. Why then is market economics so strongly supported? Why are we asked to pay such holy regard to 'the principles of sound finance'? The reason is really very simple: change from the restrictions and arbitrary authority of absolute monarchy and from aristocratic hierarchies and feudal structures was widely and strongly enough backed to succeed. Capitalism through the success of industrial production grew economically powerful; expanding trade and the power of money eroded and undermined the older social structures. Money-power became established as the primary basis of social power, and market economies were the economic environments by which money-power was nurtured and given scope. An oligarchy whose power basis was capital replaced an oligarchy of nobles and courtiers. The social philosophy that sustained the new society concerned itself with the functions of industrial workers, capital and trade instead of with peasants, lords of the manor and the produce of the land.

In short, the market system is supported because it is the economic foundation of society as it is now. Change in this foundation brings into question the balance of social power and might have far-reaching implications. Since money controls the whole economic system's manner of operation, it is the source from which social power springs. 'Principles of sound finance' are rules to preserve the authority of money; they specify that finances are to be managed in such a way as to preserve the socio economic structure in which continuing effectiveness of money – power is sustained. Those who control capital in its essential form – money-capital – must be able to continue to use it to perform its essential function as capital which is to turn money into more money. Interest must be paid for the use of money. The earning of interest is possible because capital set to work can create exchange-values in excess of the capital expended on the work process. The economic life-system of a fully developed market economy requires continuous turnover of capital – the health of this life-system finds its most general expression in the payment of interest for the use of money-capital. 'Sound finance' relates not at all to 'social usefulness' in what is produced in the course of the turnover of capital, but to the objective of making secure the payment of interest and repayment of the sum borrowed at such dates as may be stipulated. The objectives of 'sound finance' are concerned single-mindedly with putting borrowers in a position to repay lenders. Whether or not the use of resources that results from pursuit of this objective is socially good is altogether another question. It is with exploring this 'other question' that this book is concerned. Now the economy is treated as a sort of god to whom people must make sacrifice. Could there instead be an economic order in which 'social usefulness' were made *the direct purpose of economic acitivity*?

'SOUND FINANCE' – THE REALITY AND THE MYTH

We have laboured the point that Britain's economy today has become merged into a world economy. This world economy is shaken by appalling stresses and strains; it is moreover an entity in which the pace is set by very big transnational companies. This needs to be reiterated so that account may be taken of some of the practical implications. Speeches are made about 'the British economy' but it is questionable whether such an entity may meaningfully be said still to exist. Government policies are not concerned for the ends served by the economic resources that fall within its jurisdiction. The fortunes of smaller organisations and individuals bob up and down helplessly on waves which radiate from the activities of the big companies. These big companies compete with one another for profitable employment of capital in whatever part of the world and for whatever purpose best serves the logic of self-producing capital. They cannot (except in violation of the logic of their market money-motivated mechanisms) pause to ask whether what they are doing leads to the most socially useful deployment of resources from the standpoint of the community over which a British Government has jurisdiction; these are considerations that do not enter into 'the principles of sound finance'. 'Sound finance' in fact conflicts with 'social usefulness'. This conflict is felt in the stark brutality of 'cash limits' which plunge millions into the despair of unemployment, throw homeless families onto the streets or herd them into cramped soul-destroying 'temporary accommodation', deprive sick and old people of facilities needed to make life supportable. Why are not financial mechanisms used to pay, for example, the homeless unemployed building worker to build homes for him/herself and others? If finance directly allocated resources to socially useful ends, this function would conflict with financing the reproduction of capital under the guidance of market forces; money-power would be made to defer to human judgements of social value.

This clash between contradictory economic principles can no longer be avoided. In Britain currently we are only too obviously beginning to take sides. It also threatens the stability of the international financial system. It is seen in starkest form in the debt-crisis of Latin America. Most of the Latin American countries are the scene of extreme poverty. They have received loans from overseas totalling many hundreds of billions of dollars. The IMF and other financial institutions link loans to internal policy requirements. These requirements embody what the lenders regard as principles of sound finance, aiming particularly to improve the balance of payments, that is, the earning of internationally acceptable money with which to repay loans and to pay interest on loans. But this means cutting wages and social expenditure at home so as to give priority to exports. This in turn means, if feasible at all, draconian oppression at home in the face of trade competition both from other hard-pressed debtors and powerful capitalist giants all pulling against the tides of world depression.

Desperate needs dictated by internal poverty clash starkly with 'the needs of sound finance'. Giant financial institutions have been scouring the world for placement of money at their disposal where it will earn interest. Governments anywhere are generally – because of their powers as Governments – regarded as good security. Moreover the logic of capital points to the need to sustain countries of Latin America as markets, and more generally as part of the living space open to the operation of capital. Loans help to keep poorer countries within the orbit of the world system that is powered by market exchanges, money circulation and capital reproduction. However the automatisms of this system do not cause resources to be put to work and do not feed the needs of the needy. The struggle of poorer countries to comply with loan conditions gives rise to appalling tensions. Policies that might ease these tensions diametrically conflict with the 'sound finance' on which lenders insist. Already in June 1984 Latin American debtor-countries met in Cartagena, Columbia, jointly to discuss their predicaments. In time a day might come when together they might say 'Sorry, we must withhold payments due'. Were this to happen several huge banking organisations would be threatened with collapse. What then happens? The outcome certainly is not predetermined; Governments will be forced to take action and the outcome will turn on the policies pursued.

In fact, the clash between 'principles of sound finance' and 'principles of social usefulness' is not an abstract, theoretical disputation but a choice that circumstances are forcing upon us immediately. The topics under discussion at these seminars are in fact a belated briefing in which every democratic and Labour organisation needs to engage. To fail to see that decisions are being forced on us, from at home and from abroad, is to capitulate and in practice renounce all concern, for real, about democratic and socialist politics.

The difficult side of this choice is getting a true focus on the alternatives to the market principles that underpin 'sound finance'. The discussions reflected in this book attempt to see more clearly various aspects of this choice. But first it is useful to bring together what we have so far seen about the why's and wherefore's of the economic philosophy that guides our present use – and non-use – of resources. The myth of finance is that the discipline it imposes ensures the best use of resources. In support of this belief, when one takes into account the whole arena over which the financial system of the world operates, there is no empirical evidence and there also is great dubiety even about theoretical claims that this system could, even supposing ideal conditions, work more effectively. Empirical evidence suggests that the system worked *relatively* well for nations that first developed industrial capitalism – for example, Britain, Germany, France, USA, Sweden, Switzerland, and Japan. Workforces numbering a few millions supplied commodities whose sales spread out to hundreds of millions in all parts of the world. Some groups of capitalists in these countries became extremely wealthy. Some workers and salaried employees enjoyed rising stan-dards of living. Taxes and other subtractions from the wealth produced sustained powerful armies and latterly social services. But even in these countries where the capitalist–commodity mode of production grew most powerfully, much poverty and much unemployment persisted. Organised labour in these countries was able to bargain successfully for better wages and conditions and to press politically for a better 'social wage', that is, publicly provided services of benefit to the community at large.

Such organised bargaining to modify the market system was possible because the wealth production of the greatest capitalists relied heavily upon special skills and labour experience in industrial establishments in the metropolitan countries, and upon the specific social and economic infrastructure of 'the country of origin'. From the original industrial bases, trade and capital flowed out to the rest of the world under the protective care of home-based financial institutions. Now – and these are logical extensions of commodity-exchange processes – the British economy is subjected to two radical and fundamental changes: (i) its predominant and 'pace-setting' capital is now 'transnational capital' and (ii) the older industrial skills are now only marginally and no longer centrally needed by capital, many complex industrial skills having been 'externalised', that is, work-processes once embodied by training and experience in people are now, to an hitherto unparalleled extent, embodied in routines performed by machines. (Electronic data process-ing, the microchip and so forth have been used by capital to this end.)

IDEAS AS ORGANISERS OF RESOURCE USE

Transnational capital spreads its operations across the world and is much less dependent upon workforces located in Britain. Now more and more productive processes require only operatives who are literate and disciplined; they can be usefully employed after minimal instruc-tion. This means that capital's success and well-being is no longer tied up with the prosperity of working people in Britain. Capital-labour relations characteristically are less 'British workers facing British capital' and more 'members of a world work force facing transnational capital'. The political and economic consequences are profound; British workers in-so-far as they stand in a capital-labour relationship, are part of a workforce of hundreds of millions of which capital will directly employ only a small fraction. Capital originating from Britain can prosper and be actively engaged according to the motivations and discipline of the market system, whilst unemployment could well continue to mount from 4 to 8 to 12 million. This more than anything else points to the necessity of having some other principles by which to organise use of resources. We face problems that principles of 'sound finance' will not cope with. When economic cooperation based on commodity production fails – and it is failing much – prosperity for Britain, except for a few well tied in with transnational capital, requires some new organising principles. To enquire how to develop the socially useful economy is to pursue such alternative principles.

The 'myth of finance' is that sound finance opens roads to economic prosperity. What 'sound finance' in fact does is to enable money-capital to function as capital, and to sustain economic foundations for social oligarchies whose basis of power is control over capital. Those who control capital are able to dictate social behaviour – not so much directly by law-backed authority as indirectly through the authority they have over organisations on which people depend for a livelihood. Defence of market-principles is much more than a technical debate about economic efficiency, it is about changing or not changing an established social system. It is for this reason that arguments about 'developing the socially useful economy', however straightforward they may seem, often meet – if listened to at all – extraordinarily stubborn resistance. Possibly this is why almost all research and theory firmly pens itself within the assumption that economic relations are commodity relations, and that economic practice must be disciplined by money and market competition. But, as was pointed out above, if one looks at the real world one finds much economic practice for which this assumption is not valid. In Britain in the 1970s, for example, not far short of two-thirds of all expenditure originated from public expenditure (by the Government, by Local Authorities, by publicly owned industries, etc.), yet hardly any theoretical analysis, research or even discussion has been directed to the 'autonomous motivations' which lie behind public expenditure as requiring guidance by distinct economic principles. It seems to be assumed that either market principles apply or that all is wrapped up by what 'representatives of the people' decide. Criteria by which to judge the 'social usefulness' of public expenditure are rarely debated or even cited; so when the IMF's 'security requirements' demanded cuts in public expenditure by the British Government in 1976, there was no well-grounded, popularly understood case to explain the economic virtues of increased public expenditure for well-chosen social and employment purposes.

Economic concepts not only describe reality, they are also social organisers. The organising ideas that prevail in today's public consciousness are those of the market; this is an important aspect of the dominance of 'transnational capitalism' – its ascendancy is helped if capital is free to move and operate as market forces permit. But in reality the market is not the only existing mode of economic organisation: the civil society in which we live is an amalgam of modes of economic cooperation – the private household or family organises many economic activities; there are traces (extensive in the whole world but faintly present also in Britain) of older feudal, tribal or tributary social orders; public authority (over and above the military and government itself) organises industry, health, social services, communications, which since they are regulated administratively and not by market forces, one might describe as 'bureaucratic modes of economic organisation' (and these assume many and changing forms). As modes of economic cooperation these other structures are given a very low profile; it is as if all the public relations officers worked for commodity relations and money-power! But the fact of the coexistence of differing modes of economic existence is very important for the development of the socially useful economy. People cooperating with other people in relationships that are not governed by exchange-values provide starting points for change. The 'myth of finance' is an illusory tale about what the money/market economy can achieve; but the illusion will not easily be dispelled until some substance is given to alternatives. That is why non-market modes of economic cooperation need to be given a higher profile and be made the subject of deeper theoretical and research investigation. Alternatives require also alternative organising ideas.

TECHNOLOGY: THE MYTH AND THE REALITY

The second myth that obscures vision of reality is 'the myth of technology'. This runs somewhat as follows: science and technology, as is well known, have made and continue to make huge strides; obviously these new found powers make more wealth and more well-endowed leisure a real possibility, but equally obviously they must mean great changes in the labour process. New industries will rise, old industries will decline; what men and women do at work will inevitably change. Unfortunately people don't like change; fear and stupidity make them resist change and when this resistance is taken on board by unions it becomes organised resistance to progress. So runs the myth of technology.

This whole line of argument tacitly assumes that the use of economic resources as organised by the market is the best possible – in short, it has swallowed the myth of sound finance and goes on from there.

As has already been stressed, the logic of an economy disciplined by money, markets and profit requires management to perfect control over 'factors of production' so as to optimise output of exchange-values relatively to the input of exchange-values consumed as costs. Input comprises plant and machinery, materials and components, energy and labour. This logic does not demand attention to social consequences; it does demand technologies that make labour a more manageable, a more plannable, a more controllable factor of production. Productive methods that do not call for special skills are obviously 'manageable' – for a number of reasons not least of which is the queue of those who can take over the job of any who are sacked. Threat of the sack enhances discipline but the technology that enlarges this spectre also makes work itself more hateful and alienating. The logic of the market does not favour the socially best technology.

Unfortunately, the ability today to harness the electron to process information in networks of molecular dimensions and at speeds near to that of light, (all that is summarised as the computer or information revolution) subordinated to the logic of the market, horribly accelerates appalling social consequences. Automation, robotisation, computer-isation take skills from people, who, wanting and needing to join in meaningful activity with other human beings, are deprived of all opportunity of developing skills and capabilities because such 'non-manageable' work is not in demand; these technologies assume crimi-nally sinister forms and start waves of social consequences whose sombre outcomes are quite unpredictable, and drastically reduce countervailing economic power *within capitalist structures*. When billion dollar organisations, driven towards aims beyond human con-trol, can focus the sum total of human knowledge to serve automatisms of the market system, then technology is not some silly toy played with as children play 'snakes and ladders', but a lethal weapon that can destroy the human species.

Technology as developed by market forces in the context of the transnationalisation of capital obviously leads to a radical diminution in the power of organised labour. It cannot bargain toughly and win better wages and conditions within the capitalist structure in the same way as it could in the past. Then capital's greater interdependence with labour necessitated some sharing of output via higher wages and social benefits. But when controls against the logic of the market lose effectiveness, science and technology – that is, applied human know-ledge – do not serve to make social life better. Some benefits could come so long as organised labour and other democratic pressures could exert economic control against capital; but now technology is shaped by the logic of the market and by the potential worldwide labour force for capital far in excess of the numbers it is ever likely to employ. The creativity and the exciting new possibilities of technological discovery are pushed aside by the prioritised demands of capital.

Socially useful technologies can only be developed through alterna-tive structures and by the pressures that alternative employment possibilities bring against capitalist managements from outside. So democratic organisations must seek new economic structures, new ways of using resources, if they are to have any chance of making advances against poverty and unemployment – and also if conditions of work are to be made more human. Human potentialities require social coopera-tion, so we must find some better form of cooperation than those organised by money incentives. Nervous illness, tension, distress, criminality, violence testify that we are failing to use human knowledge, science and technology to ease our social ills. But as an information revolution can hardly be the direct cause of a decrease in knowledge, must we not look to the logic that *structures* our use of knowledge and, in particular, modes of economic cooperations?

'PRODUCTIVITY'

Twin sister to the myth of technology is the 'myth of productivity'. Mere utterance of the word commands respect akin to the holy words of religion. But we should dare ask what 'productivity' means. The impression one gets when it is spoken of as a praiseworthy goal, is that the pains of those who live by the sweat of their brows will be eased. But what does a manager mean when he says a new method of production increases productivity?

In a market economy there is only one meaningful measure of produc-tivity – exchange value of commodities produced divided by exchange-value of commodities used in production (labour, materials, plant). For example, assuming stable prices, if costs of producing 100 tables that sell for £1 apiece are £80 and a new technology makes it possible to produce 250 tables for £100 costs, then the productivity of each £ of capital has increased from £100 divided by 80 = 1.25 to 250 divided by 100 = 2.5, that is productivity doubles. In the commodity exchange system the only meaningful measure is exchange value. If a machine enables a worker to produce more in a given time, it is not necessarily productive for capital; if, for example, the interest payable on money used to buy machinery is more than the saving on wages, the machinery will not make the capital more productive. What is important to capital is that the money value in hand at the end of the production process should be more than the amount at the start. In our example £80 becomes £100 and then when the new technology is introduced the £100 grows to £250.

Does this reduce the sweat of the brow or tension of nerves for the workforce? Only if workers are in a strong enough position to influence choice of production methods. Social benefit will not enter into managerial decisions that aim to increase productivity. And, of course, the empirical record is pretty atrocious on this score. The immediate impact of the industrial revolution was appalling socially. Improvement in wages and conditions during the 19th Century came only as a result of stubborn struggles by organised labour and other democratic movements.

COLLECTIVE CONSCIOUSNESS AS ANTIDOTE TO MARKET AUTOMATISM

The technology myth is indeed a myth – and, when one considers the harm that may be done when powerful techniques are misapplied, an extremely dangerous myth. However, within 'the myth' there is also a 'truth' of some importance. Dislocation, unemployment, fragmented isolation, nervous tension, alienation are all fruits of market economics that declare the necessity for change; but at the same time the last two centuries of exploding market economics have brought into existence social possibilities which in earlier centuries could not be imagined. The irony is that capitalism gives birth to a sense of individuality, awareness of new faculties and new activities and new forms of intercommunication with others from all corners of the world but at the same time frustrates realisation of all these newly seen potentialities. It creates the most intricate modes of human cooperation and outlaws the humanity of participants. The individual elements in the powerful, carefully orchestrated collectivities that constitute workteams are not purposeful human beings but units of a factor of production, known as 'labour', which have been sold to capital to assist its pursuit of goals dictated by market forces, goals from which the human purpose of a human being is excluded and alienated. The human being exists as a human being 'in a personal capacity' isolated and lacking the spirit of community in cooperative social activity. Capital creates 'the collective worker', an intricate social machine for tapping accumulated knowledge and resources – but this is a creature that lacks the most human of attributes, that is, consciousness. Even the purposes of the decision-makers that direct it are not human purposes but goals dictated by markets, by commodity-exchange processes outside human control. The intricate cooperation of human beings that the 'collective worker' has brought into being is now basic to the human species' provision of its material needs. If there is to exist the kind of community through which human individuals' potentials may be realised, the cooperating groups that capitalism has created must become conscious of themselves and capable of purposeful collective control over the technological potential that they collectively embody. Some of those who took part in these discussions – from Combine Committees of Shop Stewards, from local community projects and elsewhere – perhaps, by the ideas to which their experiences are leading them, are now expressing a first groping towards such *'collective worker consciousness'*.[1]

We need to ask what part we can play as individuals within collective organisms in work and in social life (that is, groups such as those which we have above called 'the collective worker') to move back towards human community. The human community embodied in pre-capitalist society was lacerated by capitalism. Cash-nexus took over from social responsibility (albeit paternalistic and authoritarian). One aspect of the Luddite struggles was just this; no one was taking social responsibility for the jobs machines were destroying. Today's struggle against capitalist technology is also against the social irresponsibility of sightless capital. We must look where we are going; but, since technology is application of collective skills, we need collective vision, 'the collective worker' needs to become conscious. As has been said of Lucas Aerospace and other Combine Committees and of local employment plans in Sheffield, London, West Midlands and elsewhere,[1] very possibly the crucial first steps towards such consciousness are already being taken as groupings of workers in factories and in local activity begin to reject regulation of their lives by price tags and cash limits, and in so doing to acquire some awareness of their social and economic functions in the world as it is. From such consciousness immediately springs also a consciousness of what might be instead. Collective consciousness maybe is the seed from which human community can be reborn, and from which may grow shared moral purposes and the power that at present eludes us to control the economic and material resources on which the achievement of human purpose depends.

The discussions opened by the seminars on developing the socially useful economy were in themselves one expression of an awakening of this new consciousness. These discussions arose from grassroot movements that go back a decade and a half to before the Upper Clyde Shipbuilders' work-in and, subsequently, a variety of factory occupations and the like asserting, however crudely, claims by workers to control use of productive resources in new ways. The formation of the Lucas Aerospace Combine Shop Stewards' Committee was a more sophisticated approach to the same problem; but what this made clear was that, essential as were the separate expressions of grassroot movements, it was also essential to support them within a wider economic and political framework. In fact vision and wisdom expressed in the Labour movement at the level of grassroot activity have been ahead of the theorists and professionals who coordinate and speak for the movement as a whole. But one should not conclude from this that 'consciousness of the collective worker' will of itself spontaneously transform the economy. In answer to science subordinated to the logic of capital, it is essential that there should be hard thinking, planning and coordination devoted to alternative economic formations. What happens in science in the commodity system is that knowledge in individual scientists becomes a commodity divorced from the humanity and morality of those who sell their knowledge. Science, in common with economic activity generally, is a mode of cooperation in the use of knowledge and can recover humanity and social morality only through collective consciousness and responsibility for what it is doing. The conclusion to which the needs and experiences of our times point is that people have to open their eyes to the social functions of the groupings, the collective organisms in which they live and work, to develop, that is, 'collective consciousness'. The pressure of events are in many places awakening people to new forms of collective actions; it is important that theorists and coordinators (who in their own ways are pressed by events as their time-worn organisations and past certainties begin to disintegrate) should attend to these new stirrings of democracy, not by attempting to impose their own preconceptions, but by helping to shape 'organising ideas' that correspond to new aims as seen by people for themselves. Theory that is imposed on people is not democratic; democratic theory requires a democratic dimension in itself in that it responds to and formulates, gives hard coordinating power to wisdom, will, and vision emerging from the grassroot activities of democratic forces.

CONCLUSIONS

Several pressures at large in society demand that we look clearly at the motivators and constraints which exert such tremendous effects on us all. That 'economics' is now some sort of God-like phenomenon – to which we must pay homage and make sacrifices – is a profoundly disturbing phenomenon. That peoples of one race or region are now so unremittingly pitted against each other for economic survival or advantage is another awful and dangerous trend, for 'economic warfare' breeds xenophobia, distrust and isolation. The hype of technology has also been a recent phenomenon which concerns, worries and confuses most people. Not to be 'computer literate' is now akin to some sort of social disease. We are asked to believe that complex technological so-called advances, despite being totally beyond our comprehension, are somehow a vital necessity for economic survival of the nation (being at times on metaphysical or jesuitical planes of quasi-theology). We can almost talk of a second wave of technological progressivism which bedazzles and blinds in the same way as occurred in the late nineteenth century and early twentieth century.

A further pressure evidenced in the past few years has been the extraordinary inversion of 'sound money principles' by the United States of America, where the domination of the dollar has been enormously amplified by a type of deficit budgeting under the Reagan administration which flies in the face of financial orthodoxy. Thus we in Britain, sticking to our 'sound financial principles' saw the value of the pound decline by over a third against the dollar – thus raising an enormous question about the validity of our so-called financial principles.

And finally a great sea – change is being actively promoted, for us to accept levels of unemployment and treatment of the disadvantaged in ways which we have not seen for nearly forty years. Where defence of trade union principles is now regarded as being non-patriotic, where the young unemployed must be 'disciplined' in an economic sense by accepting cheap and shoddy training schemes or very low paid employment; and where social benefits, be they unemployment benefit or supplementary benefits, are now openly said to be state hand-outs, completely disregarding the fact that the income for these has been provided by our own income taxes, consumer taxes, excise duties, rates and other payments of various sorts. A deep-seated change is being wrought where the increasing proportion of income for those on average and below average wages, which is being taken up by taxes of one sort or another is now regarded as irrelevant to the *rights* that we have to good local and national services in times of need.

These conclusions have been put into starker relief by the policies and actions of the 'radical' Conservative Government that Britain has had since 1979. There is more genuine fear at large in society, more anxiety and feelings of deprivation and hopelessness. Politics has appeared to be more of a 'spectacle', with rhetoric and ideology coming to dominate most public representation of politics. This causes serious and careful study of Britain's real problems to be pushed aside, and no attention at all to be given to clear questions such as 'what *is* the economy for?'

NOTE

1. 'Collective worker' is an expression used by Marx and others to describe what is now the typical human agent of production in a modern industrial economy where organically complex teams of people combine to produce goods and the capabilities of units are realised through the collective interaction of many individuals. In a commodity producing economy the individuals who make up a team are assembled by capital and normally the team as a collectivity has little consciousness of what it is doing or why. Coordination and definition of purpose is the province of 'management' expresses the will of capital which in turn as determined by market possibilities. The predominating purpose is always to use these possibilities to produce more exchange-values; that is, the consciousness even of capital is limited to evaluation by the narrow yardstick of exchange-value or, to put the matter more simply, in money terms. If production is to put use-values, moral values, social values above exchange-value, the producing agents will need to become conscious of possibilities assessed concretely by reference to possible uses of the productive facilities. This cannot happen unless the producing agents become conscious collectively of what they are doing and could do. Combine Shop Stewards' Committees in various companies in the course of challenging threatened redundancies have found it necessary to acquire a collective consciousness of what the workforce viewed as a work team might be doing. This consciousness – frustrated though it has been by hostile or un-understanding social environments – in fact prefigures a very significant potential for developing a socially useful economy and socialists, democrats and any others who are sincerely seeking economic change should attend carefully to and foster such attempts towards developing 'collective worker consciousness' as have actually been made. (The most important instance so far is probably the 'Corporate Plan' of the Lucas Aerospace workers; an excellent account of their new forms of union activity and the problems they met is to be found in 'The Lucas Plan' by Dave Elliott and Hilary Wainwright (Allison and Busby, 1982).

2 Why We Need Alternatives to Money-Power

But in the world
children are lost;
whole countries of children
starved to death
before the age
of five
each year;
their mothers squatted
in the filth
around the empty cooking pot
wondering.

Alice Walker

INTRODUCTION

For two decades a remarkable new range of political and social intiatives
have been set up in Britain. In some respects they reflect aspects of
previous activities seen earlier this century and even back into the early
part of the 19th century, dealing as they do with new types of enfranchisement, social audits of areas and groups of people, analysis and
prescriptions about poverty in the midst of plenty, and so on. For despite
broad economic growth in the post-war years of a degree not ever seen
before, tensions, inequalities, deprivations of one sort or another
became heightened by the fact that some people were becoming very
much richer, and expectations enhanced through the ideology of never-
ending prosperity. Although the search for new values and the growth of
'alternatives' such as the environmental movements, the women's
movement, the peace movement, 'ethical' investment trusts and the

like, through the 'new politics' of the 1960s and 1970s, have been attacked with some successes by the Radical New Right, certain key changes about the way in which society should be looked at have become firmly embedded in at least one generation of people. Some years ago one of the authors quipped that the 1980s will be 'the spot your friend decade', and he now takes no great pride in uttering this crude truism, for the Radical Right has certainly driven many people who act in opposition into factions or fractions. Important ideas, such as the decentralist propositions of Fritz Schumacher, the disabling of people by 'professions' put forward by Illich, the alternative technology movement and so on have been assimilated only by some self-perpetuating fractions of people, with little or no access to or real activity in the national political forum. Others, such as parts of the 'poverty lobby' have felt it necessary to modify their modes of activity to retain political credibility somewhere in the 'centre' ground of political life in Britain. In both cases these understandable changes have weakened both particular and general challenges to the new status quo imposed by the New Right.

But the picture is mixed, the pressure of opposition from the government and its friends have forced many in the 'new politics' area to take less and less for granted and work perhaps in more fundamental ways, to think more deeply, and to act in more 'clever' ways in the broad political sphere. Some of the heritage of the last two decades has been expressed by local authorities, and with their greater resources they have obviously been seen as a substantial threat and must be rate-capped or legislated out of existence. Whilst 'the new realism' was tried in the trade union movement it is now clear that the future of a collective trade unionism will come to rely less and less on the narrow economism which was relatively successful during the 1950s and 1960s. The impact of the law upon norms and expectations in society has become highlighted to a degree not seen since the 1930s. So paradoxically the very pressure coming to maintain and enhance (if at all possible) the 'status quo' have given rise to types of opposition which are perhaps rather more firmly rooted in society and in experience. Correspondingly there is a greater than ever realisation of the need to systematically analyse society's malaise, and to be more realistic at a strategic level. Our attempt to approach the complex and half-hidden area of 'economics' and all that that implies has been prompted by the events of the last five years or so, and by the lack of an adequate oppositional heritage. And in the following we lay out some of the more obvious needs to develop alternatives – we make no apology for re-rehearsing the very real problems that we face as we move into the latter part of the 1980s, and even more importantly the 1990s when that very substantial economic cushion of North Sea oil revenues deflates.

THE POLITICS OF HUMAN NEEDS

To be critical of society is often to be accused of being negative. But the main thrust of new ideas is defined by what are the essential defects of the old. To give these ideas practical force must also imply a positive, new approach, since however bad the existing system, it must be accepted if there are no alternative possibilities and practical steps leading to the alternatives.

In the capitalist crisis of the 1930s when unemployment was on a scale comparable to today, positive new ideas were formulated and implemented. Ideas such as a New Deal, full employment, the welfare state, the mixed economy were formulated and fashioned out of the debris of the capitalist holocaust.

We are again suffering as a nation from severe deprivation. According to Brown and Madge[1] in 1982:

> roughly ten million people are suffering from poverty, over 4 million of them in families with children . . . three million are currently unemployed. One million eight hundred thousand households are living in physically unsatisfactory housing conditions in terms of overcrowding, shortage of amenities or general unfitness. Over half the adult population can be termed educationally deprived in that they left school early and have no educational qualifications.

The problems have grown to such a proportion that they can only be described as a political crisis of human need. The British Society for Social Responsibility in Science[2] states that 'Britain in the 1980's is a society that does not meet basic human needs. Many people lack adequate nutrition, satisfactory housing, a healthy environment, access to effective health services and a decent education. Most of us are deprived of the chance to do satisfying work and millions are denied any job at all.' The fundamental problem is that we seem unable to utilise the resources we have available in a way that is appropriate to the needs of our society and its members.

We maintain that the primary goal of any society is to create the conditions for the satisfaction of human needs and the aspirations of all its members, 'from each according to his ability to each according to his needs'. Instead of moving towards this primary goal we seem to be moving in some other direction or in no direction at all.

It is disturbing to observe that in an advanced country like the UK we are failing to meet basic human needs. What is equally disturbing is that we are being forced to pay a crippling price directly as a result of this failure, not just in individual terms but in terms of the costs to the community and to the nation. Many of these costs are not notional but real costs resulting from the depletion or wastage of human resources.

We can thus make no apologies for being critical of our political and social structures in such a crisis. Under the pressing necessity for change we must seek positive alternatives that give scope to new forms of social decision-making about the use of human and economic resources.

However in a crisis political positions become more extreme, as also occurred in the 1930s. We are witnessing in the 1980s the emergence of a New Right with its extreme alternative vision of society that it has so dramatically put into effect. The essence of this philosophy is to reassert the primacy of financial goals, the creation of a money power system so that the key decisions about the use of real resources are taken by those who own the financial resources and capital. Furthermore, the economic goals of profitability, efficiency, material wealth have been translated into a political and social ideology which maintains that what is profitable is good and what is unprofitable is bad, and that what is good for private enterprise is good for Britain. The social and human goals of need fulfillment, social justice, equity, service have been cast aside to be replaced by the ideology of the decision maker in business or government, which pretends that the values which can be measured in terms of money are the only ones that ought to count. This ideology in turn has been applied dramatically to sell public sector undertakings, to transfer council homes into private ownership, to move many hospital services to private firms, and to privatise local authority activities.

The success of this philosophy is based on its ability to convince people that market freedom is equated with the freedom of the individual to make his or her decisions. Thus capitalism is equated to individual freedom.

According to Michael Barratt Brown,[3] Thatcherism is a 'totality of political and economic aims which appears to have a central coherence for 80% of workers who are still employed. The core of this knot is a private income, private health insurance, private education, personal initiative, personal responsibility, personal choice of goods and services and a private morality.'

It is the failure of the Left to provide such an integrated alternative strategy that has created the vacuum which the New Right has filled and continues to hold. Although this New Right philosophy might appear to be attractive, we would maintain that because it is based on the pursuit of private profit, it creates fundamental conflict between the interests of private profit and the interests of society.

We would not equate capitalism with freedom but with the money power system. Money power means much more than rich people are powerful (which they indeed are); far more important is the fact that the use of money power is 'automated'. Humanity is, as it were, adrift in a pilotless craft, destination unknown. Those who control capital are slaves to the necessity of seeing that it is 'well used', that it produces new capital, accumulates, by engaging in such profitable transactions as market circumstances dictate. International banking institutions and transnational companies are slaves to the logic of a system that demands maintenance and enlargement of money power, the penalty for failure to obey this logic being elimination and replacement by others. In this sense those who decide the use of humanity's resources have abandoned human judgement of value and handed over to the automated decisions of the market. Such personal decisions as they take about the use of resources are secondary to the decisions that the system imposes upon them.

When profitability is the norm, the problem of satisfying needs lies in the creation of material wealth based on exchange value. What constitutes wealth is that which involves the production of goods and services for exchange measurable in terms of money. Whatever can be sold is deemed as 'useful'. Goods such as fruit machines, electronic toothbrushes, video nasties are automatically included in this total of wealth. Thus exchange value is equated with use value. The more goods and services we produce the more we are able to satisfy human needs only so long as they can be sold at a profit. Thus the market system distorts our notion of wealth by excluding many of the unpaid activities which are regarded by many as being socially useful. These activities might include domestic work, child rearing, artistic activity which are not produced for exchange and therefore are excluded from the calculations of wealth and gross national product.

Thus *need* becomes part of the ghetto of extreme poverty, such as that in Ethiopia, which must be seen to be addressed in a short term and compartmentalised manner, in this case through the provision of so-called 'aid'. Needs are seen as extremely relative, so that almost any form of paid work under whatever conditions, in the Export Processing

Zones in the Phillipines for instance, is regarded as fulfilling a need, where the interests of transnational corporations (to obtain the cheapest type of labour power) are quite spuriously related to a 'contrived need' of the unfortunate people who live there. Similarly, needs of young people in Britain are thought to be adequately covered by providing them with a weekly wage of £25 or £40 through the YTS or some other scheme, with little or no regard to family circumstances. And more profound needs, such as human dignity at work are now regarded as a luxury, something which cannot be quantified as such and  which can only be satisfied by the ideology of the 'small entrepreneur' or 'vocations' such as nursing, where material rewards are disregarded except as part of a cost within the new managerialist systems of running hospitals and other social welfare institutions. In 1946 the Labour Chancellor of the Exchequer put forward a budget which commenced with things like the actual housing needs of people in post-war Britain, quantifying the actual requirements in terms of housing space and numbers of dwellings and then, secondarily as it were, allocating the required amount to provide for this social need. The politics of need have now been transformed into market terms, where the government allocates a decreasing proportion of public expenditure with absolutely no reference whatsoever to the actual housing needs in Britain: it is not that the housing budget is viewed in purely market terms but there is now a clear separation between public provision and public need in the government's budget announcements.

THE CRISIS OF JOBS AND THE JOBLESS

The present crisis of unemployment reveals that not for the first time the market system cannot sustain full employment. The public costs of unemployment to society were recently estimated at some £20–5 billion or 20% of public expenditure. If the increasing social and health costs due to unemployment are added, it can be seen that we are paying dearly for depriving people of the basic need to earn a living.

We agree with Erick Fromm[4] when he claims that 'capitalism puts things (capital) higher than life (labour)'. People are regarded as factors of production, a raw material, as inputs which are only of use in so far as they contribute to costs and revenues. Human needs are subservient to the needs of capital.

In discussing social relations of production, Raymond Williams[5] argues that the technical and institutional changes have been introduced as part of a strategy for increasing control over the production and organisation of work:

> the purpose of these processes of centralising and rationalising production was not then and is not now the general welfare of all the people in the society. The benefits of increased production and of regular and rising wages have been real. But whenever the choice has had to be made between the true primary purposes – increases of production, reduction of costs, thus success in the market and higher returns on invested capital – and the variable secondary effects – increased employment, rising living standards for wage earners, even overall levels of common wealth – there has never been any real doubt which way it would go.

At a time of high unemployment, this process is accelerating. Investment in new technology is less concerned with job creation than with job saving. In the drive to rationalise 'the labour process', vast areas of manufacturing employment are being eroded in the name of efficiency and profitability. In the words of a Lucas shop steward the ultimate logic of the private enterprise system firm is that 'if the company could make more money by employing robots and accountants and no workers they would do it'.

The development of the means of production, its organisation, are often justified in terms of economic growth, the need to be competitive and technologically up to date. This creates a feeling among people that they have no option but to accept the necessity for technical change whatever harmful consequences may follow. The logic of production is thus pre-eminent, not the logic of need. This results in planned obsolescence, lack of repairability, and also produces technology in artifacts tending to alienate people from their environment, so they generally understand less and less of what surrounds them. This may be regarded as *real* privatisation. In so doing it fuels peoples' feelings of inadequacy. We believe that rapid technological development hasn't appreciably made anyone happier, hasn't increased artistic or any other creativity, and that communications and the computer revolution have made people more isolated. Furthermore the development of technology is resulting in the destruction of what Williams[6] calls the 'social norm of employment', which people have come to expect from the system. The Industrial Revolution established a notion of employment as the basis of the social organisation of work; the mechanism being the labour market in which people contracted to buy and sell labour. When production was divorced from consumption, people had to earn a living to buy goods. This created the fundamental need in our society for the 'right to work', the social norm of employment.

The growing feeling that long term unemployment is now a fact of life, that three and a half million is the norm, and not the high, conflicts with the crucial roles which employment has played in our society. The Protestant work ethic ceases to have any meaning especially for people under 25 who comprise 40% of those unemployed. We are creating a lost generation who have no job prospects and are being forced to adjust to the 'reality of unemployment'.

The Beveridge Report on 'Full Employment'[7] in a Free Society proposed that there should always be more vacant jobs than unemployed persons because of the

> human difference between failing to buy and failing to sell labour . . .
> a person who has difficulty in buying the labour he wants suffers
> inconvenience or reduction in profits. A person who cannot sell his
> labour is in effect told he is of no use. The first difficulty causes
> annoyance or loss. The other is a personal catastrophe.

However the market forces do not make a social distinction between the human needs of the buyer and the seller of labour, it is concerned only with supply and demand of labour as a commodity like any other good. Re-establishing the laws of the market at a time of high unemployment means that power automatically shifts from a sellers' market to a buyers' market. In the present labour market conditions there is no equilibrium between supply and demand. The market mechanism is not sufficient to sustain the goal of full employment and is under no obligation so to do.

Andrew Glyn[8] claims that the failure of the market to create sufficient jobs could be avoided, 'the fundamental point is that achieving of full employment is perfectly possible on the basis of existing resources and would be immensely beneficial in terms of additional goods and services produced'. Glyn argues that the heart of the problem lies in the determination of employment according to the profit motive, 'the fact that a plant is not profitable to the employers to operate does not mean that it is not in society's interests for it to continue in production. Society gains from any employment which yields socially useful production'.

Using 1982 national income figures, Glyn makes the assumption that the workers' average wage is £140, and average take home pay is £101 after deduction, the average income out of work is estimated to be £40. This means that when a worker moves from being unemployed to being employed take home pay would increase from £40 to £101, representing an extra demand of £61. So provided the worker is producing additional output of more than £60, then the worker's employment results in a net increase in production available for everyone else. However by the criterion of profitability a worker would only be employed if the additional output was greater than his gross wage of £140, which is misleading. Society would benefit from the additional employment at any level of productivity over £60 per week. Thus the problem of employment could be tackled differently, but not under the present market system.

The jobs crisis has other dimensions too. For, following partly in the tradition of Japan there are now significant efforts to segment the labour market and the labour force in profound ways, ways which we have not seen since the 1930s. Employers and their organisations are openly talking about a two, three or even four tier labour market within each enterprise. The first tier comprises those 'trusty' or needed employees who will enjoy the fruits of their labours in a fairly secure form of employment, jointly regulated by the employer and a trade union which is committed to the profit motive and all that it implies in terms of work practices, job design and the wages package. There is then a second tier of people that are taken on through short-term, fixed-term contracts for say three months or perhaps a year, their employment being related to changes in seasonal demand for company's products or for the duration of a particular major project, union membership is not included as part of their employment package and there would be remuneration differences between them and the first tier. The third tier comprises sub-contracted labour, either where individuals (as in IBM) contract their services on a personal basis i.e. they are self-employed but tied in essence to one employer, or employed by a satellite company which itself is largely or totally dependent upon its 'parent'. Then there is a fourth tier of so-called trainees who are in essence young people or on a scheme with their own separate lower pay rate, and who are taken on either to replace existing older workers (often on a short term basis) or employed for part of the year in particular places in order to clear specific orders or to carry out work in a marginal part of the firm. The emerging attitude towards women at work and the young people in employment supports this segmentation of the labour force. If the New Right ideologues get their way we will end up as in Japan with a *dual economy*, which is increasingly seen in action in the USA too, where peoples' job prospects and all that goes with them are increasingly determined by economic forces which have little or nothing to do with their abilities, ambitions or needs. This *is* truly a crisis, for it shatters generations of expectations and ideas about personal work which are related in some form at least to a personal sense of value and position in the labour market. It is a crisis for trade unions and collective organisation, and it well may be leading to a crisis of racial and sexual discrimination at work through this new authoritarianism enshrined in the regulation of the labour market.

INFLUENCE OF THE ENVIRONMENT

Another area of conflict between the needs of profit and human needs lies in the continual destruction and damage to human beings and their environment caused by capital accumulation. Fritjof Capra[9] argues that

> Excessive technological growth has created an environment in which life has become physically and mentally unhealthy. Polluted air, irritating noise, traffic congestion, chemical contaminants, radiation hazards, and many other sources of physical and pyschological stress have become part of everyday life for most of us. These manifold health hazards are not just incidental by-products of technological progress; they are integral features of an economic system obsessed with growth and expansion, continuing to intensify its high technology in an attempt to increase productivity.

Again as with the crisis of work, huge social costs are incurred to pay for the environmental damage caused by this technological excess. Private enterprise has little interest in paying for these costs and will try to ignore them as 'externalities', and push them off onto the state and the tax payer, and continue to create pollution for others.

However the problems of damage to the environment as in the case of pollution, is not seen as a fundamental criticism of the market by its supporters. The polluters can be made to pay by legislation they argue, but this can prove difficult in practice because as Bevan[10] points out 'the ideology of the market can undermine the fabric of society because the necessary conditions to make the system work depend upon a moral code which is at variance with the principle of the maximisation of private interests'. The cases of acid rain and nuclear waste disposal illustrate the efforts of corporations to overcome and evade legal sanctions. Use of the environment also includes use and re-use of natural and manufactured resources. At the time of writing the world has supposedly got an oil glut, yet any sane person can see that we have an oil shortage – of a precious resource that cannot be renewed, and that becomes ever more expensive in real terms to utilise as the years go by. But the 'logic' of the financial systems insists that the price of oil must come down and the consumption increases whilst in a year or two years' time the polar opposite may well be said to be 'logical'. Recycling and renovation or repair again follows no obvious logic, bar that of the marketplace, which deems most such activities to be marginal, yet the detritus of the market place is often dangerous, unpleasant, and in the long term supremely expensive.

And in broader terms misuse of the environment under the marketplace leads to very accurate predictions of quite horrendous increase in the spread of deserts across the globe (being many miles away we don't care of course), and many think that we have the beginnings of profound meteorological changes being caused by the blind pursuit of a type of economic growth which has little or nothing to do with the optimisation of resource use.

THE CRISIS OF THE WELFARE STATE

The Welfare State is also under attack. Having led Western Europe in the creation of the welfare state, the UK is now lagging far behind most European countries in what we now spend on social services as a proportion of our gross national product. The Central Policy Review Staff Secret Document 1982 proposed the further dismantling of much of the existing welfare state, including the end of all public funding for higher education; the abolition of indexation of all social security benefits; and the abolition of the national health service to be replaced by private insurance; Secretary of State Norman Fowler began implementing such measures in the Social Security field. Although this is in accordance with free market theories it will mean that only those that can afford to pay for education, for health, or to provide for old age, will get these services. The remaining population, millions of whom are already in poverty will be denied the fulfilment of basic needs.

Many basic welfare needs occur outside the market framework at present. But more and more they are falling within a framework of market values. Hirch[11] has commented on the effect of commercialisation of medicine in the United States; the weakening of the doctor/patient relationship is a matter of common experience and widespread comment. He quotes a survey of the American Medical Association which shows that one in five of all physicians in the United States had been or was being sued for malpractice.

This trend also moves attention away from the actual needs of people who do not have sufficient power in the marketplace to fulfil crucial needs. 'Welfare' is systematically being changed from an activity which a civilised society would take for granted into one which is conditional upon esoteric calculations around the Public Sector Borrowing Requirement and the management of so-called scarce resources (i.e. the reducing amount of money put by to help people). People who are disenfranchised through age, poverty, disability and the like are increasingly seen simply as a cost to the state, and little else. In this way things such as access to telephone boxes in rural areas, public transport, access to health services, nurseries and the like is now very much a secondary consideration compared to that of monetary management. Today political considerations of social justice tend to be dealt with now '*in extremis*' rather than as a natural and possible productive activity carried out on behalf of all of us through income derived from all of us; for who knows how many of us who are now able-bodied will need, through no fault of our own, to utilise the services of the welfare system.

THE CRISIS OF OUR INFRASTRUCTURE

We have seen in recent years how our infrastructure including housing, water, reservoirs, bridges, roads, transport, sewage have all been neglected by cuts in capital investment programmes which have fallen dramatically from £6.5 billion in 1972 to £1.4 billion in 1982. The Association of Metropolitan Authorities[12] recently stated 'in the absence of any action by the government it may be the last chance to produce a comprehensive plan to stop the decline in housing standards and assist the millions who are in desperate need'. Britain's housing situation is 'rapidly heading for a crisis of similar proportion that was reported a hundred years ago by the Royal Commission on Housing for the Working Classes' it added. The Association estimates that £50 billion is required to restore the sub standard housing stock and to meet the shortage of housing. The Director General of The Federation of Civil Engineering Contractors in a letter to *The Times*[13] asserted that 'over a quarter of the water that is pumped into our water mains leaks out before it reaches the consumer. As with so many other areas of our infrastructure, the failure to renew and repair is increasing cost and inconvenience today and storing up much larger bills for the future'.

In these areas of welfare, environment and infrastructure, the concept of the individual consumer fulfilling his needs in the market place seems largely irrelevant. We use these services in a collective sense as part of a network of social relationships. They should be designed to reduce individual inequalities, to provide equal life chances. We want our towns clean and free of congestion. We want hospitals, schools, libraries to be provided as part of the quality of life for everyone – not just a privileged few. We use these services collectively as well as individually. A socially useful economy is one which lays emphasis on the social and collective needs as a criterion for economic activity. The present overriding view of infrastructural services is that they are an unfortunate but necessary part of the maintenance of certain aspects of the fabric of society's needs and must be kept under tight cost controls, guided by managerialist concepts of efficiency. This is not only person-ally offensive, but also tends to preclude the possibility of more democratic control over such individual and collective services.

THE CRISIS OF HUMAN RIGHTS – FREEDOM

The advocates of the market system maintain that it is the only system which ensures individual freedom of choice to buy and sell goods within the market, unhindered by the state; which functions only to maintain property rights and the competition of markets, the preservation of internal order and the organisation of external defence. This freedom is referred to as economic or market freedom, but it is based on the private ownership of resources which are not equally distributed. Thus the freedom of the individual to earn a living is not an inalienable right, but only possible within the market system. The reduction of state spending on welfare, and privatisation could be seen not as restoring market freedom and individual choice, but increasing the power of those private interests which own the major resources, especially when it is backed up by state policies to protect those interests.

It is significant that defence and law and order are the areas which market advocates regard as being the prerogatives of the state to protect the rights of property and the market. Williams[14] states

> Thus as we have seen in recent months, the police can be used to enforce a free market in labour. The law can be used to tame institutions such as unions which interfere with free individual bargaining. Armed forces and security agencies can be used to forestall or destabilise collectivist and other socially controlled economic systems. Behind the apparent double mouth is a single set

of values, an economic liberalism, now in fact in corporate rather than any significant individual forms, actively promoted by both law and capital, electoral power and armed force.

There develops a great assymetry between political forms of democracy and an increasing centralisation of institutional power over which there is in effect no democratic control. Real economic democracy can only begin to exist when ordinary people, as workers and consumers, exercise some control over resources; but this would shift the centre of gravity of social power and weaken the money-power which the advocates of market freedom regard as central. That is why extensions of democracy have been fought against so strongly, and why today the New Right are suspicious of democracy except insofar as it preserves and reinforces the free market system.

This also accounts for the trends in trying to manage democratic choice as if it were similar to market consumer choice. Free elections are often based on choosing two or more politically packaged leaders. This is not an active view of democracy; yet historically this has been the only meaningful democracy – based on the notions of struggle, opposition and public protest.

Our economic system should exist for the satisfaction of human need; it should be evaluated by the extent to which it can be responsive to those needs. If resources are scarce then all the more reason to socially determine the best allocation of those resources according to NEED and not according to profit. The anarchistic nature of the market system with its narrow monetary criteria, its non-recognition of the physical limits to growth, its inequalities, its inherent instability, and its emphasis on exchange values result in the reduction of socially useful activity. Under such a system a person who is out of work is confined to the dust heap, made to feel useless with feelings of 'nothing worthwhile to contribute'. This system produces an asymmetry of power which renders individuals powerless with the feeling that they have no real freedom of choice or decision making. However it is the ideology of the market system which claims that is acting in the name of the freedom of individual, that it maximises freedom. Its very appeal is to the individual to become responsible for all his or her actions and not to hold the state accountable. This strategy has worked very effectively. It is significant that the government has so far managed to avoid being held responsible for unemployment. People are continually being pressured into believing that we have 'got it right', that we are passing through a transitional phase on our way to the post industrial society, that economic growth will cure unemployment.

IDEOLOGICAL FIXES

We are told that the path we are taking is inevitable, subject to the inexorable laws of technical progress. We are moving from an industrial society to an information society; a society which can produce the necessary wealth but with a much reduced working population. The electronic age is upon us but is this equivalent to developing the socially useful economy? Who has the finger on the control button? Does capitalism and its consequent ownership and control of production simply wither away? Will individuals be able to fulfill their potential and will society acquire social purposes which will act as criteria for production rather than ones which depend solely on profit?

We are urged to believe in a technological determinism which has a hidden agenda, namely that we have no real choices of alternative forms of social organisation, that we must accept our fate and deny the possibility of human intervention to alter the course of history; that there is no alternative (TINA). This is reinforced by subjecting the population to a sort of linguistic terrorism; if new technology and the development of capital accumulation are opposed, then the population is accused of 'Neo-Luddism'.

We strongly reject the notion that there shouldn't or cannot be an alternative. The belief that technological progress is inevitable has paralysed thinking in the Labour movement. Democratic activity, intervention, and institutions in fact make a profound impact. The forces trying to maintain power and provide ideological justification are meeting with resistance on many fronts. However, so far, the ways in which alternatives are being sought do not fit together into an explicit philosophy or coordinated movement, but are still fragmented reactions against the existing framework, struggle founded on protest which is not necesarily coherent. However, this miscellany of new movements is highly relevant because these are nevertheless expressions of peoples' unmet needs. They are crucial social indicators that the present framework is in need of change.

ANALYSIS OF ALTERNATIVE ACTIVITY/SOME BASIS OF ALTERNATIVE ACTIVITY

If we look around us we can see a host of efforts of this sort. Organisations with a wide popular support – unions, tenants', groups, lobbyists for the environment, youth, etc – are desperately looking to create some space and opportunity for change. What is needed is a much more open and practical climate for their development. Unions in mines, shipbuilding, electronics, desperately need some vision of the future for their members. Workers keep being promised greater participation, but they don't get it, *except* within the confines of economic structures that remain very traditional and authoritarian. Millions of people are concerned about the arms race, they know it's a waste of money, it's dangerous, and they increasingly know it is bad for jobs in the long term, it is inflationary, is volatile. Movements against arms expenditure combine moral, religious, practical, political and social elements, and now, through the unions, are increasingly questioning the economics that lies behind the arms race, and the economic consequences of the arms race.

Unions, patients' associations, doctors and nurses worry greatly about the health service. Any cut is deeply disturbing, any efforts to make hospitals run like factories scare people at a very deep level. Here we have a vast number of people who really want and need new concepts, new criteria, 'a new vision' of a more caring, open and appropriate health service. There are lots of ideas of how to make it better, and they don't all mean that a lot more money has to be spent on it.

There is a continuing tradition of concern about technological development – well known fears on bio-engineering, such as were expressed in the Warnock Commission, to consumer organisations and journals critical of the performance of many artifacts, criticisms of agribusiness, broader arguments against the technologies of communications and travel (as they are presently presented), a range of critical groups concerned with new work technologies and their effects, and much else. Critical science and technology continues a long tradition of questioning, and sometimes condemning, economics based on technical progressivism. Concern originating within scientific circles has ranged over the years from Oppenheimer's moral legacy questioning the direction of work on the atom bomb, to health and safety at work. A variety of organisations are concerned with the problems of job creation; local authorities such as the GLC have set up special enterprise boards concerned with the creation of socially useful employment. Civil liberty groups and activities have developed, there are no formal constitutional rights other than those of the 'individual in the marketplace', where fluid pragmatic practice is open to many abuses. There are people and groups worried about trading relations and economic and political stances in relation to oppressive regimes around the world.

Today the challenge to the status quo comes from protest movements which are not simply based on class (although a great many of the protest movements arise from clear class-based concerns), but represent a wide variety of social groups such as environmentalists, tenants associations, ethnic minorities, feminists, gays, nuclear disarmers. What is significant is that these groups are fragmented, they seek change for particular group or sectional interests. What they lack, as Raymond Williams has noted, is the concept of a general interest, an interconnected framework which contains within it the possibility of combining the various interests which could be incorporated into a vision of a socialist society.

It is just such a framework that we have attempted to explore in this book. It combines approaches which elaborate the connections between for instance the nuclear disarmers and interests of trade unionists who work in the arms industry. It is an attempt to find and re-create notions, ideas which have an everyday and important meaning for people, as opposed to the current spurious 'Grantham Grocer Shop' economics allied to an 'economic God' – which orbit somewhere out of reach. It is also an attempt to regain the language, to say the things that we want to say without fear of ridicule.

PRINCIPLES FOR DEVELOPING THE SOCIALLY USEFUL ECONOMY

'Developing the socially useful economy' may not sound an exciting vision of society. Yet such a vision is needed; change is not possible until the imagination of people is aroused. In arguing for a radical revision of our existing organisational frameworks several important principles can be specified; firstly, that societies cannot be considered purely as economic machines. They consist of human beings who must be considered. (Schumacher gave his book *Small Is Beautiful*, the sub-title *Economics As If People Mattered*.) Analyses borrowed from the physical sciences have often ignored the simple fact that social systems contain human beings and not just things or commodities, and that therefore they are qualitatively different from physical systems. This qualitative difference applies in particular to the ideas and actions which shape the development of social consciousness and social change. That is why a precondition of debate about choices is deeply worked out concepts of alternatives; they are themselves agents of change.

Secondly, the aims of maximising production and consumption should not be ends in themselves. According to Fromm:[15]

production and consumption must be subordinated to the needs of man's development, not the reverse. As a consequence all production must be directed by the principle of its social usefulness, and not by that of its material profit for certain individuals or corporations. Hence if a choice has to be made between greater production on the one hand, and greater freedom and human growth on the other, the human as against the material value must be chosen . . . the goal is not to achieve the highest economic productivity but to achieve the highest human productivity.

Socially useful work would create in people a feeling of worth, not just monetary worth like a commodity. Socially useful work combines the right to work with a dignity of work and preservation of human skills and creativity.

Thirdly, we believe that the principles of social usefulness can provide key linkages between production, consumption and human need fulfilment. Production and consumption can be considered as socially useful insofar as they fulfil a human need, which includes needs fulfilment at both user and producer end. This implies that employment is not wanted for the sake of employment irrespective of what it produces. According to Beveridge[16] employment 'which is merely time wasting, the equivalent to digging holes and filling them again, or merely destructive like war and preparing for war will not serve that purpose. Nor will it be thought worthwhile. It must be productive and progressive'.

Fourthly, if resources are not used in a socially useful manner, there is waste that is, then social costs are incurred. This can be seen as a result of needs not being met, or through meeting artificial or false needs. The principle of social cost effectiveness could well be developed as a means by which to evaluate resources–use decisions.

Fifthly, developing a socially useful economy involves development of social frameworks where people can effectively control their own lives whilst at the same time continuing to contribute to society as a whole. Democratic involvement at all levels is essential in order to achieve a socially useful society. Thus, developing a socially useful economy would require the extension of political democracy to all levels of decision-making.

We also want democracy to have some real practical meaning to people, to be more than vague general principles, or a speculation such as that of 18th century political thinkers. It should be a way of removing or relieving the myriad of worries and concerns that many of us have on a day-to-day and year-to-year basis, and a means of allowing frustrations and ambitions to be 'worked out' through action, and find expression as realised potentials in a much more 'transparent' society.

SUMMARY

Concepts or beliefs in new ways of using resources, alternatives to decision making by money power, that is the essence of what our existing economic order today lacks. Academic thinking about economics, the parameters within which trade unionists determine their practice, the boundaries of 'political realism' to which political parties confine themselves, all fall victims to this extraordinary spell that equates economic reasoning with assessment of value in money terms and expression of needs with readiness to buy on the market. Search for alternatives is the 'therapy' necessary to undo the spell that enslaves human beings to the laws of the system which is no longer controlled by human judgement and human values. The system's misuse of resources and failure to allow people to use resources for themselves causes despair, poverty, violence, alienation, distress, oppression, torture, starvation, and war on such a scale that the very future of the species is in peril. Under such circumstances *not* to search energetically for alternatives is nothing short of criminal negligence.

We can't assume some inevitable process of history from which the ideal society will just emerge as a consequence of all the contradictions within the present one. We have to make *it* happen. Just as Marx's ideas in the past profoundly altered the course of history, so it is ideas and consciousness and actions of human beings which are needed to bring about change in our society today.

The search for and elaboration of alternatives to 'TINA' is and should be a legitimate activity, history is not some straight motorway to the future, it never has been and never will be. The idea of developing a 'socially useful economy' is to mount a challenge within that most hallowed area – economics and all its meanings.

NOTES

1. N. Brown and N. Madge, *Despite the Welfare State* (Heinemann Educational Books, 1982).
2. BSSRS, *Science on Our Side*, BSSRS publications (1983) p. 3.

3. Michael Barratt Brown, *Models in Political Economy* (Penguin, 1984) p. 240.
4. Eric Fromm, *On Disobedience and Other Essays* (Routledge & Kegan Paul, 1984).
5. Raymond Williams, *Towards 2000* (Chatto & Windus, 1983) p. 87.
6. Ibid., pp. 85 – 90.
7. W.H. Beveridge, *Full Employment in a Free Society* (Allen & Unwin, 1944) p. 17.
8. Andrew Glyn, 'Its Profit That Kills Jobs', *Guardian,* 28 Nov 1983.
9. Fritjof Capra, *The Turning Point* (Fontana, 1982) p. 249.
10. R.G. Bevan, 'Social Limits to Planning', *Journal of the Operational Research Society,* vol. 31 (1980) pp. 867–874.
11. Fred Hirch, *'Social Limits to Growth'*, (Routledge & Kegan Paul, 1977).
12. 'Britain's Slumming It', *Standard*, 6 Sept 1984.
13. D.V. Gaulter, Letter to *The Times* (July 1984).
14. Raymond Williams, 'Two Faces of Liberalism', *Guardian,* 11 Oct 1984.
15. E. Fromm, op. cit.
16. W.H. Beveridge, op. cit.

Part II
Understanding What
Cripples Us

process of identifying phenomena that
make up the pre- basic tenets of the
economy — stating from various studies
analysis
posits

Part II breaks 'economics' into constituent parts.

(1) that it is a political practice and not simply or even mainly a scientific enquiry or endeavour that can be guided by objective and value-free rules;
(2) that technology in its widest sense is ideological, political and social, being a complementary set of activities to economics; and
(3) that social organisation is intimately bound up with the theory and practice of economics.

Chapter 3, 'The Politics of Economics' uses expert evidence to show how many crucial economic principles are in fact derived through general and particular political pressures and persuasions. This evidence is used to pose the thesis that current 'economics' is a truly problematic area, and that a quite different set of economic principles and priorities can be derived and developed if one starts with a different political philosophy.

Chapter 4, takes as its starting point the view that no technology can be neutral in social, economic or even political terms. Thus current technological developments reflect and complement existing views on economic development, and as such technologies are just as much instruments of politics as are social welfare or health service decisions. A number of key problems with the topical 'technological progressivism' trend are indentified and criticised.

We conclude Part II with an examination of social organisation, in particular that of bureaucracy, and how it is an integral part of the current political scene – in private as well as public concerns. The conventional counterposing of market democracy and command economy bureaucracy is questioned, and found wanting. Here we directly raise some quite fundamental issues about democracy and social organisation.

As a whole Part II seeks to illuminate and criticise a number of key, interlinked phenomena that make up the principles and mechanisms of the economy.

59

3 The Politics of Economics

In scientific thinking, you try to imagine a situation as accurately as possible and to think about it as logically as possible. Surely in any important issue we try to do the same.

This does not mean that mathematical thinking can answer every question. If a certain course of action would benefit one person and harm another, there is no mathematical procedure that could conceivably indicate whether it should be done or not. The choice of aims is a question of values. Once an aim has been chosen, mathematical and scientific thinking can often assess the value of various ways of working towards that aim.

The aims we choose depend, I suppose, on our experiences. For me the decisive experience was in 1934 when I returned from 4 months with Jewish professors in Hitler Germany to find the county of Cambridgeshire covered with agricultural produce that was rotting in the fields. Similar waste or destruction was occurring in other parts of the World. Ever since then it seemed to me that much of the human suffering of this century must be regarded as a self-inflicted wound. If in 1930 we had used the bounty of the earth to meet the most urgent human needs in Germany, Britain and other countries, it is practically certain that Hitler would never have come to power. We did not do so. The price of this failure was paid by those who were murdered in the gas chambers and by those who were killed or maimed in 1939–45.

There is no reason to suppose that the price of economic failure will be less in the future than it was in the past. A rational aim for economic thinking would be to make impossible a repetition of such horrifying waste.

W. W. Sawyer

(This is an extract from a letter which Professor W. W. Sawyer of Cambridge wrote to the *Bulletin of the Institute of Mathematics and Its Applications*, vol. 19, nos. 9/10, Oct. 1983.)

'ECONOMIC' VERSUS POLITICAL GOALS

Why do particular economic ideas 'have clout'? And why do certain approaches to economics get established to the exclusion of others? Professor W.W. Sawyer writes: 'In scientific thinking, you try to imagine a situation as accurately as possible and to think about it as logically as possible.' Is economic thinking scientific in this sense?

Economic ideas as organisers of social behaviour were the topic of the papers with which these discussions started. Academics often talk and write about concepts as if their only role were scientific, that is, the accurate picturing of reality. But in fact ideas live in a world of social and political struggle, much of which is about the organisation of economic activity and the distribution of its products. In these struggles economic concepts are also weapons.

Thus economics is *not* just a body of theory. It is central to the way we govern our lives and how our lives are governed. It dictates the terms of reference under which people live and work. Employment, wages, hours of work, are all treated by economists as economic factors from which moral purpose and human value have been abstracted; yet the reality is that they are fundamentally inseparable from peoples's lives and values in a practical sense. Labour is not just a commodity, a resource, a factor of production to be allocated according to economic principles. Labour is an activity of human beings with feelings, values, creativity and many other dimensions.

Like it or not, there is a political content in economics and this is crucial to economic analysis because the political and social environment permeates the framework of economic activity. This is well illustrated by the post-1945 period when the goals of social justice and equality, full employment, free education and health were politically accepted as objectives of economic activity. Now these goals are being replaced by purely economic goals such as profitability, efficiency defined as competitiveness on the market, and increase of wealth defined in terms of exchange-values. At the centre of the recent miners' strike was the notion of what is an 'economic' pit. The whole debate centred on assessing alternatives 'economically' in this narrow sense. Social benefit, social justice and impact on the lives of whole communities were excluded from the Government's and the management's calculations of what was 'economic'.

Notions of economic efficiency – again in this narrow sense – dominate the thinking of those who administer social services. For example the Health service is now being analysed in the same terms as a business with relatively little regard to the needs for patient care and attention, because these do not enter into costs measured in the way costs are measured in production for the market.

A regime that believes that purely economic motivations are superior favours an ideology that makes purely economic goals an end in themselves: 'what is good for private enterprise, is good for Britain'. The political and social consequence of this approach is reinforcement of the status quo and money-making at the expense of human needs. Unemployment is only regarded as a social problem insofar as stronger laws and police powers are required to curb consequent threats to 'law and order'. Unemployment as degradation and destruction of potential human activity does not enter into the calculations.

The political struggle is, of course, much more than competition between Political parties for Parliamentary ascendancy. Social power feeds, in the last analysis, on economic power: power to do things means having access to the resources with which to do them. So to talk about systems of social cooperation that determine how ways of using resources are decided, how goods are produced and so forth, is not only to 'talk economics' – which it is – but 'to talk power'. What is said and what is believed in itself affects power. The Heisenberg Factor, (a concept from physics illustrated by the fact that the very act of observing with a gamma-ray microscope drives the observed particle from where it would have been unobserved) operates with a vengeance in economics. Things are made to be different by the way people observe them. No wonder worthy, otherwise – tolerant citizens can be driven to frenzy by economic ideas they don't like!

Such ideas are themselves a challenge to the structure of society as they know it. Social classifications derive largely from differentiations in economic function and, insofar as this is so, the class to which a person belongs in any particular society depends on 'what he or she does' and the rights this gives in the share-out of material goods. Inevitably therefore economic concepts deeply touch the relationships between classes. This they do in various ways – they organise in the sense of saying who does what, they defend or challenge in the sense of portraying a social order as just or unjust, as efficient or inefficient. These emotionally and politically charged aspects of economic ideas may well override what one might call the academic aspect of economic concepts as accurate representation of situations. For all these reasons economic concepts and ideas play a key part in the struggle between defence of the status quo and desire to change it towards, say, forms of economic activity that would focus more consciously and purposefully on socially useful ends.

The 'hegemony' of a class, an economic system, an established order is defended by ideas as much as it is by institutions and instruments of power; so developing socially useful activities cannot be separated from challenge to the economic ideology of right-wing politics. Alternative ideas are not to be seen as preceding political action but as inherent aspects of constructing alternative economic activities, socialist forms of organisation or systems that embody a 'socially useful economy'.

'First, an economy operating on the basis of social need rather than profit (or even an extensive sub-economy) cannot be built unless state power is in the hands of the Left and just as ideas have been crucial in the Right's offensive, so they are crucial to socialist political success. The forces generated by capitalist markets and organisations (forces such as those which push, say, co-operatives in the direction of having to adopt capitalist ways of operating if they are to survive) are so strong that a space can be opened for the construction of alternatives only if the state is used to carve it out with subsidies and controls over market forces. Second, the construction of any individual enterprise or local initiative requires constant 'negotiation' (with the central state, with contractors, with banks, with pension funds and other financial institutions) and 'negotiating' requires the concepts with which to undermine the terms of discussion defined by the Right. If local initiatives such as Greater London's require expenditure from the rates it is necessary to undermine the government's arguments against public spending, to reject the imperatives that the Public Sector Borrowing Requirement is supposed to exercise. If pension funds' money is sought to finance socially useful production their managers and trustees cannot refuse, unchallenged, on the grounds that they are bound to make profits for their members; they have to be persuaded that there are alternative definitions of their members' interests which have economic validity.

The Monetarist Model

Three economic concepts have been particularly important in right-wing ideology at various times since 1945. Although they are presented by the Right as the keystones of immutable laws which prevent the development of alternative policies and strategies, they are, in fact, riddled with contradictions and weaknesses. They are:

(1) the Public Sector Borrowing Requirement (PSBR);
(2) the money supply; and
(3) professional portfolio management

The first two have been especially important at times for the macro-economic circumstances which constrain the development of socially useful economic activities and which have led through unemployment to the destruction of people's lives and the waste of their social potential; the third has been especially important in justifying reluctance to finance socially useful production.

Restricting the Public Sector Borrowing Requirement has been presented as a fundamental necessity for the state since Denis Healey's abandonment of Keynesianism in 1976. It has been given special prominence in the presentation of the Thatcher administration's policies, particularly since target ceilings from the PSBR were incorporated in the government's first economic blue-print the '*Medium Term Financial Strategy*'. The need to restrict the PSBR has been given as the rationale for the most contentious of the government's policies. Cuts in grants to local authorities, cash limits on programmes (except supplementary benefit, unemployment pay and similar programmes), and the sale of public sector assets on the stock market have all been justified on these grounds. Cuts in local authority finance hinder local policies for the development of socially useful production, and privatisation of public sector industries leads to their total concentration on profit and the abandonment of the last vestige of social service in their operation. Looking at it from the macroeconomic point of view the relative switch of state spending away from socially useful sectors like welfare services or education and toward the military and police has been pushed through on the grounds that since the latter need more the former have to have less in order to keep the PSBR within bounds.

The argument of the Right is that the PSBR has to be limited because immutable economic laws dictate that a high PSBR will be harmful. It is said that it would either lead to an unduly high increase in the money supply or high government borrowing would drain funds out of the financial system, starving private industry of funds and 'crowding out' private investment. That this is an attempt at mystification can be seen from its propagators' own policies which are inconsistent with and contradict their argument.

First, although the sale of nationalised industries reduces the PSBR (at least on a once-for-all basis in the year of the sale) it drains funds from private investment rather than the opposite. For example, the sale of British Telecom, which ultimately puts in jeopardy social services like remote rural telephones and free emergency calls, absorbs some £4 billion from the financial system and those funds are not available to finance investment in, say, private manufacturing. Second, if the Right really believed that money loaned to the state led to productive investment in British factories being starved of finance it should believe that investing money abroad creates similar harm. But in 1979 the government lifted all restrictions on foreign investment in order to encourage an outflow of funds which has, as a result, reached very high proportions.

These contradictions occur because the idea of economic laws requiring the PSBR to be restricted is wrong. The financial system is elastic and does not have a fixed pool of funds so that it has to rob Peter to lend to Paul (although it may charge higher interest the higher the demands on it). The real reasons for spending cuts and the sale of nationalised industries have to be sought in the *interests of the firms* who stand to profit from a decline in the relative size of the public sector; it is a major push in the direction of increasing the hegemony of profit as the criterion of economic activity.

Controlling the money supply has been closely linked with control of the PSBR in the Right's presentation of what is right. The argument has been that a high PSBR, if it doesn't crowd out private investment, (or if it does) will lead to a large rise in the money supply because government borrowing is akin to printing money. A high rate of growth of the money supply is, in turn, presented as unacceptable because by the laws of economics it must lead to high inflation. This argument is put over as additional support for the policy of restricting the PSBR and shifting the economy's balance toward the private sector and profit criterion.

The argument is *invalid* partly because changes in the money supply have not been systematically related to or caused by changes in the PSBR, partly because 'the money supply' has proved to be impossible to define and measure in a meaningful way, and partly because there is no strong evidence that the rate of inflation is determined by the growth of the money supply. Again the falsity of these ideas and their status as myths with which to wage a struggle for right wing ideology are shown by the inconsistencies and contradictions in applying them.

The first Thatcher administration's 'Medium Term Financial Strategy' set target ceilings for the rate of growth of the money supply and chose one measure of the money supply (sterling M3) as the main target. In a short space of time it was found that this money stock could not be tightly controlled and other measures grew at very different rates. There could be no sound basis for choosing one measure rather than another and in the end the government has had to watch (rather than target) at least four different measures corresponding to different definitions of money.

The impossibility of defining the money supply satisfactorily stems from the flexibility and complexity of the financial system. This flexibility has been encouraged by the state because *it is the foundation of the City's strength*, but it makes it impossible to distinguish 'money' from other financial assets. Yet despite being forced to abandon its own belief in its own simple prescriptions, Thatcher's government still uses the idea that the money supply has to be controlled as a whip in public debate over economic policy.

The concept of professional portfolio management has increasingly been used as an ideological weapon in conflicts that have been less publicised than those over macro-economic policy. But they have been 'at the coalface' of the struggle to develop economic activities which are not dominated by the profit criterion. When union, university or church trustees argue that their pension and investment funds should not be invested in South Africa or in the arms trade, or that they should be invested in cooperative and other enterprises for socially useful production, fund managers and right wing trustees argue that their duty to the fund's members or beneficiaries precludes this. Obliged to pursue the beneficiaries' interests, these are interpreted as an obligation to pursue maximum profits. And that is interpreted as requiring the freedom to pursue a conventional investment policy, 'selecting winners' from completely unrestricted opportunities.

One straightforward criticism that has been made from a socialist standpoint is that funds' members' interests are not best defined as the maximisation of financial profits on the funds invested in their name. When pension funds are encouraged to invest in the long-term development of local industry rather than seeking short-term profits from whatever investments seem most glittering, a socialist argument has been that trustees will thereby advance their members' interests by supporting jobs.

But challenging the idea on its own ground, even accepting that profit is the definition of the beneficiaries interests', it can be shown to be a purely fallacious defence of right-wing investment policies.

Diverting funds from the shares of arms manufacturers, for example, or companies with South African connections would restrict the number of investment opportunities from which fund managers can select. But even orthodox financial theory does not lead to the conclusion that such a reduction will reduce a fund's profitability and security. The results achieved by an investment fund depend on the combination of securities with diverse frequency distributions of returns; excluding particular investments on the grounds that they are anti-social would not preclude the achievement of sound combinations because today's capital markets contain so many securities of diverse types and with different frequency distribution of returns.

The idea that fund managers are expert at picking winners in terms of profitability and need maximum freedom of choice to do it is a myth. Although presented as an economic law it has no foundation and serves only to defend a system where social values are excluded from financial criteria. To move forward we have to do more than criticise the political role of currently dominant economic ideas. The natural question is what valid economic ideas will serve the politics of socialism and the construction of a system that serves social needs? Some answers will come up in the course of further discussion but the most significant ones will be developed out of practice'.[1]

THE POLITICS OF GENERATING ALTERNATIVE ECONOMIC IDEAS

How then might ideas that better serve social needs be generated and how could such ideas win ascendancy over the now ruling power of economic ideas geared to competition and monetary returns?

Sometimes 'alternative ideas' do little more than use orthodox concepts of economic management by government to advocate alternative government policies. The Labour movement's presentation of its 'Alternative Economic Policy' is sometimes presented in ways that seem to amount to no more than this. In contrast the approach of the Lucas Aerospace Combine Shop Stewards Committee and others in the Joint Forum of Combine Committees, local Popular Planning initiatives and bodies such as CAITS hinges on adding a further dimension to economic thinking, namely, grassroots involvement in practical attempts to use resources differently. Such attempts are in themselves a form of education by 'trying to do' which challenges accepted conceptual frameworks. However, achievements can only be meagre and frustrating unless backed by powerful state action, giving protection against overwhelming market forces and concentrations of finance in private hands.

To say that economic ideas come from scientific and academic research is to tell only a fraction of the whole story. People *learn* economics from their own experience and collective attempts to use resources for socially useful ends teach a different economics from that of individuals managing the family budget. And certainly the family budget gives rise to concepts of economics. These concepts are echoed in justifications of national policies to which they have in reality no relevance at all. For example, is it not 'common sense' that it is bad to borrow too much; so, by analogy, to restrict the PSBR wins approval as down-to-earth common sense. At the same time quelling doubts there may be about a too simplistic trust in common sense, policy-guiding ideas (such as PSBR and Control of Money Supply) are given the sanction of academic expertise. Indeed they are actively constructed and shaped by experts with sufficient precision to give consistency to their analyses. The same message is again and again reinforced by government departments, the International Monetary Fund, spokesmen for Banks, specialists from universities and others 'who speak with authority', convincing public opinion that the PSBR must not exceed limits and that money supply must be curbed.

Viewed pragmatically these overarching concepts, once accepted as points of reference, replace a host of other controls over social policy. Limitation of public spending allows decision-makers at the centre to stand back, they no longer are required to take positions on concrete specifics of social policy; without further argument a cast-iron alibi is provided for stopping workers in the field from doing this or that, compelling them to cut down in one area of social policy after another.

Economic analysis has paid extraordinarily little attention to the actualisation of economic practice. Yet the really important thing is what guides the practice of economic agents. For what is 'the economic system' but a complex mosaic of economic activities, 'a regime of economic practice'?

ECONOMICS AND THE REGIME OF THE CALCULATIVE

'There is an enormous difference between economic principle and a regime of economic practice. Economic practice requires an intersection with the specifics of economic institutions and actors which is rarely considered by theorists of almost any variety. Even the most critical seemingly are content to accept much of economic practice as we know it. Indeed in economics the world of the practical only rarely has been made problematic.

That realm of the practical in economics calls upon a detailed regime of technical economic calculations. Practice cannot be reformed without a means to actualise the potential implicit in economic conceptions. And, as everyone knows, economic calculations play a significant part in the process. They serve to make visible, salient and actionable the realm of the economic. In practical affairs the calculative apparatus of the economic makes real what otherwise would reside in the realm of the discursive. It provides an objective, precise status to phenomena which otherwise would be vague and tenuous.

Such statements have a particular significance under the present political administration. No government has placed more emphasis not only on the economic but also on economic calculation. Policies have even been formulated in the name of economic calculations. The Public Sector Borrowing Requirement, for instance, has been made into an important symbol of the economically significant. It is difficult to conceive of an admistration that has made more of the significance or, as they would see it, the realities of cash limits. And few administrations in modern history have invested more in influencing, indeed amending, the stories that might be created in the name of economic calculations. Unemployment, inflation and indices of the extent of the pervasiveness, potential or actual, of the penetration of the 'public' into the realm of the 'private' have never previously been so subject to influence and change. Economic policy-making has been a calculative endeavour in all senses of that term.

Be that as it may, the significance of economic calculation has not been subject to very much examination and criticism. Economics, per se, has been a contested phenomenon. But the means for operationalising the economic has not. Economic calculation has been seen as a by-product, a *mere* means to a wider end. Even those who would denounce what is being done in the name of the economic have not regarded economic calculation as a significant and important area. Economic abstractions seemingly have triumphed over economic practice from a diversity of perspectives.

Perhaps because of this very little consideration has been given to alternative practices and approaches. Regrettable as it is, few have invested in thinking about how alternative conceptions of the economic and the social might be realised. Ends have been seen as more important than mere means. The significance of the practical has not been recognised.

In the light of such a series of arguments it is tempting to think in terms of an alternative calculative regime of the social. What was ignored must be prioritised. What was invisible under the regime of the economic must be emphasised under the regime of the social. Social calculations at the very least must be set aside those of the economic. Social reports, audits and calculations must be given a new significance, a new priority, a new means for making the possible, the probable, the necessary into the actual and the real.

But while there is virtue in such an argument, it should only be accepted with great care. For:

(1) All calculations, social or economic, new or traditional, play a role in creating an objective domain of the seemingly factual that often can have an uneasy relationship with the contested, the uncertain and the imprecise. Social calculations may be useful but they are rarely adequate. That needs to be continually emphasised.

(2) The factual domains created by extensions of calculative practices are often conducive to management by new expert groups. When things can be known, ordered, regulated, ranked and controlled, a regime of expert administration can very easily develop. We have seen this happen repeatedly, including in areas of the social. Increasingly, however, there is a growing awareness of the different patterns of dependency, and power associated with the advance of facts and expertise. That sceptical awareness needs to be maintained. We must continue to ask questions of what is actually done in the name of the calculative rather than being content to argue only in terms of its future potential.

(3) Related to the above, we need to be much more conscious of the relationships between calculations and political process. We need to see how calculations can emerge from politics, how they can facilitate the exercise of certain political strategies and how their potential to further the culture of the expert might even limit those areas of everyday life where political process is seen to be legitimate. Calculation can, in other words, be politically enabling and politically restrictive. That needs to be recognised.

The advance of social calculation therefore is an equivocal one. It can undoubtedly help to increase the visibility of the social. The economic can more readily be made to confront its consequences. Social action can be legitimised by appealing to the calculus of the economic. All these are advantages. But, on the negative side, we nevertheless must be aware of the ways in which an extended calculative regime, advanced for the best of reasons, can serve to further an administrative regime where experts confront politicians, where 'facts' have greater legitimacy than preferences and where concepts such as efficiency and rationality take priority over social value and need. Some of the latter possibilities are very real ones; so advocacy of a new calculative regime of the social must be 'contingent, tactical and rather cautious'.[2]

The 'regime of the calculative' is in contemporary society a mode of bureaucratic practice and as such specific to the kinds of bureaucracy that exist at the present time. Its economic basis is the gigantism of transnational corporations and the huge centralised state institutions administering social life within the various national territories. The professions organise skills for the apparatuses of bureaucracy in ways that vary between different national cultures. Britain, for example celebrates its homage to 'the calculative' with a huge army of account-ants (150 000 which, per head of population, is about 50 times as many as West Germany and several times as many as the USA).

The calculative has behind it an aura of responsible impartiality and objectivity. The intellectual and scientific foundations of this objectiv-ity are rarely examined; and so altogether insubstantial concepts transmute into rock-firm belief in well-established practices of experts. These practices then lend support to emotive 'common sense' via such phrases as 'value for money' and 'proven efficiency'. The virtuous-sounding quality of efficiency, for example, when calculated amounts often to little more than a tautology: the ultimate criteria of efficiency measure the money costs against the money value of output and so prove that 'efficient firms make money' which being translated is saying that 'firms that make money make money'.

The connection between the calculative and bureaucracy is a subtle one. Obviously calculations are helpful to decision-making; but they don't give final answers. They are always and necessarily based on models that represent only partial aspects of a totality using measure-ments that are necessarily imprecise. They take from the multi-faceted richness of reality particular quantitative aspects and apply to these such measures as are available and convenient to their purposes. Very naturally bureaucracy does not advertise the limitations of its skills and the subjective judgements that enter into choice of measures. On the contrary a *cardinal rule* of bureaucratic conduct is to energetically assert that its mastery of the techniques of the calculative enables it to reach indubitable conclusions and gives it the right to make judgements on behalf of society. The calculative becomes both instrument of power and the ideological justification of how power is used. It defends both the established economic order and with it, 'occupationally' one might say, the bureaucratic apparatus that serves it.

In this environment concepts substantiated by the calculative take on a life of their own. The products of substanceless calculations become practical realities that guide decisions and govern social behaviour. PSBR and Money Supply have already been cited as calculative concepts guiding national policy. Numerous calculative concepts provide norms governing the management of institutions of various kinds, ranging from corporations or nationalised industries to social services, hospitals and local government departments. Over recent years domination of policy and justification of policy by calculative norms has developed extensively, and implementation of policy by laying down calculative limits has become the hallmark of the Thatcher administration's style.

False concepts become real. What is false in the sense that claims cannot be substantiated by verifiable fact, nonetheless becomes a real organiser of real social activities. These activities implement policies that are influentially supported and 'the scientific validity' of the concepts is, as it were, overridden by a 'validity of activities' whose proof is power to prevail in the tug-of-war of social forces. Certain ideas prevail because championed by the powerful; in the arena of political power jousting, as in feudal times, is the test of 'truth'.

A calculative concept of considerable political force, cited in justification of policies and made a target towards which nations are urged to direct their energies, is the Gross National Product. This is deemed to measure the totality of economic achievement quantitatively. But what in fact is measured? Calculative techniques combine into a single index a multiplicity of different things: carrots are added to computers and computers are added to package-holidays! How? By adding their prices. But what do prices measure? Only what you pay to buy things – and this changes from year to year and changes differently for different things. So an arbitrary *fixed-time* reference base is chosen for an index that purports to measure *change over time*. If price relativities at a different point of time are chosen as the base the index moves quite differently and may reverse its direction of movement. In fact this famous index claiming to measure the ultimate reality of economic growth, measures only, albeit in somewhat disguised form, totalities of exchange values. It says virtually nothing about how well the economy has served social needs. Exchange-values, that is, monetary values fixed by the automatisms of the market, in no way correspond, as is well known, to social needs. Can five thousand loaves be said in any sense at all to correspond to one diamond? So it cannot be for any intellectual reason that the concept of GNP remains unchallenged; it holds its ground only because in the tug-of-war of social forces, the energetic production of exchange-values that the GNP concept motivates has a lot of political weight on its side. The values measured by this calculation are the values of the money-system; it totally excludes such values as moral and aesthetic worth, creativity, health, happiness and well-being, the interests of unborn generations and much else besides.

What alternatives are there to 'the regime of the calculative'? To find these should not be a problem – but somehow the calculative and the quantitative mesmerise. Here is the domain of the expert, 'the people who know best'. Only by shaking ourselves awake from this mesmerisation, by putting aside a social psychology that has become almost second nature, can we see how narrowly this ethos now disciplines us. The ethos tells ordinary folk to stand back and let others take social decisions for them. To find alternatives to the calculative, relax and set aside for the moment the proprieties of public institutions and think of how we conduct ourselves naturally in the course of everyday life. We look about us, consult our feelings and decide what to do. We may make a few calculations but these are secondary; primarily we let ourselves be guided by a many-sided awareness. By analogy in wider social life the essential alternative to the 'calculative' is a collective consciousness (that is, a consciousness we share with others with whom we work or live) to which the realities of what is going on 'in public life' *is made clearly visible*. For all the pretences of impersonal objectivity with which weighty institutions clothe their public appearance, it is more than probable that 'great captains of industry', 'financial geniuses', 'masters in the art of management', 'leaders of exceptional ability' do not so much rely on wizardry with figures or hard-headed calculation of profit-and-loss accounts as on privileged access to wide-ranging information that enables them to see and feel situations as they are and what is likely to happen if they take one or another course of action.

PUTTING POLITICS BACK INTO ECONOMICS

How do such considerations translate into concepts that bear on the democratisation of economics? Is there then no 'scientific element' in economics at all? Is economics in reality just disguised politics? Or is economics wholly a matter of values? Clearly, in developing a critique of the calculative, there is a danger of focusing exclusively on its use as ideology instrument by the bureaucracy that today services transnational capital and the State. So to do would be as one-sided as the one-sidedness that is criticised. Since societies are many facetted organisms, democratic economics and 'a socially useful economy' have to take account of the totality as a totality. The scientific element in economics hinges upon understanding the inner logic of particular modes of production and distribution, the dynamic of the relationships between

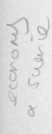

people that activates human cooperation for economic ends. (For example, in a capitalist market economy people work to get money, the substance into which economic power is distilled, defining in its use the relationships of buying and selling through which the market system lives.) Scientific analysis sharpens vision but when it comes to social decision-making, the economic and the political fuse. Since the most crucial aspect of social organisation is cooperation for economic activity, the essentials of politics more often than not boil down to justification of economic policies. Calculative justification makes appeal to some supposed objective expertise that impartially measures what is good for us. The socially useful economy in combination with democratic ideals can make its ultimate appeal to human or moral values. It no longer assumes (as did the utilitarian defences of market economics) that exchange-values coincide with social values.

The socially useful economy is grounded in social reality made visible, concretely and qualitatively, so that values – as human or moral values – may be approved or not approved. If the democratic ideal is to be sustained, the approving authority can only be the conscious, collective decision of the individual human beings that it affects. (Here 'democratic' implies that people themselves control economic activities in which they themselves are engaged or by which they are significantly affected.) Escape from the 'regime of the calculative' to the 'regime of democratic morality' implies an asking back of authority which society, as it were, surrendered to 'market forces'. How in practical terms to recover what now market-economies have in their charge, is indeed the complex conundrum underlying the development of the socially useful economy.

It is perhaps curious that the 'regime of the calculative' has been so uncritically accepted by academics and by popular 'common sense'. Once criticism starts a host of weaknesses quickly come to light and economic thought is, as it were, liberated from a straitjacket, but this very liberation carries with it dangers of rushing to opposite extremes, equating the quantitative, for example, with bureaucracy and requiring democratic economics to make only qualitative choices. But obviously social cooperation that overrides market criteria will require appropriate quantitative measures as instruments with which to help the planning of exchanges between units and sectors of the economy. Quantitative measures are necessarily partial and limited models of reality; but just as maps of rail connections represent the reality only as caricatures represent faces, they are nonetheless practically useful, provided their limitations are well understood. The danger is not in quantitative measures as such, but in allowing their validity and limitations to be lost to sight and turning them into camouflage to disguise the real consequences and social significance of economic policies. If quantitative measures are used it is essential that their meaning and limitations are open and clear. For example, the GNP as a measure of 'economic progress' is highly dubious because its meaning is obscure and it misinforms human motivations. By contrast to count the number of 'unemployed' defined as people who want jobs and can't get them (despite some ambiguities also in this measure) is to produce a measure whose meaning is much more open and clear. If employment and unemployment were taken as central measures of economic activity, they would not, of course, take account of energy, skill or effectiveness of organisation, but what they do measure would be clearly understood and they would direct economic thinking towards the use of human resources as a goal of policy. To boycott the quantitative from democratic economics would be to trade one fetish for another. The point is to clearly assess the meaning and limitations of quantitative measures, to consider also their practical implications, the motivations and consequences to which their use leads, and to beware of allowing them to take on a life of their own.

Economics itself is a body of ideas whose significance is practice, political and moral as well as scientific and representational. To present economics as no more than objective scientific analysis of sociological situations (how people cooperate, what motivates them, laws governing economic processes and so forth) in itself implies that practical responsibility lies only with experts who are required to make sound analyses and with 'rulers' – be they elected politicians, princes or dictators – who 'govern' the mass of people. If democracy is more than occasional votes to delegate authority to representatives and if economics is more than accommodation to self-regulating markets or plans determined by authority at the centre, then economic decision-making has to pass down to people at 'the base'. This necessitates before all else the democratisation of information. Only so can individuals and groups at the grassroots make sound, realistic choices. They will also need shared concepts of the working of the economy as a whole to guide and motivate cooperation. General understanding of the purposes that economic activity serves and the inter-relationships between people in the economy as a whole is the starting point of democratic consciousness. The first step from subordination to a system that seems external to us is understanding of the collective organisms, in industry and in the community, of which we are ourselves part. Heightened consciousness of the situations and organisations of which we ourselves are part immediately generates desire for change and a vision of possible directions of change. (This in fact was the experience of the Lucas Aerospace Combine Shop Stewards' Committee in the decade from 1969.) The practice of monitoring and seeking change teaches understanding, explores means of controlling the use of resources and defines aims to be pursued.

It has been seen how economic concepts of dubious scientific validity become powerful social organisers in the implementation of monetarist policies. To effect change from such policies towards a socially useful economy requires more than a critique of monetarist ideas and the economics of market competition. It requires the development of economic understanding adapted to and shaped by the experience of people themselves in the basic social organisms, in industry and in the community, where the living practice of economic cooperation produces and distributes the goods that keep society alive and give substance to its distinctive characteristics.

NOTES

This Chapter has drawn heavily on papers by Professors Harris and Hopwood.

1. Extract from Paper by Professor Laurence Harris to Seminar held on 28 February 1984 (with very minor editorial changes).
2. Extract from Professor Anthony Hopwood's Paper to the Seminar on 28 February 1984 (with very minor editorial changes).

4 The Politics of Technology

Such is the world in which we find ourselves – a world which, judged by the only acceptable criterion of progress, is manifestly in regression. Technological advance is rapid. But without progress in charity, technological advance is useless. Technological progress has merely provided us with more efficient means of going backwards.

Aldous Huxley, *Ends and Means* (1937)

INTRODUCTION

The myth of technology is that science and ingenious applications of sophisticated engineering or chemical skills will make life better for everyone, once we have adjusted ourselves to the new style of work and work organisation that 'new technology' makes necessary. The reality is altogether different. New technology only incidentally, indeed only accidentally, brings social benefits. The dynamism by which it is developed is an urgent pursuit of success dictated by competition; the main thrusts of new technology are chosen by those who manage the major international conglomerations of capital. They seek – and by the logic of competition to survive they are compelled to seek – greater and greater commercial strength and to this end the question they ask the technologists to answer for them is 'How can we make our control over the resources we possess more effective?'. The same question is asked by autocracies in so-called socialist countries to an increasing extent too. For whilst conventional 'commercial strength' may not be the ostensible reason for seeking to develop new technologies in such countries, the global pressures of transnational capitalism certainly do impinge heavily on their technologies and their economies, and 'technological progressivism' is used as much as a defence as an offensive tool in world markets. Many countries which are not ostensibly in the league of so-called developed nations feel that they *have to* import current technolo-

78

gies simply in order not to slip even further down the international league of economic strength, and thus political significance.

So technology is aimed at devising productive processes that management can control with precision; and this means processes in which managment is not dependent upon labour and can make good use of any literate, disciplined workers in more or less any part of the world. New ways of organising production that simplify the labour input, often will so reduce costs as to make consumer goods available to lower income groups. In this sense the new methods may be 'socially useful'; but any gains for society at large that capitalist competition may generate are only incidental to its motivating purpose. By the same token the new technology also 'incidentally' generates much that is socially harmful.

The vast technological potential of our times may be a great force for ill every bit as much as for good. But around new technology an ideology of 'progress' is exhaled, encouraging the false belief that new technology is *in itself* good. The style and external atmosphere that emanates from the technologies introduced by dominant institutions colours more and more aspects of social life – creating blindness to the real meaning of the uses to which they are in fact being put and to their consequences and side-products. This false ideology of 'advanced technology' is extremely dangerous. It encourages the belief that all we have to do is to give technology its head, encourage limitless expenditure on the invention of new devices and await humanity's glorious future. The whole difficulty of our present situation is that what needs to be done is precisely the opposite – every new technical 'advance' needs to be questioned and only accepted, if accepted at all, when the ends it is serving are well understood and when it has been adapted to suit those who use it and those whose needs it meets. The problem is to find a starting point for action that develops collective consciousness of technological purpose and that exerts control over it. Most obviously one point from which to begin is trade union negotiation over technical change.

TECHNOLOGY CHOICE

The influences that trade union negotiation and workers' reactions had on choice of technologies were the subject of a good deal of discussion, reflecting the views and experiences of negotiators, technologists and theoreticians. Robin Williams' paper explored this:

'Views of Technology

The traditional left-wing perspective on technology has been criticised for conceiving technological change as either a 'progressive' force (which would increasingly reveal the social contradictions of capitalism) or as a neutral and inevitable process.

In contrast, the 'New Left' analysis saw technology as embodying 'social relations', and indeed as reflecting the needs of the ruling class (in the spheres of military, industrial process and consumer goods technology alike). For example, Braverman saw in the current round of technological change the means for deskilling, routinising and controlling labour. Such analyses tended toward political/economic determinism. It is no coincidence that this tendency was strongest in the USA and was associated with particular strands of fundamentalist political thought.

Neither approach is adequate. The latter has been of value in stimulating debate, but was of little help in getting to grips with the increasing number of political struggles on technological issues that were emerging during the 1970s. The most significant of these concentrated on 'single issues' – the environment, military technology etc. The concept of social need (or 'socially-useful technology') would appear to offer a means to integrate these separate concerns and counterpose them to the 'needs of capital'. However there is a severe problem in assuming that, in any given situation, an alternative technology exists which embodies different 'social values' – some sort of alternative, utopian technological universe, paralleling our own capitalist world. To address this issue adequately, a more complex model is needed which avoids a deterministic approach, and gives weight to both the opportunities and the limits to influencing technological development.

Limits – to Determination and Choice

It is necessary to avoid economic (over) determinism. Technology must be recognised as a means of conducting production (etc.) processes with given labour and material inputs, as well as a part of (capitalist) society. New technologies produce use values as well as achieving profitable production. They are subject to technical as well as social constraints and promoted by scientific developments. It is not sufficient to make the teleological assumption of identity between 'the needs of capital' and the steps of technological development in a capitalist society. For example, a technological advance which allows a production process to be operated with a dramatic reduction in the labour and materials input required is likely to prevail (albeit with some variations) under a range of social and economic systems. Similarly, it is not very useful to dismiss the development of new consumer goods which have achieved mass markets as 'production for profit' while ignoring the 'social need' for the products, expressed in people's willingness to buy.

I am not arguing here for a return to the 'traditional' Left view of technology as random or independent of social forces, but merely for a model which is adequate to understanding the social process of technological change in all its complexity, and is therefore able to guide our attempts to control this process. This involves recognising the means by which we can influence the process of technological development and the scope for technological choice. Here we come up against the problem of selectivity of the technological process – with the result that one technological model will tend to predominate. Future technologies are typically built on the foundation of earlier technological development and thus may be affected by the existing 'technological trajectory', as well as market forces, corporate strategy, state intervention, 'popular' pressure, technical problems etc. In certain circumstances (e.g. competition between capitals, market fragmentation) divergent models for a given technological application may continue.

It is important to distinguish the different phases in the technological process and the timescale of influence. The location and controlling forces of technological development will vary from the innovation, development, diffusion, and application of a technology. At the 'application' end, there may appear to be a high degree of choice in the short-term (e.g. between different manufacturers' products), which operates within the broader (and less visible) constraints of the longer term development of the technology. The scope for immediate choice in technologies is not uniform – for example there is clearly much more flexibility of application of computer-based information systems than for new production equipment.

Notes on a Strategy for Technological Choice

A central theme of this talk is that there are a wide range of opportunities to influence the process of technological choice in the interest of popular need/objectives, and that the political process in general, and the politics of technology in particular, require that the progressive movement adopt a 'hegemonic' strategy for dealing with technology:

(1) that intervenes across the variety of sites and phases of techno-
    logical development;
(2) that goes beyond polemic and develops a concrete and (technically
    a well as politically) viable policy; and
(3) that develops through a set of alliances between different social
    groups, with the objective of constructing a counter-hegemony to
    'corporate technology'.

The important role of the state in shaping technological development
– by regulating the potential hazards of technology, by conducting basic
scientific research and education, and in funding military and industrial
R & D both in state and private establishments, provides opportunities
for democratic political influence. The 'old left' strategy was criticised
for centring its perspective on winning formal control over state
apparatuses/policy (which sections of the 'new left' conversely dis-
counted as impossible). A hegemonic strategy would in addition seek to
influence the technological process through the direct involvement of
those groups affected (e.g. workers or consumers) as well as through
broader social institutions (e.g. the professional organisations of
technologists). In addition to direct control longer-term and informal
means of influence would be sought focussing in particular on the key
role of technologists and their relationship with society (for example, by
shaping the political attitudes to technology at a societal level or the
training of technologists).

It is interesting to note in this respect the policy developed by the
Swedish Trade Union movement to make a comprehensive intervention in the development of research policy – not only by seeking
enhanced representation on the national state research agencies, but by
representation on the governing bodies of universities etc and very
importantly, by contact with the academic researchers themselves.
Industrial democracy legislation was called for to extend union influence to include corporate R & D.

A variety of opportunities exist for exerting political and economic
pressure regarding the application of technology within private
industry. However, the traditional methods of exerting popular power
may not be very effective. For example shop-floor bargaining can be
characterised as reactive, short-term, focussing on a narrow range of

issues, acting on 'line' rather than strategic management levels, and divorced from the processes of technological design. It is frequently 'sectional' – directed towards a particular group of workers, let alone other groups that may be affected. The weaknesses have been stated rather baldly – certainly attempts have been made to overcome some of these limitations. Other methods of popular pressure are much less well developed.

Any attempts to control the application of technology must build on those channels that already exist, but need also to be informed by an alternative vision of technology, and a longer term strategy that for example links the needs of the group in struggle with those of other groups (e.g. workers, residents, consumers) and with the general social interest.

The recent response by the TUC to the current round of technological change based on microelectronics can be seen as an attempt to develop a 'hegemonic' strategy. The trade unions had a major influence over the early development of the 'employment and technology' debate. The TUC policy not only sought to articulate workers interests, but also posed the trade union movement as representing a general social interest surrounding technological change – in contrast to the narrow economic approach of companies.

Thus far the discussion has dealt with the control of technology in general terms. The remaining section will look more concretely at the problems that have surrounded attempts by trade unions to influence a specific aspect – the introduction of computer-based technology in the workplace.

The Design of Computer-Based Systems in the Workplace

In 1979 the TUC and many individual unions developed policies for dealing with the introduction of microelectronic-based technology at the workplace. A major plank in achieving their objectives was to be via an extension of company/plant level bargaining to include technological development. Specific safeguards and procedures were to be established by negotiating 'New Technology Agreements'. (It is worth noting that the original TUC policy sought tripartite agreements with companies and the state by an extension of the idea of 'Planning Agreements' – however this idea seems to have evaporated after the election of a Conservative government.)

This was a radical development of union policy. Like traditional union policies it sought government and employer action to 'ease the transition' by retraining displaced workers, etc. However in addition the unions sought to influence the process of technological decision making itself – to safeguard workers against some of the more negative effects that had been predicted as arising from new technology (e.g. on jobs, health and safety, work pace, etc.) and to ensure that the benefits of new technology were 'equitably' shared.

Five years later, it is clear that the actual achievements have been far more modest. Formal technology agreements have been negotiated in a minority of companies and have typically been signed by four white collar unions (APEX, ASTMS, NALGO or TASS) on their own or in combination. A major reason for this uneven distribution would appear to be union policy. Whilst workers in many companies have established the principle of some form of consultation in advance of the introduction of technological change, both the scope of union involvement and the safeguards achieved fall far short of union objectives. This state of affairs must be seen in the context of the rapidly worsening economic and political circumstances, but cannot be reduced to this.

'Thatcherism' and the acute process of industrial restructuring in Britain have been accompanied by the promulgation of a model of industrial development based on economic and technological determinism, with minimal involvement by trade unions in decision-making. There is widespread assent to this viewpoint – that total acceptance of technological change is necessary for industrial recovery. Corporate plans for technological change go largely unchallenged; attempts by affected workers to refuse change are seen as backward looking and sectional, and are typically defeated (if not at first, then in the long run). Some accounts would appear to suggest that the process of technological change is going ahead with no influence by unions/workers.

Less attention has been given to a significant development in the approach amongst certain professionals concerned with the design and implementation of computer-based systems. They have emphasised the need to take 'social' considerations into account in introducing technological change, and consequently stress:

(1) the potential for choice in the design of computer-based systems; and
(2) the need for worker ('user') involvement in their introduction.

Whilst this approach is doubtless in part an expression of the social/ political concerns of the practitioners involved, it also reflects some of the real problems of the process of technological change.

This paper suggests that union and radical policies for controlling technology in the workplace are informed by a misleading model of technological change and have consequently failed to utilise important opportunities for influence. Case studies of decision-making and negotiation of technological change in a range of industries have diverged substantially from the 'deterministic'/'Thatcherite' model. In particular it becomes clear that, although trade unions have not been able to articulate and implement their own objectives for technological change, winning the consent of workers to the change remained a central managerial objective. Underlying this 'need for consent' was management's reliance on worker cooperation and skills in implementing the new technology and achieving productive goals. The need for consent was not uniform – for instance it was focused on those groups of workers who had strong trade union organisation as well as necessary skills and experience for operating the new technology, and was least marked *inter alia* with low-skill workers or those to be declared redundant.

There were substantial differences in the decision-making and negotiation process according to the social and technical difficulties of the change being implemented – in some cases management was able to plan the introduction of change on a five year time scale, in others an ad hoc implementation and negotiation strategy was necessary. Either way, the model of technological change that pertained was far removed from Braverman's view of technology as essentially certain in its implementation.

Equally it is clear that there were often substantial benefits to workers from accepting technological change (in contrast to Braverman's view of technology as an instrument in management attempts to deskill the position of labour) – sometimes these benefits were sectional (e.g. improving the grading, job security or skills of current employees, possibly at the expense of other workers in the firm, or those outside the labour market). In contrast, trade union policies (following new left analysis) emphasised the negative aspects of new technology and failed to grasp the benefits available. In some cases, union negotiators seeking to regulate the rate or conditions of introduction of technological change found themselves outflanked by their members who were keen to get their hands on the new systems.

Problems in Applying Union Strategy

In the cases examined, the difficulties experienced by the trade unions in developing and implementing their perspective over technological change were substantial. We can distinguish problems of union structure/organisation, policy/access to expertise, and legitimacy of role.

The trade union organisation was built (i.e. divided) around the pre-existing division of labour/technology. Different bargaining groups exhibited radically differing strategies for achieving their objectives – especially where the basis on which union organisation was built differed. The differences of approach between different groups of workers had a long tradition and were extremely deeply rooted in the daily activity of the union. (For example attempts in two of the plants to develop a joint forum for handling technological change that spanned the division between 'white' and 'blue' collar workers, by signing a technology agreement with the company. In both cases these attempts broke down when put to the test of real life.) Within this fragmented structure and divergent basis of union organisation, the interests of different groups of workers are often counterposed. This is particularly problematic where a division of labour/work organisation established under one production technology is replaced by another technology embodying a different division of labour. This union structure may constrain the policies that the unions are able to develop.

The unions only rarely made a fundamental challenge to the basis of management decisions regarding technological change. What was needed to challenge the management proposals, but was largely absent from the union response, was an alternative vision of how technology might be introduced, and the information and other resources needed to sustain and apply that vision. The union representatives did not have access to technical expertise and information available to management, and lacked the time and facilities to develop their own responses. In most cases they did not have alternative models or criteria to assess or criticise management proposals for technology. National union policy documents might provide general descriptions of union objectives regarding technology, but concrete policy was in the main lacking. The major exception here was on health and safety – over which a consistent union intervention was achieved. However it is possible to define safety guidelines on a central basis that will be appropriate to a range of working situations, whereas it is much harder to codify union objectives for other aspects of technology. Such an approach would require a substantial increase in union resources and expertise and might only be possible at local level. These problems have been discussed in greater depth elsewhere.

Whilst it is easy to identify a range of 'structural' obstacles that might frustrate attempts by union representatives to develop an alternative vision of the technology, it is not clear that these factors constituted a barrier in any practical sense on a day-to-day basis. Although union policies for technological change called for representation and influence by union members in corporate decision making from the earliest stages, there was much more ambiguity amongst union members and representatives about the role that unions should adopt. This seemed to stem partly from direct assent to the lines of managerial prerogative, supplemented amongst union representatives in particular by a desire to remain 'at arms length' from the managerial function for fear that the union would become incorporated within management's outlook.'

In such a many-faceted situation the problem facing organised labour is to see what means it has of controlling technological change – and this is a far from easy problem to solve, involving as it does the weighing of short-term advantages, or advantages for a few against long-term consequences for the movement as a whole. The problems that arise include the long-term direction of the economy as a whole at one end and day to day working conditions at the other. Moreover, since effective action includes understanding and conviction on the part of the grassroot membership of organisations through which action is taken, the Babel of conflicting ideologies with which the media invade the deliberations of workers' organisations, does not make matters easier. Indeed the media have become the 'Fifth Estate' of modern politics. This is a terrain in which Labour has to start building almost from scratch to create democratic means of communication capable of shaping a collective will and winning allies from society at large in support of resistance to the established oligarchies of wealth and administrative control over the economy.

LANGUAGE OF TECHNOLOGY

Rather like Public Sector Borrowing Requirement the term 'technology' has been a relatively recent introduction to everyday political, social and economic language. It has somehow come to mean more than technical change, more than automation, it has come to embody a very wide ranging phenomenon of technical development. Indeed technology itself somehow seems to imply something which is changing and progressing at a rate which is vastly 'superior' to that described for instance by 'technical change'. In going back to its linguistic roots technology is in essence supposed to be the study of the art of technics (note the 'art'). Perhaps, just as mechanics and mechanisms were used in that other era of technological progressivism in the late nineteenth and early twentieth century, so has technology come to denote step-function increases or changes in the applications of science in post-war years. Thus is technology now reified; it has come to mean more than the mechanisms and the way that things work, it has almost become a *philosophy* to many people. So, just as mechanics are somehow regarded as outmoded, something from another age (e.g. Dr David Owen's contention that 'smokestack industries' have to give way to 'sunrise industries'), so has technology come to encompass and denote types of material progress which are supposed to bring in the dawn of a new age of prosperity or whatever, i.e. the import from the USA of the idea of sunrise industries and sunrise technologies.

Within this new ideology of technological progressivism there are several segmentations, such as high technology, new technology, appropriate technology, leading edge technologies and the like. The power of the language is indeed significant, for 'low technologies' come to denote backyard enterprise, whilst Hi-Tech is firmly embedded in rich and 'progressive' organisations. Great difficulties are caused by this and there has been much discussion about appropriate technologies for the Third World for instance. (It is interesting to note that appropriate technologies are thought to be good for those people 'over there' but not for us in Britain, or the West, or the rich North.)

The day-to-day separation of technological alternatives from social or political choice is a profound one in itself, and is largely achieved through the developing ideology of high-technology progress. For to engage in high technology or new technology endeavours is to imply access to substantial resources, usually money or so-called experts, in order to produce equipment and systems for satellite communications, defence electronics, or the (largely unknown) fruits of bio-engineering. Yet we as 'ordinary people' deal with technologies of a completely different order to that proposed by the ideology of technological progressivism.

A one-bar electric fire may be a simple though expensive technology for heating a room in a house, but the electricity that drives it may come from a nuclear power technology which in real economic and political

terms has absolutely nothing to do with our actual end-use of technology. We may own a new car which has been sculpted to provide an
extraordinary low drag co-efficient and which contains a range of
electronic gadgetry and is thus regarded as 'Hi-Tech', but which
provides us with a range of very difficult problems in use, such as lack of
easy repairability, or very high nominal cost of spares etc. The technology of road travel itself is basically two hundred years old or more which
means that our latest 'Hi-Tech' car may well spend the majority of its
time travelling at less than 20 miles an hour, where the drag co-efficient
is absolutely irrelevant and the electronic gadgetry is to all intents and
purposes useless.

WHOSE LOGIC?

In truth, the 'logic of production' is an innate determinant of the level of
technology employed in a particular artifact, where use value or the
'logic of use' may often be very secondary. The outer limits of
information technology for instance are very unlikely under present
circumstances to provide any significant gain for ordinary telephone
users; what we have is a whole new range of business services –
technologies to serve big business and finance, and it's only if it's
'convenient' in conventional market terms that 'us ordinary people' will
gain any significant benefit from satellite telecommunications or the
like. In the so-called advanced countries technology has been essentially hi-jacked by money power interests and has lifted-off from the
realities of everyday life to the extent that even some quite large
corporations now regard things like engineering as being unnecessary,
unprofitable and undesirable (it being an 'old technology').

We are told that what we are witnessing is an Information Revolution,
that we shall become information workers in the 'Post Industrial'
Society. Information it is agreed is a resource more precious than oil and
gold. The significance of new technology is that it is not just creating new
products. It replaces human mental processes with 'electronic intelligence', and makes access to information instantaneous. But the
channels of *communication* through which information of any kind must
flow remain in the hands of bureaucratic institutions. The ability of
vested interests to collect, organise, distribute information and to
control the flows of information confer enormous power of social
control, not social use. Information technology can be used to deprive
people of information, not necessarily to provide better information.

The new powerful hardware systems which make up the 'wired' society provide 'one way power' through which the daily activities of industrial citizens can be monitored without permission.

There is of course an economic reality under present circumstances of high technology or new technology providing a product/market base for very highly profitable endeavours. Of course much of the direction of technological change is determined by that simple fact. In some senses high technology is supposed to mean the creation of more from less, thus do silicon chips provide mathematical-style manipulations with miniature components, but at the same time we must remember that major parts of those components depend upon very low paid womens' work in the Far East, where the actual costs in terms of poor health and safety are immense. Therefore what can be seen as 'getting more for less' perhaps in terms of the amount of material used may have a very different meaning if looked at from a point of view of other interests, such as that of labour.

It is wrong to reduce all aspects of high technology or new technology to the sole interests of those who wish to increase value-added or surplus-value through the exchange value mechanism, but much of the practice and all of the ideology of technological progressivism can reasonably be laid at the door of those private interests. This is supported by the extraordinarily uneven development of different technologies in society. We are still building houses whose living characteristics are in many ways inferior to those built a hundred years ago or more; we still assume that partially sighted or blind people should have only a white stick to guide them and not some version of sophisticated radar and related technologies which are so important in the defence sector; we have the extraordinary hype of home computing but according to many studies the vast majority of these are used solely or mainly for variations of the 'space invaders' types of games. Professor David Noble in his book *America by Design*[1] clearly shows up the way in which the chemicals and tele-communications industries developed in the USA through the self-interest of just a few corporations (that also ruthlessly stole and suppressed certain inventions and applications if they did not fit in their current policies).

Bearing in mind the extraordinary impact of technologies on just about every sphere of human activity it is remarkable to say the least, that Technology Policy, as such, simply does not exist in national political life.

At the very least it is clear that we have to start trying to find ways of talking about technological choice and options in as many areas of life as possible. Production technologies may suit the interests of a corporation but be damaging in a great many respects to the labour force, for example. A new process may throw thousands of people out of work and the costs of keeping those people unemployed then falls upon the State, whereas the same corporation may well be receiving large amounts of income from the public purse in the form of orders, regional grants, tax concessions and the like – so the question of technology choice and production is clearly part of the wider economic and social scene. The adulteration of food through the 'logic' of the requirements of agribusiness causes, according to a lot of unimpeachable opinion, enormous health problems in the population, which obviously has economic consequences as well as grim social and individual implications. Energy policy, the choice between differing technologies in energy generation is a crucial issue in respect of fuel costs, and obviously has enormous long-term economic consequences for every aspect of life, including the extraordinarily troublesome issue of resource depletion in the longer term and all that that implies, not only in terms of the nation state but also in terms of international relations and even international tensions.

TO APPROPRIATE A TECHNOLOGY?

As Robin Williams pointed out, it is however important for us to separate out conceptually and through practical means the difference between technological choice where technology is deeply embedded in the private interests of the money power, and technologies that are thus derived but which may be liberatory. Very few technologies are politically or socially neutral, and side by side with a critique and criticism of existing technologies we must find means of re-appropriating certain technologies to maximise their social use – completely new and useful applications of information technology is a case in point.

While recognising that modern science, engineering, chemical and biological applications of knowledge, and contemporary modes of the division of labour integrated into vast systems of social cooperation, take many widely varying forms, it is nonetheless right to see that what is essentially new and technologically revolutionary is the harnessing of electrons as instruments to transmit, process and store information. This new thing is reified and symbolised in 'the Computer' – the qualitative leap in this new instrumentation derives from:

(1) speed of operation (typically measured in 'nanoseconds' i.e. in a thousand millionth of a second);
(2) smallness of size (typically some thousands of 'logical units' using molecular structures, assembled on areas of 1mm square); and
(3) economies of time and material in manufacture (e.g. photolithographically) and of energy in use.

This key technology was discussed from the standpoint of the industry today – producing computers and computer systems, and also from the standpoint of trade union organisation negotiating about its introduction and impact. Martin Stears addressed this in his paper:

'Definition and Demystification

Much of the discussion on ' New Technology' leaves people in some confusion as to exactly what this 'New Technology' is. So I will start with a definition of what I shall be talking about:

I take New Technology to be 'Any process or system controlled or assisted by computer, which is in turn controlled by a company of human users.'

The second part of the definition I take to be necessary for an understanding of the essential nature of computers and, by 'company' I mean the organisation which owns and uses the process or system. I have chosen the word deliberately because I believe that any discussion of New Technology must involve a discussion of the structure of the group of people who own, control and operate it. I rejected the word 'community' as implying a common interest which is not necessarily present.

Computers on their own can do nothing; they are *Tools* of human beings. I have heard computers described as supremely efficient idiots. There is something in this, which draws from their origins as very fast calculating machines, which have the nasty habit of doing exactly what you tell them to do.

But this is misleading. A better description is that there are certain human processes that can be extended by programming a computer, such as memory, calculation, sorting, following a plan, etc. The key difference is that a computer can't do what it wasn't told (i.e. programmed) to do.

That is not to say that computer programs can't be so astonishingly complex that they are impossible to follow. (Whether humans are also programmed by their environment is not part of this paper, but anyone interested in the philosophy of human and computer intelligence could read *Computers and Thought* by Feigenbaum and Feldman, McGraw Hill, 1963.)

Computers, to labour the point, are the agents of their controllers.

A further point on New Technology. I prefer the title Computer Systems or in some circumstances Information Technology, to New Technology in that the latter tends to be used to describe the hardware developments which have enabled greater speed and capacity with reduced size at a cheaper price, while leaving out the equally important developments in Computer languages and software.

In order to talk about Computer Systems in a way that keeps what we are saying anchored to reality and as far as possible free from jargon, we need a simplified model (see figure) of what a computer can and can't do. We all have a role to play in de-mystifying technology. In essence computers are simple to use and their use can be taught step by step. That's why they are taking off with children faster than with adults. I would suggest this is potentially a good development as an accessible

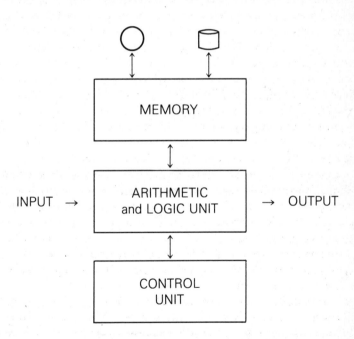

FIGURE   A simplified model of a computer

technology is more likely to be socially useful than one hiding behind a high-priesthood of computer professionals. So we must develop a non-technical language of discourse ourselves.

A computer is a general device for processing and storing information. As I have said earlier, computers started off making calculations until it was discovered that you could generalise this process into any manipulation of symbols. If the symbols represent real things in the outside world they become information.

A computer's memory may be as large and as complex as the available storage and may be structured as a database to allow easy and consistent retrieval of information.

Its input may be readings on values in an oil refinery or bar codes on a tin of tomatoes read at the check-out of a supermarket or a line of type on a VDU. Its output may be an instruction to the arm of a robot or a precise drawing on a blueprint or a line of type on paper or VDU.

The arithmetic and logic unit may be asked to select information or make a calculation or a choice depending on the value of its input.

The control unit reads the program, which is also an item of information stored in the memory, and operates the other units.

That quite simply is a description common to every general-purpose digital computer, from the smallest micro to the largest mainframe.

The Economics of New Technology

There are two basic messages I want to get across:

(1) The introduction of Computer-based systems confers the power on its *owners* and *controllers* to get more done for less work expended and in particular to eliminate in turn particular types of work. Since in general the position of all groups of workers is based on a particular type of work (i.e. there is a division of labour) there is no protection in holding a particular currently scarce skill. That has been the basis of craft Trade Unionism and before that of the Craft Guilds. It is however not the only basis of Trade Unionism and has always been extremely sectional.
(2) The potential is there in the Information Technology based on Computers, and parallel developments, for people to be liberated from useless toil, either to increasing opportunities for leisure, consumption, education and so on; or to poverty and despair.

Put simply the introduction of New Technology brings to a head the contradictions of capital accumulation and the profit-based market system. 'Who controls what for whom?' is given increasing weight by the change in relationship between the owners of capital and the providers of labour. The basic contradiction must be faced that the market still requires them to be consumers after it has apparently ceased to require them as producers. *That is why the constantly re-emerging theme in this seminar series of workers realising their power as consumers is so important.*

A training in Systems Design has led me to believe that it is necessary to consider the Economic System as a whole as well as the sum of its parts. It is interesting to note in this connection that people with as different a perspective as Stafford Beer, an advisor to Salvador Allende, and John Hoskyns, an advisor to Margaret Thatcher, have also taken this view and a study of their work would be instructive.

I am no economist however, although I believe we have to make economics more accessible if popular planning is to become a reality. It is therefore with trepidation that I present the following diagrams as my attempts as a non-economist to understand what is happening economically in terms of two alternative models of what might happen.

Current factors + Computer Systems – Less work, Same surplus (or use) value
Less work → less consumption
Less consumption → less value *therefore* downward spiral

Current factors + Computer Systems – More Surplus (or use) value, Same work
More value → more consumption
More consumption → more value *therefore* upward spiral

Why then do we seem to be following the first model and not the second? I should like to make two propositions.

First, the current factors are not stable, but are changing. Multinational corporations are using the opportunities given by technological change to shop around for cheaper labour thus producing less consumption leading to less work, etc. In other words things are already on a downward spiral.

The computer industry is a prime example of this. The silicon chips required for the great leaps forward are produced most often by the grossest of exploitation of the weakest groups of workers, such as young women in Malaysia who are cast on the scrapheap at 28 through failing eyesight. The first industrial revolution was paralleled by the growth of empire and a particular type of exploitation of raw materials. The second has its international dimension also.

The second proposition is that the latter process is more difficult than the former. You can, if you like take the first model as the 'maintenance of existing production and service' model and the second as the 'maintenance of full employment' model. The latter requires investment to be transferred to new production or services to enable more consumption to take place.

I can remember being told in my O-level Economics course that an increasing number of people would be employed in Service Industries as less people were needed for Productive Industries. *In pressing for socially useful products and services we must not underemphasise the need to massively expand services.*

Perhaps incidentally, a way out of our dilemma of finding measures of use value is to start from people rather than from money, as economic measures do. A 'use value' measure should start from a concept of full employment and be a means of fixing priorities for the services we might provide on some cost-benefit scale. (See Chapter 2 for instances.)

The final point is that *our requirements must include control of multinational corporations.* We should, in my view, propose measures to tie them down which can be copied by other, particularly Third World, countries and help the development of transnational Trade Unionism.

The Impacts of Technological Change

It is important to realise from the start that technological change is a complex process without the benefit of a plan or a conspiracy. Management have problems introducing Computer-based processes and are often as much in the dark about the impact as the workforce. The managements that survive however are those that have learnt from their mistakes.

Members take up technology eagerly in the belief that if they don't their firm will go bust, which is worse than losing a few jobs. Where managements come up against resistance they learn to bide their time and introduce new processes in brand new factories, eliminating the old as surplus to requirements.

These processes lead to so-called 'restructuring' with not only redundancies but also the removal of people from one part of the country to another with subsequent disruption of their lives. In my view, and speaking with some feeling, the acceptance of Mobility of Labour as a right of management runs totally counter to developing the socially useful economy. It has been far too easily accepted by the Labour movement.

Often also there is overkill in redundancies in the hope of requiring less workers later, or, for the same reason, 'anticipatory non-recruitment'. This leads to high overtime of a temporary (permanent) nature.

In summary, existing relations of production, exchange, distribution and consumption are embedded in the design of Computer-based Systems as they are introduced, but the impact of the introduction changes those relations to develop, in particular, different requirements for labour and for skills.

In this environment straight opposition is counterproductive. There must be an alternative or alternatives to hand to successfully argue against a particular change.

In order to point the way to how alternative systems, appropriate to developing the socially useful economy, could be put together, I want to describe how Computer-based Systems are designed.

If we want to constrain the development of Computer Technology to a more socially useful direction, then our designs must be more accessible and must take full account of the human user. I am therefore drawing here on material I used recently on a talk on the design of human centred computer systems.

The Design of Computer Systems

In theory, the Systems Analyst analyses the overall system, including the users, and produces a solution based on the requirements of both users and the overall system. In reality the Analyst looks at what is required and either the nearest similar system implemented elsewhere or what software/hardware products are available – already designed of course without taking account of the users. The users, being more flexible than the existing computer products, are then tacked on to the system.

So to get at the place where Human Centred Design should take place we must look at the initial design and development of the software or 'systems'. It is here that the users' needs should be taken account of. One problem is immediately apparent. The designers have absolutely no direct contact with the users. This makes any inclusion of users' requirements at best a matter of guesswork based on experimentation and certainly not a matter of participation.

The TUC in 1979, following a congress decision issued a checklist for negotiating New Technology agreements, one of its requirements was that there should be negotiations over Systems Design. Below are some suggestions for Ground-rules for Human Centred Design, which might also be used as Guidelines for negotiating purposes.

Some Suggested Ground-Rules for Human-Centred Design

(1) Each human user should control (either individually or collectively) the part of the system with which they interact.
(2) Systems should be flexible enough to enable human users to develop their skills and in the work environment to develop their careers and gain increasing responsibility.
(3) Users must not be monitored by or paced by the system (except for the purposes of self-monitoring).
(4) The design of the jobs undertaken by the human controllers must be an integral part of the design of the system at an early stage and must cater for other basic human needs. Most particularly these would include Health, Safety and Job Satisfaction.

Existing design fails to meet these ground-rules. It takes place in an environment of severely restricted resources, where effort is directed to those aspects that will sell.

Let me emphasise this. Does ICL marketing take account of the users when giving the development divisions a statement of market requirements? I asked that question and was told specifically 'no'. *We sell to purchasing managers, not to users.*

Users are not included in the design process as participants. Designers do not control the way their designs are used, and also pass on insufficient record of their designs. This is of particular concern where the products may be used beyond their limitations, for example the horrendous possibility that speech recognition might be used in Air Traffic Control.

Also there is a tendency to design out any flexibility so that users are told what to do, unless they happen to be managers – who will only use non-directive systems themselves.

A Note on Job Design and Deskilling

I want to briefly comment on this because there does seem to be a certain lack of clear thinking on this. We should not be claiming that skills must always be protected, if they do not contribute to the job satisfaction of the person concerned. We must be careful to distinguish between skill loss, skill change, variety as against monotony and responsibility.

Towards the Socially Useful Development of Technology

I want in this final section to tie in with some of the other themes which have emerged from the seminars and make some suggestions for some action and hopefully some progress.

I want to agree fully with the views of John Ball, expressed in an earlier discussion, that Technological change should be used as an opportunity for national campaigns for a Shorter Working Life and for Freedom of Information. It occurs to me that the first industrial revolution led to a Workers' Charter. It would not be inappropriate to look for a Charter appropriate to the second.

I would seek within the first point to include the need for legislation limiting overtime and I would add two demands: the right to socially useful work and the right to democracy and accountability in industry (in this context because control of technological change is so vital).

Alternative proposals for the use of technology are also vital as means of bargaining as well as symbols of the alternative possiblities. We should therefore publish guidelines and checklists.

We should encourage producers of technology to talk to consumers as fellow Trade Unionists (e.g. ICL Combine members have talked to Lucas Aerospace and Metal Box Combine meetings).

We would encourage the formation of a Computers and Telecomms Combine. We should show how technology can be designed in a human-centred, socially useful way.

The problem of the bureaucratic hierarchy has been mentioned as standing in the way of design which takes account of users. Cooperatives have in some cases non-hierarchical structures. A Technology for Cooperatives project would be interesting in this connection.

Technology at the service of the Labour Movement? We should be able to develop Information and Decision Support systems for Trade Unionists and for progressive local authorities.'

POLITICS OF TECHNOLOGY

While the introduction of new technology does not necessarily entail the deskilling of workers, the overall tendency is for management to use this technology as they have always done, to reinforce their control of the work process. Skilled work can be fragmented and then centralised away from the shop floor. New technology provides opportunities for management to accelerate this process especially in work involving hand and brain. Cooley[2] has shown how this occurred in the replacement of the draughtsmen skills by 'computer aided design' software which management can then control. The worker becomes even more alienated from work.

Mumford[3] has pointed out that skilled machinists could be trained in programming so that the whole machining process remains in their hands. Rosenbrock[4] has argued that old and new skills can be integrated in a much more effective way than by simply replacing human skills with new technology. The possibilities are summarised in his image of the 'computer-aided craftsman'.

Technology is the hand maiden [sic] of Economics and also one of its increasingly important ideological representations. The design of technologies is adapted primarily to serve those 'who pay' rather than those who have to work with it or who have to try and use the end results of it. In so doing certain possibilities in wide-ranging social fields are cut off, others are distorted, and yet others are promoted. Furthermore, as we have pointed out elsewhere current production technologies increasingly favour the practices required by the internationalisation of capital, both through the routinisation etc., of labour tasks, and through the corporate and finance-based use of new information technologies. It alienates people at the production and consumption ends by removing skills, subsuming consciousness and experience under so-called objective systems. It is increasingly weakening the bargaining power of organised labour by changing the very ground upon which the bargaining contract between the employee and the employer is based. And it contains seeds of extremely important anti-democratic movements, such as current uses of computing and information technology to privatise work and many other social activities. This is also so because most of us 'ordinary' people are increasingly led to believe that wondrous new technologies will provide us as consumers with untold new artifacts and services. At the same time much is done to make sure that we accept them without question and indeed we are unable to question the basis of these technologies because they are too esoteric or complex for us to understand.

However as we have seen there *are* great possibilities for us to develop information technology, for example through a Freedom of Information programme which would provide significant means for us to start to reverse the current balance of power in society. There may be many other routes that we have to pursue apart from this. Our single most important task perhaps is to raise at least *one issue of technology policy* at a national political level in an effective way.

Democratisation of design and implementation of new systems could well provide us with a strong 'cutting edge'. Why can't we *all* have access to information via a Prestel-like service, that comes with our TV Licence? Such information could and should include people's rights to housing and social welfare provisions, the real level of renumeration of Company Directors, and so on.

The provision of trade union terminals for convenors, stewards and officials who operate in large, multi-site corporations is another possibility of key importance.

Thus could Freedom of Information be bought from an esoteric activity of 'expert' researchers, right into the workplace and the home. It requires dedicated R & D, new investment profiles for computing/ telecommunication operations – but could probably be achieved through a 'diversion' of 5 per cent of current military electronics expenditure! In organisations such as Electronics for Peace, and throughout trade union organisation in the computing/electronics/ telecommunications sector there are a great many people who would readily embark on such a project.

NOTES

1. David Noble, *America by Design* (Oxford University Press, 1979).
2. M.J.E. Cooley, *Computer Aided Design – Its Nature and Implications* was published in 1972 by AUEW TASS of which Mike Cooley was President.
3. Enid Mumford and Mary Weir, *Computer Systems in Work Design – the ETHICS Method* (Associated Business Press). (Ethics stands for Efficient Technical and Human Implementation of Computer Systems.)
4. H.H. Rosenbrock, 'Social and Economic Design for a Flexible Manufacturing System', paper for CAITS seminar on new technology and trade unions, 1984. Professor Rosenbrock's approach to technology is also to be seen in 'The Future of Control', *Automatica,* vol.13, 1977 and *Computer Aided Control System Design* (Academic Press, 1974).

5 The Structure of Authority

God made the wicked Grocer
  For a mystery and a sign,
That man might shun the awful shop
  And go to inns to dine.

G.K. Chesterton

INTRODUCTION

As market forces grew in importance they gradually took economic and some political decisions out of the hands of the feudal lords, absolute monarchs, generals and landed gentry. Money power started to speak instead of bloodlines – the blood of birth and the blood of the sword. Money power also began to *buy* the sword, and many of Britain's earlier trading endeavours were part and parcel of military domination of many countries. As such the development of money power was thought to be a genuine alternative to the old aristocratic oligarchy, but almost from the very beginning it was clear that the money system did not necessarily satisfy democratic hopes; it fostered new oligarchies, of money.

State agencies and bureaucracies have had a very mixed relationship to the systems of money power. In many instances there was a confluence of interests (e.g. between trading companies in new countries and the military), in later years some of the obvious negative consequences of the effects of the factory mode of production (etc.) started to be alleviated through new state agencies. So, money power has been both enhanced and constrained by state bureaucracies, the mixture and balance of which changes almost continuously. However while money power was in some senses liberatory it was also elitist; the power of a few turned against the many. The power of money had dislodged aristocratic power but money itself was not evenly spread (as John Stuart Mill hoped it could be). Nor (as Marx argued convincingly) could it be evenly spread if the logic of commodity exchange ruled.

102

Money power does not of course exist in a vacuum, by and large it derives from organisational activity; organisations themselves express this power; people's positions in organisational structures frequently determine the extent of their money power. As we go on to show, the organisational aspects of power take many forms. Organisations are adept at controlling information and knowledge, and thereby take on authority, for 'knowledge is power'. Organisations combine individual expertise into authority structures based on the idea and practice of 'professionalism' or expert bureaucracies. Organisations embody and promote the authority of managerial prerogative, they reproduce objectives through their internal practices, and they create new elites. And of course the economic power and political force of conventional economics is very substantially represented through organisational authority.

What options *do* exist in moving beyond a market and a money regulated economy, and in particular what foundations are there for conceiving a model of economic organisation governed by bureaucratic regulation alone or principally? These sorts of questions are centrally important for the development of a socially useful economy, for historically bureaucratic administration has been the only other model of organisation counterposed against that of market-regulated activity.

In more recent times it is obviously clear that an economy organised by commodity exchange and money has existed on the base of state power, legislation and administrative apparatus. Whilst the *laissez-faire* model of economics depicts an economic order and certain social consequences, a 'parallel' *political* free-for-all, with individuals acting to further their own interests by whatever means they see fit has nowhere been seriously contemplated. Historical reality shows political power deriving from several bases being quite ferociously used to create social and economic environments favourable to the market/money economy. The notion that political and social freedoms *automatically* go with market freedoms has not been borne out by history. There nevertheless exists an illusion, an ideology which equates social freedoms to market freedoms, most ably expressed in the USA, which emphasises a type of economic advancement supposedly available to all of us; and such advancements have frequently brought overt political power and state recognition. This ideology says that every purchase is a de facto vote for the product bought, but against this others also point out that the 'voting power of money' is so unevenly distributed as to be anti-democratic.

The laboured efforts of market theorists to demonstrate that all rational choice in society is in essence like a market process, even if well-founded (which they are not), cannot disguise the fact that resource-use guided by conscious and specific assessment of the purpose to be served is qualitatively different from resource-use guided solely or principally by profitable sale on the market. At the very least the gradual development of state-resourced and state-organised activities to supply clean water, sewage, transport infrastuctures and the like has been a very mixed phenomenon; in some instances the state has had to intervene simply in order to avoid enormous dysfunctions of market anarchy (such as has happened in the railways). Both general social and economic causes have been served by maintaining and developing state-based military establishments, in yet other areas state expenditure has been regarded as necessary to provide certain infrastructures to support private economic interests. Motivations have thus been very mixed, dependent upon many specific political decisions – many of them taken in crisis situations. However, the bureaucratic/administrative mode is not only found in the state and its agencies but within companies and corporations themselves, where very substantial elements of internal administration are necessary which may not be easily determined as 'productive' in terms of capital accumulation. There is in fact one line of thought which seeks to quantify the 'transactional costs' of adminstration of enormous corporations.

The bureaucratic structure is typically a hierarchical organisation in which there are distinct gradings of power and 'knowledge'. This is true for both market enterprises and state apparatus. In reality of course there are many other possible forms of organising economic activities, but contemporary economic and political thinking tends to assume that the only alternative to 'the market' is to hand decision-making over to these conventional types of bureaucracies. The seminar discussions vigorously challenged this whole train of thought and led to some important insights into associations and inter-dependencies between market economics and bureaucracy (in contrast to the widely held belief that they are opposed and incompatible). The seminars also indicated the huge importance of information communication in determining the nature of economic structures; bureaucracy was seen as being centrally a system of restricting and controlling information flows, from which decision-making arises in often very unclear ways.

INFORMATION AND CONTROL

The discussion of bureaucracy, most notably in seminar 5, was heavily based upon the issue of information and control and was formally addressed by John Ball's paper, which concluded as follows:

'The final point I want to make is that on a series of fronts, the demand for freedom of access to information does embody a different notion of how society can be organised.

All hitherto existing changes in the administration of either production or government have brought about an *increase* in bureaucracy. The labour movement has, unfortunately and through its own doing, become identified with support for aspects of bureaucracy, when its early years were years of bitter struggle against bureaucracy. It has lost the 'democratic' component of its social democratic (in the best, nineteenth century sense) past, and even surrendered it to the right wing from whose lips it falls as rank hypocrisy.

The most fundamental thing which the labour movement has stopped saying to the world is that bureaucracy is not *necessary*. We educate the public in the false belief that really, when the chips are down, you need bosses. You need people in charge. You need to give your administrators literally power of life and death over the individual. Is it any wonder, then, that the labour movement is unable to inspire confidence in its long-term aims? How can anyone fight for popular control whilst simultaneously accepting that there is a permanent social need for control by clerks and soldiers?

On a series of fronts very fundamental to the whole thesis of socialism, the development of new information technology offers a *potential* for reversing this. In this sense, I think the labour movement should approach information technology in a different way, say, from nuclear technology, which it should oppose *as such* and try to stop. I don't believe there is such a thing as a socialist nuclear power station. A socialist database: perhaps that's up to us.'

One of the key facets of structured inequality in and through bureaucracy is the organisation of information, its gathering, manipulation, presentation, restriction and so on. Further, information is not homogenous like grains of sand, what information is sought depends on certain interests and concerns (for instance we really have no measure of the number of people with disabilities in the UK, whilst the measurement of amounts paid out in social security benefits is usually extremely accurate). Certain 'facts' are aggregated, disaggregated and quantitatively manipulated/processed according to certain interests; thus trade unionists who try to glean operating information from annual financial accounts frequently find the 'information' entirely inadequate for their purposes, as it is organised primarily for investors and banks. In fact major obstacles for those who oppose substantial state or corporate bureaucracies are the enormous problems of assessing the 'information' conventionally provided. Similarly they find that the information required by them to mount an opposition cannot be easily obtained primarily because it is presented in a form which is appropriate to others' interests and not their own. However, a primary part of the structure of bureaucracies *is* concerned with the dissemination, and more commonly the withholding of information. For knowledge *is* power, and the fact that enormous amounts of state information are regarded as 'secret', and commercial information is regarded as 'confidential' disenfranchises most people. Frequently they can only ascertain certain aspects of information and its meanings through managed news of one kind or another.

Yet information is in reality spread throughout society, for instance the collective knowledge of a workforce if harnessed (of which more elsewhere) represents a substantial amount of real information about most aspects of the corporate enterprise. For despite all attempts to de-skill labour the collective knowledge that people obtain through the labour process is still very substantial, as is that contained within the collective consumer. 'Counter-intelligence' of this type is however unorganised at present, indeed it is used by market intelligence organisations and others frequently as a feedback mechanism for private or public organisations. The organisation of information is, therefore, very closely related to organisational structures and the more 'successful' organisations tend to utilise information control as a major source of power.

ORGANISATIONAL STRUCTURE

What we *mean* by organisational structure tends to mirror social concepts that prevail in society overall. So in contemporary society 'organisational structure' tends to be assumed to be *hierarchical* organisation. This of course fits in with the reality of a social oligarchy, where the ruling decisions are taken by a few for the many; it also fits the structures of capital; the owners of capital decide how it is used and tell employees what to do. There has been much discussion about types of organisational structure both within private and public institutions, but the common denominator is effectiveness in terms of *managerialism*.

Thus the existence of hierarchical structures are taken as read. Contrasted with that is the extraordinarily difficult nature of discussions about how nominally democratic organisations should work, in what way, and for what purpose. Some sorts of democracy are so deeply embedded in hierarchical organisational forms that it is extremely difficult to separate the two. The social and political dominance of hierarchy tends to make us assume that it's the only type of organisational form which works, which is the 'most practical'. But how one organises, no less than what one organises for, expresses social and political values. So pursuit of new values against the grain of the old is fraught with difficult practical problems, some of which are explored below.

BUREAUCRACY AND 'EXPERTS'

The hierarchical organisational form that is twinned in practice with bureaucracy tends to promote the concept of the expert, in a political sense, that is quite different to the individual expert who is for instance a specialist scientist. Bureaucratic 'experts' surround us as an everyday fact, which is accepted as it is so difficult to counter. So, if the market for instance is not to take economic decisions, is it not pure 'common sense' to have decisions taken by experts? But in reality this is a procedure for fitting the use of social knowledge, and the decision making made on it, into hierarchical structures. And these structures are self-reinforcing, since command of knowledge reinforces status. The whole knowledge, the knowledge which guides responses in action, that is decision-making, is closely confined to those at the top of the heirarchy. Those who have access to knowledge are ipso facto 'experts'. The question for whom, for what ends is knowledge to be used tends to be lost sight of. And imperceptibly, but now very definitely, an 'expert' in so many fields of life is in reality a *manager*. For the bureaucratic expert is, more than anything else, a controller.

MANAGEMENT'S RIGHT TO MANAGE

This is the sacred dogma of economics which is organised through bureaucracies, whether in the public or the private sector; it also points up the bureaucratic model described in aspects of economic organisation, within as well as beyond the market economy. But what 'divine right' has management to manage, any more than kings have a divine right to govern? Divinity was never too explicit about rights divinely granted to those who rule and, for those who try to penetrate the mystical dogma of royal privilege, the heights of abstraction are speedily abandoned for the more earthly persuasion of practical arguments. This, is for example how Samuel Johnson argued with Oliver Goldsmith about kings; 'it is better in general that a nation should have a supreme legislative power, although it may at times be abused' and, curiously, added 'if the abuse is enormous, Nature will rise up, and claiming her original rights, overturn a corrupt political system'. Most curiously, the mystery of kingship is buttressed by the mystery of Nature and the stability of social heirarchy whose cornerstone is the blood of royalty is buttressed by appeal to social revolution as the ultimate sanction against abuse of power!

Is the sanctity of managements' right to manage any better? In the small privately-owned company this right derives from rights of ownership, and this right is in its turn sanctified by belief in the market system as the true regulator of economic life. Even here private ownership may well have within it much more general legitimate rights, rights of those who labour in such an organisation, rights of those who may be adversely affected by its product, etc. But perhaps more importantly, what is the status of all these arguments when ownership of capital no longer lies in the hands of an individual or a few associated individuals? For today the greater part of capital is 'socialised' in the sense that numerous shareholdings, investment and loans from financial institutions and many other sources collectively constitute the formal ownership of most major companies. And what is the status of these arguments about management's right to manage when an institution is not even 'privately owned' through the remote control its shareholders exercise?

So where does the concept of management's right to manage come from? Solely from the fact of appointment by representatives of the state in the case of 'publicly owned' agencies and supposedly by representatives of shareholders in the case of 'privately owned' corporations. In the former case appointment by so-called representatives of the state is commonly an opaque process, dependent on 'being somebody' in one of the major hierarchies – there is still what is known as the 'List of the Great and Good' which are called upon by senior civil servants to serve as managers of one sort or another in the public sector. In the latter case it is of course the directors of a corporation that tend to have the overwhelming power to appoint managers at all levels; it is rare indeed for shareholders to effectively object to an appointment or to propose an appointment. On both counts it is assumed that 'if you want good management, you must give the manager a free hand'. There is the enormous assumption that management's right to manage is a basic necessity for the 'proper functioning' of any reasonable sized organisation. Criticism of this oligarchical power is usually refuted by an appeal to the necessity of oligarchic social structures because such social structures 'work' and hence if a social structure is to work it needs to be oligarchic. The tautology is obvious. Whenever the authority of the manager is challenged from the outside as it were, the whole apparatus of social power springs to 'his' defence, since the innermost principle of bureaucracy is under attack – it is being suggested that others, outside the elite fraternity of professional decision makers, are capable of making social decisions . . . So whilst managements' authority is defended as a cardinal essential of efficiency and good order (within laid down parameters which determine what is meant by efficiency for example) – to look for rational grounds for 'management's right to manage' means to run back to divine rights of kings to govern. Indeed, excessive deference to managerial authority is, as many have noted, actually a cause for much inefficiency, since then the only recourse that employees for example have against abuses is, to quote Samuel Johnson again, for 'Nature to rise up . . . to overturn the corrupt system.' This implies that criticisms of bureaucratic management can only usually express themselves in strikes, sabotage, working to rule, social violence, artful pursuit of narrow interests. Bureaucratic authoritarianism expressed through managerialism often constrains people who are adversely affected into dissidence, when they are simply trying to alleviate some of the worst aspects of what is being visited upon them. The very question of what constitutes efficiency, what the real purposes of an organisation are, are firmly taken out of the arena of rational or logical argument.

Yet why should not the values and collective wisdom of all who work, for instance in a work team ('the collective worker'), be used to decide aims, style of work, methods of monitoring for waste, methods of giving work meaning, purpose and scope for skills, and so forth? Moreover why should not consumers also have some effective say about what, after all, are their needs? The usual objection is that this would be 'anarchic', with a lot of people wrangling about what to produce and how to produce it. Actually people allowed to decide for themselves do not behave in such a manner: it is in fact very *offensive* for managers and bureaucratic elites to assume on the one hand that people at large are so muddled in their thinking, so unintelligent when, on the other hand, they expect people in the market place to make very complex decisions about what to buy. The assumption that democratic organisation leads to chaos is in part created and recreated by bureaucratic control, which for example severely restricts peoples' rights to information and knowledge. Simultaneously experience of having 'sufficient space' to refine and develop democratic organisations has been very severely restricted historically. Nevertheless even assuming there were some muddle and failure in the short term through developing and actuating democratic organisation, there are more than enough examples around to show that muddle and confusion exists at large in all the major institutions in society – those which supposedly embody the essence of 'rational' decision-making. Nevertheless some form of management/ coordinating *function* cannot be denied as an important element in democratic organisation; but as Mike Cooley has frequently pointed out there is a great difference between management as a function and management as a command relationship. So, control, which means the removal of influence, knowledge and even interest from others is a quite different aspect of management to that of coordination. The latter in a democratic organisation, as opposed to a bureaucratic and elitist organisation, is the essential function of management.

AUTHORITY

So, by focusing firmly on the controlling and dominating elements, of what we mean by managerialism, it is clear that very substantial blocks are placed in the way of development of democratic organisational forms which have some measure of effectiveness in political, economic and social life. It is a self-fulfilling ideology, that hierarchical forms of organisation, with which we are so familiar, are the *only* effective or 'efficient' forms of organisation. The issue of authority is in fact a central one here, for it is a form of power that is embedded in the very structure of the organisation, rather than being a real or actual feature of an individual's or group's expertise or creativity or ingenuity. Indeed, a current strand in industrial relations investigation is that of 'authority conflict'. This assumes that structurally-determined 'authority' is the root cause of so much dissatisfaction and frustration in society, as people feel that they have to 'battle' against unseen enemies that determine important aspects of their lives, where tools for countering such obscure power are historically absent. Thus bureaucracy, 'Big Brother', is almost universally feared and hated, and the oft-expressed view that bureaucracies do crazy and inefficient things in unproductive ways quite effectively and conveniently misses the point that such inefficiencies (from the 'outsiders' point of view) may well in fact be the source of the parameters of what is regarded as internally efficient, i.e. managerialism. So, authority is often exercised through the use of managerialism in bureaucracies simply because such sources of power are not amenable to change from anywhere, but actually arise from inside the organisation itself.

The organisation of the labour process built upon structures of authority and control is often justified on the grounds that it is 'scientific' and therefore 'efficient'. 'Taylorism' or scientific management places the expert in a supreme position to decide the best methods of payment and bonus, the working conditions of labour, and amounts of investment and production. However these activities carried out with the authority of management, only serve to underwrite and perpetuate this authority. Thus democracy within industry is repudiated by management because of the so called 'scientific' basis under which, they claim, their operations are carried out. The denial of self government in industry as being 'unscientific' has been one of management's most powerful ideological weapons.

THE BUREAUCRATIC TRADITION AND SOCIALISM

Bearing all this in mind one finds that the most generally acceptable definition of socialism, that of 'common ownership of means of production in order to plan production for social use', frequently assumes, unfortunately, a bureaucratic basis. With the absence of other adequately developed forms of social organisation, the bureaucratic form slips in, as it were, to become the mechanism by which policies are implemented, even when those policies are themselves intended to democratise society – and so an enormous contradiction is given birth! The assumption that planning production and use in ways which enfranchise people to a much greater extent than before, must be hierarchically organised, underlies both western ideas about socialist planning, as developed by Beatrice and Sidney Webb in particular, and Soviet planning as developed by Lenin, Stalin and their successors. Superficially this approach seems to 'work', seems 'realistic' insofar as it carries forward organisational ideas familiar to capitalism and also to other pre-existing social orders. And it fails to work for the same reason! It does not foster the changes on which the strength and viability of a democratic alternative to market economics depends. What the bureaucratic interpretation of socialism misses is that democratic control over resources (which alone gives meaning to 'common owner-ship') necessitates new forms of economic and social organisation and new ways of accessing and using social information. Analogous cri-tiques can be made of Keynesian planning, but Keynes very openly and deliberately sought instruments of economic control such as would not disturb the organisational structures of the market system at the microeconomic level. This contradiction is the very kernel of much of Labour's post-war planning procedures and structures. Barrie Sherman described the current alternative economic strategy (AES) as 'less than the sum of its parts', thus referring to the self-defeating nature of mixing incompatibles, democratic-orientated policies and anti-democratic structures. And this is far from being a theoretical point, for planning so handled becomes a dead thing, something to be feared as a further bureaucratic intrusion on peoples' lives. It is electorally disastrous, and contains nothing of vision to excite or even interest people at large.

THE REGIME OF THE CALCULATIVE – CONGENIAL IDEOLOGY FOR BUREAUCRACY

The fallacy of 'leaving decision making to experts' is not that there are no experts; the fallacy is that to surrender ultimate power to decide to others is to surrender democratic power itself. Bureaucracy frequently tries to defend itself against this charge by claiming that its decisions are guided, not by sectional interest, but by 'scientific objectivity' or some similar formulation. Measures may indeed be made 'objectively' but the meaning of the measure, that is the action to which it leads may be far from 'objective', such as when the measurement of PSBR becomes an integral part of programmes to cut social expenditure – looking at expenditure crudely as costs and ignoring benefits of such expenditure Action taken on the basis of scientific knowledge can never be objective in the sense of not being motivated by anybody's particular purpose. All actions seek to serve the purposes of those who decide to take them. Before agreeing to decisions based on 'objective measures' people need to understand and accept the practical meaning of the actions to which they give rise. This regime of the calculative further disenfranchises people as they are normally deprived of crucial information about aspects of the calculation itself. On the opposite side, the 'calculative' is the life blood of bureaucracies.

THE BUREAUCRATIC ELITE

Apart from embodying authority through managerialism and 'expert decision making', the bureaucratic elite are often overtly regarded (by themselves in particular) as being the rightful guardians of 'correct endeavours'. In one of the seminars Mike George explained that when he was in industrial relations management his task and that of his peers was clearly laid down as that of being the 'thin blue line of management defending itself against the barbarous hordes'; industrial relations management is quite overtly expected to 'protect' all the central areas of the corporation's commercial activities against 'outsiders', in which the workforce itself figured largely. Self-perpetuating elites *do* exist everywhere today, the mechanisms by which 'the succession' is ensured are complex and often subtle. The authority of elites is bolstered by an enormous range of social and political activities (such as the use of 'professionalism'), not only making the means of accession to the elite quite opaque for most people, but also providing a veritable arsenal of measures with which elites defend themselves and attack those who question their legitimacy and/or authority.

CAN BUREAUCRACY BE MIDWIFE TO DEMOCRACY?

The bureaucratic forms of institutions that surround us cannot be simply wiped out at a stroke, and in truth the process of developing democratic organisations requires legitimacy and authority which in part may have to be derived from those existing institutions. Furthermore, there are countries, such as Britain, in which it *appears* totally unrealistic to organise economic life in such a way as to obviate the need for some form of bureaucratic organisation – for whilst 'small is beautiful', its' practical limits seem very definite. Certainly some state organisations (which may well exhibit bureaucratic tendencies) will continue to be necessary to carry out certain administrative functions in a socially useful economy. We may also have to depend upon such organisations, at least to some extent in the short to medium term, to provide the necessary 'space' within which we can embark on the long and difficult road of creating wholly new democratic organisations. But at the same time it is clear that bureaucratic forms, as we know them now, cannot be anything other than antithetical to democracy in a real and active sense.

In several seminars Mike Hales and others provided illuminating

examples of the processes required in large local government organisations to rearrange, redirect and in some instances circumvent existing
bureaucracies whose 'common interests' were and are in opposition to
the policies being pursued under popular mandate. Such bureaucracies
embody great power and are in many respects unaccountable to all but
the most questing local councillor or group of councillors. One option is
to surround them as it were with new organisational forms, such that the
functional importance of existing bureaucracies is undermined and
direct challenges are made against them. Another approach raised in
the seminars suggested a systematic reorganisation and restructuring of
existing bureaucracies, to effectively isolate certain key areas and thus
diminish their importance, whilst redirecting other organisations in a
conscious and planned way. The latter course of action is the more
difficult, it has been tried both here and in other countries, but whilst
being an uncertain and time-consuming activity, it would appear that it
is the preferable course of action. An increasing input from 'grass roots'
activity is a necessary and key part of the process of change. But this at
the same time raises new and extraordinarily complex problems about
the relationships between democratic organisations, on the outside as it
were, and the 'new activists' operating within the sphere of existing
organisations, (such as the Greater London Council). What emerged
was that bureaucracies and all that they contain and represent *demand* a
much greater emphasis, of analysis and action, than has been historically accorded to them by those who wish to nurture democratic
organisations.

Part III
How We Can Reconstruct

then the
more from eds to
weary -
is SUE realist proporti
guin the present contiberacy of
social fones — Bodd as answer with
yes & illustrate this answer
examples of ...

final.

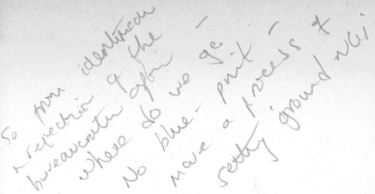

So from identical the reflection of the bureaucratie where do we get No blue-print more a process + setting 'ground' rule

In Part III we move on to consider in some detail what might be done to achieve our Socially Useful Economy, and to meet criticisms that this idea may be inadequately grounded.

First, in Chapter 6 we try to lay out some 'ground rules' for restructuring political economy which can provide a sound basis for a Socially Useful Economy. The reader will see that many of the issues raised in Chapter 2 are dealt with again, but from a position in which we pose practical alternatives.

We then move on to discuss the all-important means by which negotiation over such fundamental changes may be developed and operated. Our position here shows that a reasonable consideration of the motivations of existing and developing social forces in society can quite easily create a real negotiation; that it *is* a realistic propostion to contemplate ways of creating a Socially Useful Economy.

Chapter 8 poses in some detail institutional means for developing and maintaining all the major elements of a Socially Useful Economy. In so doing it deals with the social organisation of existing institutions in society, primarily viewing them as political phenomena – and thus amenable to change.

Finally we deal with the important issue of how we can finance a Socially Useful Economy – for this is often the most damaging form of criticism employed against those who would see any form of fundamental economic change. We demonstrate that there really is *no* overwhelming reason why we couldn't 'afford' a Socially Useful Economy, in fact we show the very reverse is true, and demonstrate the possibility of making 'social usefulness' an alternative principle to guide financial control mechanisms that we have already developed within capitalist societies.

6 Restructuring Political Economy: Social Needs Versus the Needs of Capital

> The task I am trying to achieve is to make you see.
>   D.W. Griffith

Orthodox economic ideas, theories, and practice present us with a fundamental paradox. On the one hand they tend to dominate our thinking, social values in society and our way of life, while on the other hand, for most people, they appear woefully inadequate as a method for understanding or tackling urgent questions concerning the economic management of our economy. For example there appears to be no available economic theory, within orthodoxy, which could decide upon how to allocate the £50 billion of oil revenue which accumulated from 1979 to 1985 – and which has been largely used to pay for the costs of rising unemployment.

But we must remember that what is currently orthodox was at one time radical, the restructuring of political economy is a continual process. The task posed in this chapter is not therefore impossible, as historically there has been a regular restructuring throughout most of modern human history. Restructuring political economy reflects as well as instructs changing economic and social conditions in a society. The theories of political philosophers and economists essentially mirror the prevailing economic and social circumstances of their era; there are of course exceptions to this. Marx, whose work did so much to deepen our understanding of the interplay between ideas and historical conditions, maintained that dominant ideas reflected the interests of the groups which were dominant in society at any one time; becoming 'an ideology', a framework of linked ideas (possibly false) which sustained and furthered their interests.

119

Joan Robinson[1] argues that economics itself 'has always been partly a vehicle for the ruling ideology for each period, as well as partly a method of scientific investigation'. Galbraith[2] also puts the view that

> economics, as a discipline has extensively and rather subtly accommodated itself to the goals of the industrial system. Conclusions which are not serviceable to these goals – which minimise the role of the market and profit maximisation, accord importance to effects of advertising, and cast doubt on consumer sovereignty, or look candidly on the close association of the mature corporation with the State – have an aspect of heresy.

Over the last two hundred years there have been many changes in the ways economists have explained and justified the capitalist system, ranging from the theories of Adam Smith, Ricardo, Jevons, Marshall, Keynes and Galbraith, to those of Milton Friedman. There is not *one* theory but a succession of theories reflecting changes in capitalism and its power structures, as well as criticisms and pressure against capitalism and, countering these, attempts to make the unacceptable face of capitalism somewhat more acceptable.

What links these theories of capitalism is that, however different they are, they all regard the capitalist system as a desirable system of organisation – or at least as the only *feasible* one. They do not criticise the social relations of production within the capitalist structures; but for *us* criticism of the social relations of production, distribution and exchange is inescapable, since these are central to any discussion about restructuring political economy. Samuelson[3] in his *Treatise On Economics* defines the subject as the 'study of how people in society end up choosing, with or without the use of money, to employ scarce productive resources that could have alternative uses, to produce various commodities and distribute them for consumption, now or in the future, among various persons and groups in society'. The problem underlying this line of reasoning is that not a thought is given to *who* ends up having a right to decide how scarce resources are allocated, and whose interests the allocations serve when they are made. These questions – and they have profound implications – are seldom if ever asked. Social needs, as the very basis of practice in economics, has obviously been accorded very little thought in the current theories and propositions concerning the way that political economy should be pursued.

IS ECONOMICS A SCIENCE?

It is very important to recall that the term 'political economy' was replaced about a hundred years ago by the term 'economics', by W. Stanley Jevons and others in order to put it on a 'scientific' basis. In so doing, the subject matter was narrowed (a very important issue in itself for our endeavours), and although the ideas that were subsequently developed were powerful, they had severe limitations as explanatory tools. The subject of economics now claims to be devoid of value judgements, that is, it claims to be 'positive' rather than 'normative'. As anyone who is familiar with the philosophy of science will appreciate the advantages of a 'positive' approach to investigation have their limitations – the most obvious being the topical issue of the advances in bio-genetic engineering.

The explanatory theories of micro and macroeconomic phenomena have certainly produced some powerful understandings of economic organisation, *but* they are based fundamentally on acceptance of the underlying structure of economic relations in society. The theories of the early economists such as Adam Smith assumed the values of self interest, of private property and of *laissez-faire* – that is, minimal interference by government in the conduct of economic affairs. However, support for certain political aims is inevitably implicit in this view of economics; this remains true today, it is implicit in the work of most economists today, as indeed of other scientists – there are fundamental assumptions which accept the directions and goals of the economic system that sustains the prevailing structure of poiltical power. In using the term 'socially useful economy' we are deliberately trying to make *our* assumptions, directions and goals explicit; we are requiring that attention be paid to the purpose of economic activity, that is, trying to direct the economy towards socially useful ends.

While 'economics' claims to be a science, attempts to use methods of natural science run into several problems. For example it is very hard to validate economic models by setting up experimental tests under control conditions. There is a more fundamental problem also in that 'objectivity' debars orthodox economics from fundamental criticism of the underlying capitalist structure, as that very objectivity is a reflection of what is currently regarded as 'true'.

The separation of economics from political economy can be seen to be an approach which separates some of the *real politics* of the capitalist economic system from political representations of society which are based on ideas such as 'one nation', welfare capitalism, the 'end of ideology', a classless society and the like. In several respects this characterised the post-war political settlement in this and other countries, which was sustained through a certain amount of economic redistribution 'allowable' as a result of very rapid economic growth for a generation. It is significant however that there is now a re-emergence of political economists of the Right, such as Milton Friedman.[4] These political economists are reverting to their predecessors, away from the narrower approach of 'economics' and advocate again Adam Smith's original model of a *laissez-faire* economy, and support the principles of the pursuit of self interest, maintenance of private property, and re-establishment of so-called unfettered market mechanisms. The political strength of classical political economy was its appeal to individualism. Capital was equated with the freedom of the individual, and according to Friedman, any departure from this market model would undermine such freedom to pursue self interest. He goes further by asserting that economic freedom through the market mechanism is an essential prerequisite for political freedom. But what he fails to take account of, of course, is that the structure of capitalism has changed out of all recognition compared with the structure of two hundred years ago. Political freedoms no longer rely upon the means of getting out from under the yoke of the landed gentry and aristocracy. And as Marx pointed out, even in the early development of capitalism there was a fundamental loss of freedom for those who lost control over their means of production. Furthermore the pursuit of self interest produces fundamental conflicts of interest – and these conflicts have been intensified over the past two hundred years. The very fact that the so-called neo-classic political economy is re-emerging may be seen as evidence that these conflicts are intensifying despite the general growth of available resources and the consequent redistribution that has occurred, in particular since 1945.

Orthodox economic theory does not provide an overall understanding of the workings of our economy. Edward Nell[5] argues that

> orthodox theory is a theory of markets and market interdependence. It is the theory of general equilibrium and exchange, extended almost as an afterthought to cover production and distribution. It is not a theory of a social system, still less of economic power and social class. Households and firms are considered only as market agents, never as part of a social structure. Their initial endowments, wealth, skills,

property, are taken as given. Moreover the object of the theory is to demonstrate a tendency towards equilibrium; class and sectoral conflict is therefore ruled out almost by assumption.

The capitalist system of production is based on private enterprise which means what it says, enterprise which is not collective, not social, but private. Enterprise used to be based on the individual owner–entrepreneur, but in today's world, capitalism takes many forms, whether it be transnational companies, public corporations, or small businesses. In essence however the decisions concerning the use of resources and to what ends they are used, are made not in the public interest but in the pursuance of private interest, e.g. for the 'good of the corporation'. The social relations of production assign the power of decision making to those who control these companies and corporations. Management's right to manage locates the centre of power with the owners and/or controllers of the means of production (and of distribution and exchange). The question here is whether the powers are exercised in a manner that is consistent with promoting the needs and interests of society, or whether there is a fundamental conflict of interests which cannot be reconciled until the structure of private enterprise is fundamentally altered; and this must of course include the private enterprise 'approach' to public sector endeavours.

It therefore takes a great deal of 'imagination' to accept that all that goes under the term 'economics' is in any sense scientifically valid, except insofar as certain, narrowly-defined, mathematical relationships can be determined within certain aspects of the money system.

THE DIVISION OF LABOUR

The principles of scientific management, as first portrayed by Frederick Winslow Taylor were and are of course just as far from being scientifically valid as the rest of capitalist economics. Adam Smith in his famous book *The Wealth of Nations* argued that a prime source of increasing wealth was division of labour – as indeed it was; but orthodox economists today accepting this as, almost, an axiomatic principle, have ignored the crucial changes that have taken place in the nature of labour. As the wages system developed the nature of work was more and more dictated by the needs of capital to control the labour it employed. Human skills more and more failed to be developed in a human way, work was evermore fragmented, workers were more and more alienated from the collective labour process – becoming machine-like parts of an apparatus, doing what they were required to do by the system from which morally and emotionally they stood apart. The struggles of the labour movement testify to the conflict generated by the incompatibility of the needs of capital and the needs of the human beings employed by capital. There is a wealth of well-researched material which attests to this fundamental conflict of interests caused by the division of labour; for this then to be assumed to be part of some sort of scientific 'principle' is a supreme fallacy.

Quite obviously the socially useful economy has to move in the direction of recovering the creativity of the human individuals who cooperate in productive processes, and enable them to develop conciousness and purposeful control over the ends their work is to serve, and the means by which they do their work. This indeed may be said to be true scientific endeavour, as the basis of objectivity is grounded in human experience, rather than in an abstracted ideology and political practice.

WANTED – A THEORY OF TECHNOLOGICAL INNOVATION

A further significant omission in orthodox economic theory is the lack of a theory of innovation and invention. Chris Freeman[6] in his book *The Economics of Innovation* argues that

> a large body of economic theory was concerned with short term analysis of fluctuation of supply and demand of goods and services. Although very useful for many purposes, these models usually excluded changes in the technological and social framework from consideration, under the traditional 'ceteris paribus' assumption (other things being equal). Even when, in the 1950s economists increasingly turned their attention to economic growth, the screening off of other things was largely maintained, and attention was concentrated on the traditional factor inputs of labour and capital, with technical progress as a residual factor embracing all other contributions to growth such as education, management and technological innovation. This is significant in that technology is always assumed by economists to be a given . . . the uses to which technology might be put are therefore never taken into consideration.

This is a striking omission since in reality most firms are under severe pressure to produce technological innovation in order to remain competitive. Because economics tends to treat technology as neutral it legitimises the ways in which technology is used and ignores the impact of technology in de-skilling and de-humanising the labour process, amongst other human consequences.

Galbraith in his book *The New Industrial State* argues that the organisation of big companies is geared towards making the best use of available technology, to retain the power of organisations within the techno-structure.

The general climate of economic opinion that the media and prevailing economic ideologies foster, is that anything likely to *impede* technological change must be bad. Thus the involvement of technological innovation is taken as an assumption, rather than made explicit. In reality technological change is almost entirely dictated by 'the needs of capital'; which basically amounts to the power to compete and use labour effectively to this end, and in more recent years to reduce other factor inputs as well. This means looking for technologies that reduce the cost of labour and increase the control of capital; the cost of labour and the control over labour is increasingly seen as part of the same thing.

Relations of production – capital competing against capital, and workers dependent upon capital for a living – tend to determine the way technology is used. Marx focused attention on the economic importance of production relations and stressed the tendency of more and more people – now an overwhelming majority – to lose control over the means of production. Workers depend on employment by management, but management is governed by the needs of capital to reproduce itself and expand. So workers are employed or made redundant regardless of their wishes or those of society. In this arrangement 'improvement of productive capacity' means cost-saving, which in turn means reduction of labour costs in most instances. Reduced labour requirements and increased managerial control weaken labour's bargaining position, and make labour evermore dependent on capital. So the assumption that technological change is *in itself* good simply reinforces underlying productive relations, and puts capital in an even stronger position to enforce its interests against the interests of employees, and often society at large. For these reasons the whole question of innovation and invention has to be looked at in a new way. The technological change to which 'the natural working of market forces' leads cannot be accepted uncritically; it has to be looked at from the standpoint of social usefulness. A new, deeper understanding of innovation and invention is essential if existing potentials of scientific and technological knowledge are to be developed in more socially useful ways.

One of the most obvious ways in which labour has tried to deal with technological change and new technology is to take a larger share of the greater productivity (in capitalist terms) that has usually resulted. This has meant bargaining for higher pay of one sort or another through productivity deals, and more recently in the reduction of the working day and week. In both respects employers are resisting any encroachment on higher returns through technological innovation, with for instance the substantial strike in West Germany, where the metal workers tried to reduce standard weekly hours from 40 hours to 35 hours; the Confederation of British Industry in the United Kingdom has resisted efforts to reduce the working week – reductions that have been obtained have unfortunately often been at the expense of deals which include greater 'worker flexibility', which in effect has meant increasing the working capacity of each individual worker, and reducing their collective power by schemes such as 'employee involvement' or Quality Circles.

The significance of the Lucas Workers' alternative plan, and similar struggles by others has been that technological innovation is tackled much more directly, by questioning the very purpose to which technical innovation and technological development have been put. In some instances this has included the actual end-product of the process, in others it has questioned the overall means by which work is organised (which includes the application of technologies); these sorts of initiatives have clearly shown the quite enormous possibilities that exist when technological innovation is taken out of the sphere of narrow capitalist concerns and into the rich area of human and social needs.

WHAT'S GOOD IN MARKET THEORY IS NOT THE SAME AS 'SOCIAL USEFULNESS'

Orthodox economic theory *seems* to take account of usefulness. Is not its foundation stone 'marginal utility'? Marginal utility is the theory that consumer preferences 'at the margin' determine the exchanges that are or are not effected, and hence the rates of exchange, the prices 'on the market'. However what *we* mean by social usefulness – what gives socially good results from all points of view – is bypassed in this theory.

As we have already stressed, the orthodox economic theory deals only with the allocation of scarce resources within a structure of economic relations and 'given' technologies that is assumed to be unalterable. Moreover, actual allocation of resources depends upon the distribution of purchasing power, and there are no mechanisms in the orthodox model that in any way match purchasing power to needs. Clearly 'utility' in this theory bears little resemblance to the social usefulness about which we are concerned, that is, ability to satisfy human needs – individually and collectively.

Very powerful criticisms of this so-called marginalist theory, striking at its very foundations, have been made from within the economic faculties themselves.[7]

To the theoretical case against orthodox economic theory must be added massive and obvious evidence from human practice and experience. The mounting problems to be seen all about us, to which many references have been made, attest to the profound dysfunctions of utility in market theory. We have massive amounts of unused or misused resources, of which the number of those who are unemployed is perhaps one of the most clear measures. Environmental pollution, which may prove to be extraordinarily expensive in the medium and long term is another neglected external cost. The exploitation of scarce raw materials is yet another. And of course the quite extraordinary and systematic dehumanisation of work, the constriction and restraint of peoples' abilities and potentials, is perhaps the biggest evil of all. These voids in economic know-how and in orthodox economic theory, of which there is so much evidence, urgently need to be filled; this is what restructuring political economy is about.

The development of a socially useful economy firstly requires us to face up to and define the social dysfunctions of the overriding use of utility within market theory, and the profound economic consequences of such rigid adherence to conventional market theory. The development of a socially useful economy requires the devising of new, widely shared understandings that motivate democratic action, people acting for themselves, discovering new procedures, criteria and concepts that make headway against the patent defects of the economic theory and practice that at present govern decisions about how we use, or fail to use, the resources available to us.

RE-COMBINING PRODUCTION AND CONSUMPTION

Conventional markets provide *a* mechanism for bringing together buyers and sellers and thus provide a form of social interaction, but because of the way in which production is organised it is clear that there is a divorce between the *meanings* of production and consumption. This has a profound importance for the dehumanisation and alienation of people in our society *both* as producers and as consumers.

We need to consider – the thing that orthodox economics altogether fails to do – where it may be socially (and economically) advantageous to bring production and consumption closer together. It is not necessary to choose between entire dependence on the market, or a reversal to some form of self-subsistence. This dichotomy is entirely unneccessary. We have to move from situations in which we now find ourselves towards more fruitful interaction between, on one side, large-scale social provision (the legacy of the public, impersonal economy dominant in capitalism) and, on the other side, household or local provision. This is indeed essential if, for example, economic and political demands of the women's movement are to be met.

A huge proportion of society's work, childcare, meals, washing, the 'keeping of houses' as living places and very much else besides is currently done mainly by women; women within or near 'the household', mostly unpaid and ill-supported by resources, technical advice and facilitating social relations. Is it not evidence of ideological bias towards the hegemony of the market that this extensive field of economic activity is almost totally neglected by 'economic science'? There is much here for socially useful economics to explore. Furthermore, if we could but admit it, very substantial areas of 'work' of people at large, and not only women, fall into this area.

Should mass production provide better for local maintenance and repair? Are throw-away products and replacement in lieu of repair socially or economically acceptable? Should not design by producers be undertaken in much closer collaboration with users? Analysis and research into such questions need to interact with practical testing and experimentation. This also means giving people opportunities to try out their own ideas in practice. In this connection a great deal of importance should be attached to the work which various local authorities (Sheffield, Greater London Council, West Midlands Council, and others) are initiating to encourage new kinds of workers' cooperatives, popular planning units, technology networks and the like. And lest we be accused of creating a new type of anarchy (inefficient, unwieldly, 'irrational') it must be remembered that a quite extraordinary amount of experimentation takes place within the portals of major institutions in the land; in a number of industrial and commercial areas it is quite common for only one or two products to be brought to market, from a basis of perhaps one thousand original research and development ideas.

Galbraith[8] has argued very powerfully that the era of consumer sovereignty has been fundamentally altered to one of *producer* sovereignty, that market forces favour the multinational companies who maintain their sales and products through the 'management' of demand. Galbraith argues that this has to be undertaken because of the inherent complexity associated with the accumulation of capital, and the need to ensure that the capital and technology employed is effectively translated into sales of products and services.

Thus the market mechanism, assumed by the theorists to be a sort of universal clearing house, is replaced in practice by managerial planning and control of consumption. Orthodox economic theory has of course paid little regard to this trend, with the forces of supply and demand still regarded as essentially independent. On the assumption that demand is a relatively independent 'fact', the successful entrepreneur simply organises ways of supplying demand. This is the ideology commonly used in political circles. Yet text books on marketing and management clearly show that demand must be managed, that market niches and market positions have to be created. Thus so-called orthodox economic theory, as applied to the issue of supply and demand, is contradictory to say the least, and, being so, it is perhaps not unexpected to find enormous mis-matches, supreme waste of resources, and truly illogical plans for the use of resources, both human and material.

Furthermore while resource and allocation problems are dealt with (in some way or other) by economic theory, they seem to be inadequate in providing a basis for the *full* employment of resources by the operation of purely market forces. This question was of course taken up by Keynes in the 1930s when he advocated government intervention in order to alleviate unemployment. The important point here is that it required government intervention, and that full employment of resources could *not* be guaranteed by market mechanisms. Equilibrium in market theory can be achieved at less than full employment of resources. And this is now being increasingly accepted and even promoted in political circles, and the old idea of 'natural' levels of unemployment is being paraded in front of us, following over a generation of partial or total rejection.

However, when market criteria do *not* apply, what criteria are to govern expenditure designed to bring resources into use? If the fundamental criterion in choice of economic strategies is to be the full use of human and other resources, then this would require planning at all levels in order to establish priorities in terms of production of goods

and services (both within the conventional paid sector and outside it).
What principles are to govern these priorities, by what procedures are
decisions to be implemented? These are questions, neglected by
orthodox economics, which the socially useful economy needs to tackle.

THE NEED FOR BETTER PLANNING THEORY AND PRACTICE

Although orthodox economic theory does not supply a coherent set of
ideas about planning, in practice planning is very widespread under
capitalism, both in relation to state or local government, and within
corporations. It is apparent that the market mechanism is, usually at a
micro level, related closely to various kinds of planning. We have
argued that the need for planning is paramount in organisations in order
to create stability and to avoid uncertainty associated with the risks of
advanced technology for example. This is why much of the advanced
technology is underwritten by government, and investment strategies
throughout the world are becoming subject to planning mechanisms
used by big businesses and governments. However, the role of planning
in *this* context is to ensure that the needs of capital are satisfied.
Generally speaking, the state is primarily used to keep the existing
economy running, that is to meet the needs of capital. In establishing
institutional frameworks necessary for fulfilling the needs of capital, the
possibility may however arise that these frameworks could be used to
fulfil other needs. Planning mechanisms are employed in order to
provide essential services such as education and health which are not
normally provided within the market sector. The objectives underlying
planning are of profound importance. For instance there were the
planning mechanisms used during the Second World War (not just for
arms production but also for food), or today planning for land use, in
contrast to, for example, planning within a large corporation for a new
product range.

The technical aspects of planning, as a fairly narrow methodology,
have to be separated from the purposes of planning – and even to some
extent the *broader* democratic methods of planning. We must not
confuse these issues. For example, is it not possible for a local rural
community to have extremely 'expert' proposals for land use in their
area? Can employees in a factory not plan the way that their skills and
resources might be used? In short, can there be such a thing as

democratic planning, in which the purely technical aspects of the process can be separated out from the much more important broader methods and purposes of planning? In restructuring political economy towards the socially useful economy, planning is a key issue, but it cannot be planning which simply mimics the 'top-down' approach that historically has characterised this process.

To plan an economy in which the needs of capital are not paramount is to challenge the very idea of economic viability (or otherwise) of decisions made by those with money-power. Economic viability is a key political issue, it is used politically to support certain endeavours and to dismiss others out of hand. For example in earlier days the Lucas Aerospace shop stewards' plan was dismissed as being economically unviable. Yet after a number of years of elaboration of their ideas, it is quite clear that what was being proposed was much more positive than the policies pursued by the company management. Plans to reduce unemployment are ipso facto of positive value. Similarly to plan for medical equipment for elderly people in order to help them live in the community rather than be hospitalised or institutionalised in some other way, is of profound positive value. New ideas for energy conservation and new forms of energy generation and use frequently have beneficial economic effects – although usually in the medium and long term rather than the short term. Therefore planning for economic viability is a quite feasible activity, politically it is a radical demand, but in terms of social and economic benefit it vastly outstrips narrow criteria of economic viability which guide those who pursue private interests within the community.

WHAT IS ECONOMIC VIABILITY?

The Lucas Aerospace initiative is in many ways a classic example of the way in which a socially useful economy can be brought about. The shop stewards and employees of that company found that the company obtained most of its income from public sources, from public procurement (principally from the Ministry of Defence), from government investment and regional grants, and from massive tax concessions. Yet at the same time the company's corporate policy was clearly aimed at reducing the UK workforce by over one third, producing a public cost of unemployment of some £20 million. Thus, in order to make the company profitable for its shareholders, Lucas used public money, mainly under government contract, to 'rationalise' its production and marketing. This created enormous social and economic costs in the community. Looked at in this way the company as a whole was not an economically viable entity for the UK. Even with reductions in unemployment benefits and social welfare provisions brought about by the Conservative government in recent years, the total costs of unemployment *are* extremely high. In 1979 the Department of Employment estimated the average cost of unemployment to be over 90 per cent of average earnings for nearly a year's period of unemployment. This has perhaps reduced to something like 80 per cent today. Within this context the Combine Shop Stewards' Committee felt entirely justified in proposing a set of alternative products and different research and development programmes which could save and create jobs in the company, whilst meeting a range of short- and long-term social needs in society.

Lucas is by no means an isolated example of the economic viability equation used by private companies leading to decisions which definitely would *not* assist economic viability for the country as a whole. Lucas, like so many other companies, is not socially accountable for the economic strategies that it adopts. Indeed, the determinants of viability within a firm are often quite overtly based on political decisions; for example, Lucas produces advanced technical military equipment. Orders here depend upon overt or, more often covert, decisions to support certain sectors and certain companies for ends that are nothing to do with economic viability as defined by the market ideology. This being so, in Lucas Aerospace the employees felt quite justified in pressing the positive social and economic effects of implementing their alternative product proposals. For instance certain medical products proposed by the workforce were fully discussed in quite new ways with medical practitioners using them, and sometimes with the users themselves; e.g. advanced portable kidney machines (allowing people to be de-hospitalised), and the therapeutic 'go-cart' for children suffering from spina bifida. In the energy field there were dozens of proposals emanating from the Lucas employees for products which would create net economic benefits at the individual level and at the nation state level.

By identifying the *political* nature of viability the field is opened up to develop alternative criteria which would, in effect, make unviable whole areas of market-stimulated activities, whilst making viable other activities which could be stimulated by public expenditure, and through structures which are not conventionally market-based. For in fields such as medical equipment the so-called 'free market' simply does not exist.

Need and the satisfaction of it are quite often entirely divorced from each other. The same applies in the field of energy, housing, and many other basic services. The conventional criteria of economic viability are clearly detrimental to growing numbers of working and non-working people (or should we say unpaid people . . .). The major problem about effecting change towards new criteria is that labour organisations are currently unable *to take on board the question of production*, rather than just distribution and redistribution.

Historically it is through struggle that what is or is not viable must be worked out, since in this way specific possibilities may be tested concretely and new economic principles evolved. No one struggle and no simple formula will provide all the answers; for instance, workers in the oil and petro chemical industry have moved, quite logically, from their job-saving campaigns at site level, to considering economic and social issues of North Sea Oil exploitation in its broadest sense. Workers in the computing industry are starting to relate to their job prospects the actual end-use of their labour power, and may thereby create a new agenda from microelectronic applications and related designs – these having profound social implications and economic consequences for society. Once trade unions go beyond their traditional sectional interests (wages and conditions) to question what is produced, a new and fertile field will open up for the labour movement. This reintroduces political economy in a new way. The Lucas shop stewards worked with potential users, (for example, patients and workers in the Health Service), in preparing their products and R & D proposals. The development of this approach can both strengthen the trade union struggle, and place more firmly on the agenda the question of current ideologies which restrict trade unionism to economism, and political parties to distribution economics.

Broad issues of political economy are opened up, quite naturally, through these approaches to labour as a *resource* rather than a *cost*. Such issues include new ways of servicing people, vast ranges of new products and services, new alliances between producers and consumers, and reformulated relations between exchange and distribution. This approach to the problem, emphasising political viability as much as economic viability, (*and showing that the two are inextricably mixed*) leads naturally into existing needs of people for jobs; for jobs that mean something to them; for products and services that support people's needs, for those which provide pleasure without guilt, for some sense of natural justice; for personal and collective activities which *open up* the future through democratic practice.

THE EVOLUTION OF NEW ECONOMIC VALUES

In attempting to develop a socially useful economy it is instructive to examine the historical relationship between exchange value and use value. In pre-capitalist situations goods were produced and consumed by the user, or simply exchanged for other goods (this is illustrated in the Table). Goods were also exchanged via money; but the producer was still in total control of what he or she produced and use value predominates.

These models which lay emphasis on value in use have their modern-day counterparts; for example, the production and consumption of

TABLE   *Evolution of commodity production*

Type	Description	Present-day equivalent
1. C*	Production for use value only, consuming what you produce.	Self sufficient communities; Domestic work.
2. C–C'	Commodities exchanged for use value only.	Bartering.
3. C–M–C'	Exchange of goods with money as a medium of exchange: no surplus value.	Informal economy: market based on the social division of labour.
4. M–C–M'	Commodity production, starting with M money to obtain money M' greater than M; Commodities C produced to achieve surplus value rather than use value.	Capitalism based on the division of labour, and a market economy.
5. M–M'	Abstract Exchange, starting with money M aim is to create more money M' – no goods produced or exchanged, money simply being lent for another's use or exchanged from one money form to another.	Money markets.
6. M–C	Money used to create commodities and services on the basis of need.	Public provision of goods and services, e.g. hospitals & schools.

NOTES

C = Commodities (goods and services); M = Money.

(Technically 'commodities' means 'goods' or services produced for exchange.' C* in Type 1 indicates simply 'goods and services'. The C' indicates 'different' or 'more'.)

goods is to be found in areas of unpaid work, self sufficient communities and community work. Estimates have been made that the number of hours devoted to these activities are roughly equal to the number of hours that are spent in waged work. Commodities for exchange can be found in the informal sector of an economy, where people 'informally' make personal arrangements with others, or where, as in many Third World countries, people in a neighbourhood do work for one another, not being able to afford to use 'high street businesses'.

In a wage-based economy under capitalist production, the emphasis shifts to the predominance of exchange value, M–C–M; industrial society depends upon a division of labour, where the goods produced do *not* have a use value for the producer. Money is required to start the process of economic activity, in the form of investment and purchase of resources, and the end product is Money, M'. For the process to be worthwhile there has to be more money at the end that at the beginning i.e. M' has to exceed M. The greater the hoped for M' the more likely it is that the investment will be made. The commodities, C, are produced in order to create exchange value. This has to be measured in money. This leads on to the assumption that the only valid measure of wealth is the exchange-value of goods and services produced for exchange. This excludes the vast amount of activity devoted to goods and services (C*) which must be regarded as socially useful, such as child-rearing, but which are unpaid. On the other hand items that are included in production for exchange are automatically counted in the total of wealth-created, whether they be fruit machines, or electric tooth-brushes, or video nasties. Because the goods produced do not have a use value for the producers, the economy is only directed towards the production of exchange values. This process is intensified when we consider the investment of money, simply to create more money where no goods are exchanged and therefore no use value can be created by the investors. The built in 'automatic' nature of these mechanisms neces-sarily causes the emphasis in capitalist practice, and in the orthodox theory that goes with it, to be on exchange value rather than use value.

People have found relief from consumer capital in forms which Bahro[9] has described as 'compensatory' needs as opposed to 'emancipa-tory' needs. Exchange of money for goods appears to *represent* freedom, in contrast to the lack of consumer goods and choice in the Eastern Bloc. But what is a commodity? 'It' has created its own need in people like a drug; human beings being regarded as machines for producing exchange values, and treated as machines for consuming exchange values.

The definition of need has passed into the hands of producers; they tell us what we need (i.e. they dictate use values when in fact they are exchange values). Their clamour for growth and material goods has little to do with needs and everything to do with the production of exchange value.

Market economics looked at in this way, as an exchange-value producing system, is seen to be flawed *precisely* because a use-value only has a dependent status, and so economic activity loses touch with real needs – responding only to the distorted pattern of 'needs' that is reflected by money-backed demand (what is usually termed effective demand).

Economic decision-making controlled by the criteria of the socially useful economy has to address itself directly and positively to needs, giving needs first place in the definition of economic purpose. Ways of defining needs are dealt with elsewhere in the book. However it should be clear by now that human need is not necessarily an 'unviable economic proposition' but maybe in all instances, by definition and by practice, an extremely viable one. This approach will give scope to the need, stifled and frustrated, of human beings to express their humanity. It will give scope also to needs such as work that one controls for oneself, and so can make purposeful and creative; needs, such as material security, aesthetically pleasing shelter and sustenance that is in tune with the environment and other human beings.

Money is used in order to provide public goods and services such as hospitals and schools through state enterprises. This, in effect, restores the ability to create use values by an appropriate investment strategy. We believe that a great deal more investigation could be undertaken in order to establish criteria for *directly* creating use values. Such investigations could look at the areas of resources, production, means of exchange and consumption. If we take the area of resources we find that by treating them just as a cost in order to maximise exchange value, we certainly do not maximise use value. We often find that resources such as fuel are simply destroyed in order to get energy; whereas by recycling a resource we retain its organisation and can add to its use value. In other words, the principle which we should operate with regard to resources, for example, is to be able to create indefinite utility.

MEANS AND MEASURES TO INCREASE USE VALUE

To this end it should be possible to develop allocation principles which enhance preservation of resources. For example, a tax could relate to the percentage lost to future use, or how much of a resource is left at the end of a process compared to the amount at the beginning. For example in the case of burning a fuel, a 100% tax would be applied, but in the case of recycling of bottles where there was an 80% return rate the tax would be 20%, i.e. 20% is the proportion of the resources lost and not recycled. This is simply one straightforward example of how 'socially useful fiscal policies' might be developed. In this case taxation would be directed to the re-creation of resources for the production of goods so as to retain them as a perpetual, or near-perpetual resource.

In treating food as a resource one aspect of use-value could be measured in terms of nutritional value, and steps could be taken to avoid the extraction of those nutritional values which are currently used to create added exchange value; for example in the case of bread, the bran and vitamin B have been extracted in order to increase the value-added. It is significant that the wholefood movement is growing rapidly in an attempt to maximise the nutritional value of food, rather than the exchange value. In the area of production it is significant that the use-value of meaningful work is disregarded by orthodox economists, except in the distorted form of 'negative disutility of units of work at the margin'. Labour is regarded like any other resource, whose price should vary according to laws of supply and demand. Even Keynes didn't care what people did when he advocated public works to cure unemployment; they could, for the purposes of his model, be employed in digging holes in the ground and filling them up again. One point here is that technology is always assumed to be a given, and that work has to be organised around the latest available technology. However it is extremely important that work should be of value to the producers; for it to be creative people need to see the end products of their work in use. Today, much producer alienation clearly exists, with interest in work being limited to interest in wages paid. But wages historically have not always been the prime and only consideration for working people. A socially useful economy would seek to directly provide for and to innovate for non-alienated work. This would require more than mere changes in the ownership of enterprises.

We under-value peoples' wish to be involved in their work, be proud of what they do, witness the numerous 'industrial sub-cultures', in which there is the very common view that people could do better than their managers for example. Actual practice belies the words of many middle class and other professionals who advocate the end of work, when they themselves would die of stress if they weren't allowed to work hard as advocates of what they believe in. We fail to tap into the strong identification that people have with their jobs and various other aspects of work, even under capitalism. Pride in skill is not just false consciousness, witness the strength of feeling in occupations such as shipbuilders and engineers, but also of hospital ancillary workers, of midwives, etc. We mustn't confuse the *fact* of exploitation with consciousness and the need most people have to find personal meaning in their working lives.

People do identify with their work and its meaning in terms of social effects. That is a supremely important use value in and of itself.

BUILDING BLOCKS OF SOCIALLY USEFUL PRODUCTION

Use value construed in this way will not be generated by policies directed only at ownership of the means of production. Nor is it sufficient for workers to participate in the management of undertakings whose aims are limited to increasing the exchange-values produced – which is the main weakness of 'reformist' and other policies for participation within an unchanged capitalism.

A labour policy needs to be reconstructed in response to commonly held and deeply felt attitudes that people have towards what they do, even under capitalist social relations. In this way use value can have meaning for people in production and opens vast new areas for power, control, invention, and policy developments in a great many areas of social life – and not only in those areas of social life which are involved with paid work. This brings into the purview of socialism swathes of, currently, alienated people, nurses and ancillaries, teachers, car mechanics, clothes makers, etc.

Since use-value is obviously what most matters about consumption, it will be helpful to have some means of measurement. At present we are dominated by restrictive measures in terms of exchange-values. If the use-values created by alternative policies could be more adequately measured and assessed it would hit conventional money resource constraints pretty squarely on the head, e.g. assessment of social usefulness would most probably point towards putting money into education . . .

The static view of availability to which assessment by exchange-value criteria so often leads, needs hitting hard. Of course we can't simply ignore or discount market-based consumption. However if we start with the aims of meeting essentials for all, regardless of income, we can give the goods required for this a high use-value rating; they provide the basic building blocks of a socially useful economy. For artifacts which people are generally used to, such as TVs and washing machines, it is necessary to plan supply so as to provide for all reasonable choices. The concept of use value will also need to take account of consumption over the longer term. Also why shouldn't we strive for efficient and rational energy policies which would mean stressing certain types of consumption as against others, e.g. a one-bar electric fire is horrendously expensive to run and terribly inefficient. Such costly types of energy could be replaced with other types which require small investments of capital but which are very much more efficient – at both the individual level and at the state level. Meaningful use value constructions for both production and consumption would highlight vast amounts of social waste and indicate the economic cost of sustaining social structures based on money power. They would also sharply distinguish between economics of supply and demand as bearing on the real experience of peoples lives *and* the economics of money markets on which the power of financial institutions depends. Insofar as exchange value is considerably modified to take account of use values, it may come to serve as a measuring tool in allocation of resources, and the monetary system which at present is a source of unaccountable power may begin to be adapted to socially useful purposes. Money would then lose its universality, and become separated from the all-pervasive market concept. Exchange-value would certainly have to remain but in what form? International relations is one sphere where the actual price for goods and services would be one type of exchange value. Within our modified consumption concept exchange value, as price, might be *one* supply-based motivator or constraint. Currency value would express *one aspect* of exchange value. Rates of exchange could reflect the social usefulness or otherwise of trade with particular countries, or in particular goods.

We have pointed out that orthodox economics does not provide any adequate theory of innovation. It is a significant fact for which there is empirical evidence, that much product innovation does not emanate from large firms, but from small firms – which are subsequently taken over by the large firms. It is somewhat surprising that in the development of microcomputers, for example, it was the one-man businesses which was first able to bring these products onto the market. It appears there is immense scope for providing resources for individuals to develop ideas which may lead to important economic innovations. Such activity for example is currently being promoted by the Greater London Enterprise Board's technology networks. It is time that we started to look directly at the social utility of research and development. At present this is stimulated less by market forces than by government funding, and the bulk of government money goes to military and related programmes. However, Freeman[10] has pointed out that there is ample scope for government to stimulate research and development directed into other channels which are more socially useful, such as health, education, and introduction of products which conserve energy, such as electric cars. This is not to say that the socially useful economy relies simply on the conventional individual entrepreneur. Most of the conventionally successful entrepreneurs are simply interested in money, not in product innovation as such; meanwhile individual inventors are either starved of development funds, or have to make over their inventions to private money-power interests. One of the key building blocks for a socially useful economy is to make inventors of us all, in one way or another – where the success of implementation is not to depend on one's own relationship with a bank manager, whether one has a house to sell, or whatever; the aim is to provide mechanisms to support *ideas* which show some promise in meeting social needs and in thus having positive economic benefits.

The capitalist system encourages limitless expansion of those material needs which capital can most easily satisfy through the market. Its function is creation of exchange-value and profit, rather than meeting social and human needs. As Freeman points out

> producers are almost exclusively oriented to product differentiation and a brand image, rather than to imaginative technical innovation or to social needs. For example, efforts to design safer cars and a relatively pollution-free car are very obvious social needs, but the R & D effort which went into improving safety or preventing pollution was negligible until recently. Interestingly enough, the stimulus came not from the R & D of the producers but from outside circles and public regulations.[11]

The same is even more true of designing a generally satisfactory land transport system, particularly in congested urban areas. Thus whilst economists emphasise the importance and power of the market mechanism, they have ignored what lies behind that mechanism, i.e. the power of the producers, and inequalities in the distribution of wealth.

> The market mechanism which theoretically was supposed to ensure correspondence between consumer wishes and in supply, no longer performs this function adequately if it ever did so in some sectors. This means increasingly the political mechanism must restore the lost consumer sovereignty which the autonomous market mechanism can no longer assure.[12]

Freeman raises a crucial point about the importance of replacing the market mechanism with some alternative politically-based system.[13] However, in the non-market sectors, such as health and housing and education, fundamental questions have to be posed about criteria used, and the purposes and interests that are served. In the absence of clarity on these questions public funds may well favour the interests of 'professionals', the planners and the people working in those sections rather than the interests of the users. Palmer[14] poses the question: 'it is relevant to ask therefore, as a number of people are beginning to, whether an increasing proportion of the costs of the welfare state is going to those doing the welfare rather than those needing it'. This is a key question, even in the midst of a Conservative government pledged to reducing 'waste' amongst staff in the Department of Health and Social Security . . .

At the same time, through a deep departmentalisation of bureaucracy, manifestations of needs are dealt with separately, whereas a coordinated attack on the causes would be more socially useful. Goodman[15] argues that the danger of planning in both the capitalist and socialist countries is loss of personal control. Planning can only make sense to us when production is generated by our needs and not by the norms of those in power. For example if the community decides between a better architectural environment or better education, its way of measuring the usefulness of these alternatives would be by evaluating the effects of a better architectural environment or better education on the quality of peoples' lives – which would probably include the lives of those people directly involved in the production or servicing of those two activities.

This leads to the all important question about the forms of social organisation which enable people to have more control over the economic means necessary to satisfy needs. Bahro[16] describes this as a major task and calls it the overcoming of 'subalternity'. At its core this means abolition of the traditional radical division of labour, and, bound up with this, a revolution in the entire structure of needs. It proceeds by radical change in all our customary institutions and modes of procedure in society and in the economy. According to Bahro a redivision of labour would be based on the principle that everyone should share equally in activities at the various function levels. The establishment of social equality between those carrying out necessary labour would make it impossible for some people to be restricted to subordinate activity. Bahro's ideas are typical of much new thinking that is going on in the ecological movement, in the women's movement and elsewhere, as well as amongst socialists and trade unionists. He recognises that for

economic change to be effective it will need to go hand in hand with
changes in social life and social morality generally. The problem is to
find paths of development that lead forward from the present historical
scene. Criticisms of the present government's economic philosophies
need to lead on to positive alternatives, and these will require grass roots
democracy to exercise control and qualitive judgement of social need,
to ensure effective use of resources specifically and concretely 'at the
base'.

We thus see any major change in the economy, such that its goals are
related to the satisfaction of needs, requires major political changes and
will fundamentally alter the nature of social decision making. Community organisations 'at the base' will have to be more involved in making
decisions about consumption, as well as about production. Producers
and consumers will have to collaborate much more closely in the
decisions about what is to be produced, how it should be produced, and
how it should be distributed. Although this is a very difficult task, social
experiments with new ways of living together, consuming, producing
and cooperating can, as Gorz[17] stresses, have an important influence on
our understanding. Hence it is also important to develop alternative
technologies which will make it possible to do more, better and with less,
whilst at the same time increasing the autonomy of individuals and local
communities. But Gorz thinks that it will still remain essential to
socialise production of necessities and to have centralised regulation of
distribution and exchange. He argues that the function of centralisation
is economy of production time for the social system as a whole (and
hence in each person's lifetime) combined with extension of autonomy
for individuals and groups at the base, which should be seen as an end in
itself. However, both distribution and exchange are themselves profoundly altered by this proposition; just how much regulation of these
must remain centralised, and what criteria are to be used, are still open
questions.

A THEORY OF HUMAN NEEDS

Doyal and Gough took up some of these themes in their paper on 'A
Theory Of Human Needs' in which they define basic individual needs as
those goals which must be achieved if any individual is to achieve any
other goals.[18] They argue that these fall into two pairs, survival/health,
and autonomy/learning. 'Whatever the society, culture or subculture all
people need a minimum level of satisfaction of these basic needs in order

to be able to function as human individuals. With any society this will necessitate a certain level of other, intermediate needs such as housing, nutrition, nurture, self respect etc. The prime prerequisite here is to maximise individual or collective choice over ways of meeting basic needs utilising the best available contemporary, theoretical and practical understanding'. They discuss the importance of individual and group participation, in order to determine specific needs, but here they emphasise the importance of education in the broadest sense, and substantive democracy in the sense of political rights and economic means to participate in such debates. They argue strongly that a rational approach to social needs implies a dual structure, i.e. a society with maximum decentralisation and participation, alongside a society with a strong central state with extensive functions. 'The society organised to meet social needs involves a greater degree of both centralisation and decentralisation of decision making.' This requires clear criteria for settling who is to take decisions at different levels. Thus in housing policy, subsidies and access are inherent in the right to decent housing, but may have to be determined at the national level, whereas questions of housing amenities, management, etc. are appropriately settled at the most local decentralisation level. It emerges from this analysis that the appropriate role of the state is not so much to centrally direct, plan and control the activities and patterns of consumption of its members, as to try and maximise the areas of decentralisation and self reliance and autonomy in order to ensure that specific needs can be translated into socially useful products and services.

Thus in developing the socially useful economy, we are primarily concerned with extending the ability of people to control their own lives and to be involved in decisions concerning production of goods and services to meet their specific needs. The state should be concerned both at the national level and at the local level with actively pursuing, encouraging and creating the possibilities for such a transformation.

NOTES

1. Joan Robinson, *Economic Philosophy* (Penguin, 1962).
2. J.K. Galbraith, *The New Industrial State*, (Pelican, 1974).
3. P.A. Samuelson, *Treatise On Economics*, (McGraw-Hill, 1973)
4. M. Friedman, *Capitalism and Freedom*, (University of Chicago Press, 1962)
5. E. Nell, in R. Blackburn (ed.), *Economies: The Renewal of Political Economy* in *Ideology in Social Sciences* (Fontana, 1972) p. 77.

6. C. Freeman, *Economics of Innovation* (Frances Pinter, 1982).
7. For an excellent compendium of such criticisms see, E.K. Hunt and Jesse G. Schwartz (eds), *A Critique of Economic Theory* (Penguin Books, 1972).
8. J.K. Galbraith, op. cit.
9. R. Bahro, *The Alternative in Eastern Europe* (New Left Books, 1978).
10. Freeman, op. cit.
11. Freeman, op.cit.
12. Freeman, op. cit.
13. Freeman, op. cit.
14. Introduction by J. Palmer in R. Goodman *After the Planners* (Penguin, 1972).
15. R. Goodman, *After the Planners* (Penguin, 1972).
16. R. Bahro, op. cit.
17. A. Gorz, *Farewell to the Working Class* (Pluto Press, 1982).
18. L. Doyal and Ian Gough, *A Theory of Human Need* (unpublished paper presented at Seminar 3 by Ian Gough).

7 Negotiating for the Socially Useful Economy[1]

. . . The modern ultra-rapid computing machine . . . has unbounded possibilities for good and evil. For one thing, it makes the metaphorical dominance of the machines, as imagined by Samuel Butler, a most immediate and non-metaphorical problem. It gives the human race a new and most effective collection of mechanical slaves to perform its labor. Such mechanical labor has most of the economic properties of slave labor, and is essentially slave labor, although, unlike slave labor, it does not involve the direct demoralising effects of human cruelty. However, any labor that accepts the conditions of competition with slave labor accepts the conditions of slave labor, and is essentially slave labor. The key word of this statement is *competition*. It may very well be a good thing for humanity to have the machine remove from it the need of menial and disagreeable tasks, or it may not. I do not know. It cannot be good for these new potentialities to be assessed in the terms of the market, of the money they save; and it is precisely the terms of the open market, the 'fifth freedom', that have become the shibboleth of the sector of American opinion represented by the National Association of Manufacturers and the *Saturday Evening Post*.

Norbert Wiener, Cybernetics (1947)

What is or is not negotiable, and the problem of who you negotiate with in what forum is a common experience in society. A social security claimant may for instance not be able to negotiate with the DHSS directly, but may be able to obtain a semblance of negotiation through obtaining support of a Welfare Rights or Legal Aid organisation. Active trade unionists well know that certain issues are amenable to negotiation in the normal forum, others are the 'prerogative' of management and can only be *discussed* through a non decision making consultative forum. Community pressure groups will know well the difficulties in protecting their interests through the contingent structures and processes of planning inquiries. The ways in which one can negotiate for the development of a socially useful economy must of necessity reflect all of these problems and more. Moreover the very issue of negotiation in this area is a profoundly political one and therefore however hard the task may be it cannot be shirked. However, as the seminars demonstrated and as this book hopes to outline, the very first stage in the process requires the delineation of subjects, notions, ideas and ideals which are desirable, necessary.

As we have said before the paradigm commonly presented by government, management and most of the media is that those currently in power 'know' how to govern and make decisions which are in the best interests of everyone. Any criticism of opposition from 'below' – and that *is* how most of us are viewed – is taken as a direct attack on management's right to manage, be they in the senior civil service or in large private corporations. We are currently exhorted by government to look after ourselves, to pursue our own self interests, to be entrepreneurial in a variety of ways, yet at the same time are treated by the very same people as semi-idiots who like so many sheep or cattle must be cajoled and prodded into doing the 'right' thing.

When decisions are challenged our leaders' response is usually to limit or suppress the impact of the challenge. Using superior access to the media and usually having vast resources at their disposal, those dominant in society always seek to show that any opposition is misguided, non existent, 'extremist' and not based on any sort of popular support (despite the fact that governments are frequently elected by a popular mandate from no more than 30 or 40 per cent of the voting population). In spite of these efforts to curb the effectiveness of popular movements for change, mobilisation of peoples' power, to challenge the decisions and power of vested interests in dominant positions in society, has been historically the crucial prerequisite for the fulfilment of a great many human and social needs. The history of the labour movement, the struggle for political and human rights, the peace and women's movements, alternative movements in technology, food, health and the environment is a long, full and important history. This history has often shown that what is needed is a change in the economic philosophy that guides decisions, so as to judge overall community advantages qualitatively and to subordinate money and profit measures to measures that access social usefulness in one form or another. Therefore, to negotiate for change to develop a socially useful economy is part of an honourable and long historical tradition, however much its opponents try to belittle it.

In the struggle to achieve effective change many organisational forms have emerged over the years, such as trade unions, rank and file organisations in the labour movement, community-based pressure and action groups, cooperative and mutual organisations and networks. The sheer energy and amount of (often unpaid) time devoted to these causes and organisations clearly puts paid to the myth that people have to be told what to do through hierarchical means. As Mike Cooley argued

> either we will have a future in which human beings are reduced to a sort of bee-like behaviour, reacting to the system and equipment specified for them; or we will have a future in which masses of people, conscious of their skills and abilities in both the political and technical sense decide that they are going to be the architects of a new form of technological development which will enhance human creativity and mean more freedom of choice and expression. The truth is that we shall have to make other profound political decisions as to whether we intend to act as architects or behave like bees.[2]

So that we can be the architects of our own destiny, we have to seriously consider how 'the base' can gain negotiating power and negotiated positions to express their interests often against those private interests enshrined in money-power. Finally we must remember to be aware that the base is not 'the mob' – so beloved of the kings and aristocracy in former years. It is comprised of existing and new organisations which express the wishes and requirements of people in work, out of work, in their homes, in the market and in the community.

CURRENT BARGAINING ARRANGEMENTS

Negotiations between employees and employers in the present economy and under the present government are unlikely to bring about the fundamental changes needed to make business and services responsive to more socially defined needs. Current forms of negotiation cannot by themselves change the interests of the owners of private capital, nor can they change the standards by which the public sector is judged, i.e. cost effectiveness rather than social benefit. This is because the ultimate control of investment and of other basic decisions about what is produced and what services are provided remains in the hands of capital or those who operate clearly within its purview. Capital employs Labour for the benefit of Capital. However although conventional employer/

employee negotiation cannot change this basic relation to any great degree, it *can* help to educate participants about its nature. Collective bargaining in industrial relations can and often has been an extremely educative process; the problem remains however that employees are precluded from bringing a great number of important issues to the bargaining table because both their organisations and the employers are unwilling and sometimes unable to cope with them. This currently leads to a tremendous amount of frustration amongst employees, directed both at the employer and their unions.

Nevertheless it is wrong to assume that the activities of collective bargaining are firmly stuck in a cul-de-sac. A recently published study[3] from a survey of over one thousand work places showed that while 95% of manual workers and 92% of non-manual trade union representatives believe the length of the working week to be negotiable, only 39% and 36% respectively believed the same of capital investment. However in areas like major changes in production things were quite different with 88% and 84% respectively believing that negotiations were possible and meaningful in this area. Thus despite the steady and heavy onslaught against trade unionism in recent years there remain strong pressures amongst employees to have a much greater say in some of the principal issues in the world of work. This survey also reported a growth in 'joint consultative committees', which at the very least shows that the general centralising influences of authoritarian government and increasing authoritarian management are being resisted. We are of course aware that what we mean and others mean by consultation makes this finding quite difficult to interpret; on the one hand joint union committees and combine shop stewards committees continue to press at the margins of what is currently 'allowed industrial activity relations', whilst on the other hand some trade unionists have felt forced to accept pseudo participation schemes as a trade off against real or potential job threats. The study did cover the possibility and actuality of discussion or negotiation over product ranges and concluded that this was not a significant area for consultation or negotiation . . .

What such a survey does not and cannot reveal is the substantial amount of often quite difficult discussion and decision making occuring within a variety of union organisations about employers' 'employee involvement schemes', new technology and changing work practices, accountability and democracy within their own organisations, and even corporate strategy in some instances. It is true to say that despite efforts to constrain and contain trade unionism within ever more narrow boundaries the very experience of the employers' onslaught, the collapse of the 'new realism' in trade unions is leading to an increase in pressure for change in the boundaries of negotiation; though few would argue that possibilities for adequate expression of these pressures can be realised in the next year or two. Whilst the reality of much present day bargaining is constrained to 'bread and butter' pay and conditions negotiation, the level of discussion about how to increase trade union- ism's influence and role is definitely on the increase. One obvious result is the much-publicised stresses and strains between different unions. Some accept the philosophy of their employers and simply bargain for what is immediately possible. Others see no future for unions unless key managerial prerogatives, as currently accepted, are firmly challenged.

CHANGES FOR BARGAINING TODAY

Any active trade unionist knows that the fear of redundancy has been used as a very effective weapon against strong employee organisation. Shop stewards' posts remain vacant, strikes have become more difficult to organise and maintain, and many people 'keep their heads down' as they see jobs being lost all around them.

Nevertheless in the field of new technology there is perhaps now a much greater understanding than ever before of the true nature of change in work practices and work organisation that accompanies technical change. Perhaps a majority of the trade union movement no longer goes along in reality with the notion that new technology is invariably or ultimately in the employees' interests, though the rhetoric may remain confused and appear to indicate that unions wholeheart- edly accept technological progress. At the moment the major area of opposition to new technology remains that of productivity and the gains from higher productivity engendered through certain types of new technology. The issue of the shorter working week and the shorter working year just will not go away, despite very solid employer resistance. And it is noticeable in the USA and many other countries, unions have now rejected so-called 'quality of working life' and similar programmes that employers have used to try to get employees to accept new technology. As one shop steward put it 'we do not want to be involved or participate in decisions about the colour of the paint that is used on the bars of the cage that contains us'.

Despite the study previously referred to there is, if anything, an increase in interest and level of demand for information about em- ployers' markets, products, technology and investment decisions.

Resources and methods to satisfy these demands are not yet properly developed; yet the idea of 'shadow planning' and other concepts which indicate a vast change in the boundaries of trade unionism continue to grow in importance. At the very least the work that is going on at the moment in research units is helping to fuel peoples' desire for more real and undoctored information about what their managements are really doing.

As previously mentioned the very issues of union organisation and democratic forces within the trade union and labour movement are very much on the agenda at conferences and meetings of all types. Some of the pressure for this undoubtedly comes from employers' desire to marginalise trade unionism, other motivations come from pent-up frustrations within groups of employees as they see that their organisations are often being out-manoeuvred by employers. For even in such traditional areas as pay bargaining the experience of the last five or six years is showing people that to obtain a decent settlement means taking on quite fundamental issues such as how employers prepare and present their financial accounts. This is especially true for employees who work in multi-national corporations, and for those in the public sector whose employer is the government and whose pay bargaining framework is laid down by clearly political decisions. Conditions of employment in general also have a higher profile than they have had for many years, as vast changes in work organisation and technologies bring into question the very notion of permanent employment, the historical status of jobs (e.g. craft occupations), the position of the increasing numbers of part time, temporary and sub-contracted employees, etc. A gut-level understanding of Tony Hopward's contention that there are more accountants per square inch in British industry than in any other part of the world is very much in evidence as corporate development comes to express itself more and more in narrow financial terms. Thus those who imagine that they are in work to produce things rather than money are a dwindling force. Last but not least the sheer viciousness with which employees, and trade union activists in particular have been treated by employers has been a profoundly important education for the trade union movement. It brings in train a very stark choice between being truly adversarial, making few if any concessions to the interests of capital, and believing that one's only 'salvation' lies in accepting managerialism in all its guises. The differences between true negotiation, consultation, participation and employee involvement on one hand, and managerial authoritarianism on the other, are being heightened in a way not seen for many many years.

In many respects this experience can be seen to a greater or lesser extent in other organisations in society which seek to forward the interests of people who are disadvantaged through race, sex, age, and other circumstances over which they have no control. Of particular note must be the initiatives in recent years by Local Authorities which in aggregate have mounted a challenge to economic orthodoxy of a scale never seen before in this country. They have been in a truly adversarial bargaining position with central government and in some cases employers too. The very fact that the popular media now talk of a 'divided Britain' underpins the contention that whilst the New Right in both government and employer organisations has exerted itself in an extremely vigorous way, people in vast numbers of organisations have resisted and have attempted to lay down some form of alternative to the current status quo.

In struggling against an increasingly virulent money-power trade unions and other organisations are *having* to seek new allies, often as a quite organic and 'natural' development for specific or general campaigns. Thus workers in Britain are equating their own job interests with the quality of the services they give, maintaining through joint sessions with 'consumers' that privatisation will be a tremendous threat to both producers and consumers. For example, this confluence of interests is being defended by the National Communications Union, and hospital cleaners in the NHS around the country are fighting privatisation because of the decline in health and safety standards that it leads to. Meanwhile the number of rank and file trade union activities which are of a truly international nature are on the increase as the reality of transnational capital is being brought home in ever more vivid ways.

WORKING PEOPLES' POWER, VISION AND CONFIDENCE

Increasingly objects of struggle are expressed in terms of social justice, echoing the very powerful calls of the trade union and labour movement in the last century and the early part of this century. Many issues are becoming clarified following the break down of so-called consensus politics that characterised the post-war economic and social settlement. But the mechanisms and frameworks for properly expressing current notions and realities of social justice are under-developed. Some would maintain that this is the direct consequence of a generation or more of economic settlements that left major policies to management and Government. Paradoxically the time is perhaps ripe for the creation of a whole new agenda and a set of new mechanisms for developing active democracy in pursuit of interests which are different to those of money-power. For when so many of the 'old' remedies against injustice, be it economic, social or political, are being seen to fail in the face of the New-Right's strategies and tactics, people quite naturally start to turn to other means and ways of attaining their requirements. It would be tragic indeed if they allowed their demands to be once again subsumed within a framework which gave the illusion of common interests throughout all layers of society. Perhaps the biggest challenge today is to the upper echelons of the British trade union and labour movement: will these organisations come to fully understand the burgeoning of new ideas, new experiences, new activities *at the base* and will they accept that it is this new creativity at the base, that can give them the power and vision to resolve the great economic and social problems now confronting them?

MANAGEMENT'S POWER, VISION AND CONFIDENCE

Much has been written about management theory and decision making by managers. The assumption of this theory is that a corporate hierarchical structure is the norm where accountability is always 'upwards'. Responsibility is taken primarily at an individual level and managers succeed by making alliances, and isolating those whose 'face doesn't fit'. Power is generally conferred from above and thus may be removed from above, whilst peer group competition is encouraged with members fighting each other for shares of resources, and approval from superiors. Managers may be consulted in the decision process but the superior manager will normally make the decision, and whilst there may be grumbles about decisions, all managers will tend to defend the process of decision making. The whole thing is overlayed by a spurious 'objective' view that managers really are the servants of the market place. The reality of management in both public and private sectors is that of a rather narrow world view, constrained by fear – the motivation of career enhancement, a crude satisfaction in the exercise of power over others, a quite understandable protectionism around individuals' areas of expertise and competence, and an acceptance of organisation goals and behaviour, often played out as a form of game-playing. There are exceptions to this, sometimes characterised as 'sharks' in certain types of management literature, who are the 'high-fliers', totally absorbed and involved in the exercise of power on their own behalfs – be it expressed through a rapid rise within the ranks of the civil service, or through clever manipulation of financial or business organisations at large.

It has often been said that lower and middle managers' interests are objectively similar to those of all other employees in an organisation. But the reality is that few can personally afford to admit to such a possibility. Collective organisations that exist for managers are single mindedly organised to keep them 'in the fold'. It is only in individual cases that some movement, some possibility of change may exist.

Managements exist within and as a part of an organisational dynamics whose aims are in one way or another tied to the interests of money-power. Vision is similarly constrained by organisational interests, and by personal interests which are themselves organisationally determined to a large extent. Confidence is currently at a high-point as management is almost forced to accept the cascade of rhetoric about a new-realism and 'enlightened' self-interest as being the only basis for running an economically successful society. Therefore to enlist the support of management in any wholesale change requires a very clear-headed understanding of their currently-determined interests, and the beginnings of the removal of the 'pseudo-theory' of managerial importance and competence. There is no easy route to this, and it is the job of those who would propose the development of socially useful economy to develop forms of argument which are awkward, difficult to dispute. Confidence can certainly be shaken for instance where trade unionists come forward with information in a bargaining framework which is entirely unexpected, and which has a powerful force of argument behind it. To expand and change management's vision of what it should be doing requires a substantial ideological effort which in effect says that their current exercise of power and responsibility is not in the common good, nor is it even in their own interests. Their power must be challenged by a thorough-going rearrangement of the terrain on which they operate. None of this is impossible.

CHANGING THE FRAMEWORK

Certain key tasks lie before us here. Perhaps the most obvious would be a change in the law which fully recognises legitimate interests of employees and transfers the relevant powers to them, and which at the same time would have to provide certain constraints on managerial power. Rights to information, analogous to a Freedom of Information Act, a workers' right of veto and so on would also be necessary. As one of the active participants in the seminar put it, we also have to ensure that there is a vast increase in the numbers of people having the right to 'paid think work'; in London capital has some 35 million hours each week available to it for 'think work'. He went on to say that it would be far more effective and meaningful if the Greater London Council's work can make it possible for time to be released and reappropriated by workers in their workplace 'whether at work or at home' and organised by them for the purposes of becoming their own planners in and against the market.

A key to this is what we have called 'socially useful productivity', that is, using technical advances in production and administration to open up spaces within the tight and oppressive relations of the market. If such spaces can be liberated within the structure of a working (and non-working) community their effect can be amplified by additional outside support through a variety of organisations in the trade union and labour movement – which themselves should be given adequate funding for this purpose. To be proactive rather than reactive begins to address a way of changing the framework in which negotiation for a socially useful economy becomes a reality. Similarly substantial research, support and promotion must be given to other models of activity, including shop stewards who develop 'alternative plans' for their enterprise, cooperatives and other mutual associations, be they in the workplace or outside it. For objectively workers' alternative plans, campaigns for creches and better child care facilities, for better health facilities and so on reflect in the main the priorities of a socially useful economy, the interests of those currently disenfranchised in one way or another are, almost by definition, opposed to the interests of money-power. We also need a substantial examination of organisational forms which are not hierarchical. This applies both to existing organisations in the trade union and labour movement and to organisations operating on behalf of money-power.

As several of the seminar contributors noted, we require a different agenda for the development, design and use of micro-electronics. Information technology, if well funded and well-supported could provide an extremely important infrastructure for the development of new plans and for their implementation. Even in the production sphere the work of Professor Rosenbrook, Mike Cooley and others has clearly shown that it is possible (technically and socially) to develop high-technology plant and equipment which enhances the human element rather than diminishing it.

Many of these issues are discussed in more detail in Chapter 10 and elsewhere in the book. The fundamental point remains that ideas for a more socially relevant use of people's time, be it paid or unpaid at the moment, of people's experience, skills and ingenuity lie all round us, largely untapped, largely frustrated. Changing the framework in which we can negotiate for a socially useful economy requires at root the *freeing* of people to construct, discuss and implement a vast reservoir of practical ideas about how to make society more civilised, and how to make a process for human development.

BARGAINING FOR A SOCIALLY USEFUL ECONOMY

We return to some key points in the bargaining process for the development of a socially useful economy. First with respect to socially useful products and services, the relationship with consumers is currently entirely under the control of management. This has to change, we have already seen the beginnings of a 'natural' confluence of interests between producers and consumers and this needs to be encouraged, if necessary supported by adequate financial and other resources. The meeting of producers and consumers in a common forum has been proved as an extraordinarily fruitful crucible for the development of new ideas and practices. (This occurred in the health field between Lucas workers and a variety of practitioners, technicians and so on during 1979 and 1980.) As an adjunct we require the elaboration of popularly available measures of community profit, use-value, and opportunity-cost; these are measures of 'how well are we doing' in terms which reflect the reality of people's facilities and gains – quite separate from the values used by money-power. Obviously people's requirements will cover issues such as low pay, skill, training, as well as purchasing power and ability to lay claim to resources and services by consumers. One very obvious example is in the direct labour organisations in local government, where both producers and consumers have an obvious interest in housing policy and control over building, maintenance and repair. At the moment the whole 'privatisation' debate makes enemies of those who work in these local authority departments and also of council tenants.

Secondly we *do* require to place a much heavier emphasis on socially beneficial working conditions – *both* for currently paid and unpaid work. Alienating and frustrating conditions of work stupefy consciousness, create cynicism and despair. The opposite of this, which is to provide a creative, pleasant and socially interesting environment, in and of itself encourages people to be involved with the meaning and purpose of what they are doing. This emphasis has to embrace *all* the conditions of work which relate to child care, to the conditions of the very many women who are currently forced to work part time, and of course to people from ethnic minorities who are perhaps even more disadvantaged in the job market. Job-sharing, which is not simply an employer's excuse for reducing influence and pay, needs to be addressed in a much deeper way. Our notions of what we mean by training and education for adults in and around work has to be re-evaluated, and of course we need to start a process of change in the relationship between technology and the human worker.

Thirdly the environmental effects of production can often result in conflicts between workers who need continued employment and people living nearby or downwind of the production site or near a toxic waste dump. This applies not only to the immediate effluent of production but also to waste associated with throwaway products – which is a longer-term problem. On the other side, as has been mentioned previously, there is resource depletion and the nature of raw material extraction. The environment 'writ large' is not simply the concern of those who live in pretty rural areas; it is also the built environment. Environmental policy has to cover housing, factory and office buildings, traffic and technologies of travel, the current depredations of agri-business and their remedies, the health and safety of artifacts used in and around the home, and much else besides. There have already been many instances where producers and environmentalists have found common cause, and the aim of developing a socially useful economy is intended to make 'environmentalists' of us all – for the environment is, quite simply, the place in which we live our lives.

MAKING THE LINKAGES

Through the 1970s there were a number of 'workers' plans' developed by rank and file trade union organisations in companies such as Lucas Aerospace, Vickers, parts of the car industry and the machine tool industry, Dunlop, Metal Box, International Computers and many others besides. These plans sought to lay out alternatives for producers and consumers alike – they were first of all *administered out of existence* by the then Labour government and subsequently pressurised out of existence by the Conservative government. These various shop steward committees made common cause at a practical level with health service workers, tenants' organisations, local authority and community organisations, and environmentalists. However the linkages so produced proved too weak to hold out against the forces ranged against them – government, employers, and even some trade unions. Despite these defeats workers' plans, albeit presented somewhat differently, continued to be developed and a great deal more thought has to be given to the types of linkages and structures which need to be developed to support these and similar initiatives. One obvious example has been provided by the various Labour-controlled local authorities in recent years. So, one of the primary tasks is to undertake an effective 're-think' about planning which addresses local needs, the needs of those in a particular company, even the needs of those in particular industries.

In a report entitled 'The Knowledge Economy' by the Economic Policy Group in the Greater London Council two opposing approaches to forging links with planning and implementation are presented. One approach accepts the 'Metropolitan' framework of existing institutions and thus sees a local authority's role as being mainly to make market mechanisms work better' or to seek competitive advantages for the local economy within the larger market. The other approach recognises that *any* locality is marginal in a metropolitan framework of knowledge and industrial practice. It therefore attempts to build a strategy which accommodates itself – in its ideas and in its practice – to this inescapably 'provincial' role of any local authority which seeks to *directly* meet local needs. Such a strategy is faced by the challenges of working both in and against the market.

In order to develop a 'provincial' approach in London the Greater London Enterprise Board created technology networks (TECHNETS) in an attempt to bring together community and workplace groups with academics and researchers. The main ideas in the original (Spring 1982) GLC proposal for Technology Networks were: a number of geographically-based centres phasing in the introduction of new technologies so as to give new life to declining industries (mainly engineering); maintaining overall employment levels; development of 'socially useful' products (non-alienating production and use, skill enhancing, energy conserving); centres to have banks of alternative products; banks of reconditioned machines, technical support units and new-enterprise support units for co-operatives and similar enterprises; networks to liberate the 'wasted' resources of academic institutions, and enabling workers' organisations and communities to get access to technical development resources financed with matching investment from academic institutions or borough councils (in opposition to the elitism and self aggrandisement of university-linked Science Parks). Centres were to have a small staff (exploiting the research time or spare time of national-state funded academics and student projects). Enabling work in the networks began in late 1982 but workshop premises were not occupied until mid 1983 or 1984.

An *important* underlying principle of this is that any restructuring of local industries must be based on the provincial planning approach and does not entrust the future of a local economy to metropolitan interests in which the forces of the market are allowed to define the patterns of investment, employment and growth.

This requires the development of the practice of "provincial" planning which can identify social 'market' needs and provide a set of mechanisms for linking research with action. These mechanisms in London range from centralised organisations such as the GLC's industry and employment branch and enterprise board, through Technology Networks and the networks of resource centres, Co-operative Development Agencies and so on, to the most local peoples' planning initiatives. At the same time they cover a range of different working mixes of people who are paid to think and people who are not. This complicated range is necessary in provincial planning, involving local state funding and investment. So is the range of autonomy which has to be allowed for in building such a set of arrangements. However, accepting these points it is necessary that the fragments should now be linking increasingly together into an overall network which, for the sake of a label, we have called "research city". (Paper from Mike Hales of GLC)

Although the local authorities have obviously been under attack from the Government the Labour Party is now planning to produce Regional Development Plans as part of its process of developing industrial and economic policies. These could become the focus for bringing together local plans and enterprise plans and giving renewed vision and confidence, and eventually power to working (and out of work) people.

SOME CONCLUSIONS

A key point in negotiating for social usefulness is the sheer excitement and interest that has been demonstrated by the vast international, as well as national, concern about the implementation of workers plans,

environmental initiatives and the like. This should not be underesti-
mated; for example in the Scandinavian countries the Lucas Aerospace
workers' initiative has in fact led to some quite substantial changes in the
industrial infrastructure of Sweden and Norway in particular; in West
Germany, in Australia and in a number of other countries workers'
plans have been taken up as an integral part of trade union campaigns to
protect jobs, and to advance workers' interests in the longer term. The
whole peace movement, environmentalism, women's movement and so
on also have an international dimension which has in some instances
proved to be of sufficient significance to affect political processes and
decisions in a number of countries. Perhaps, thankfully, optimists, on
balance, outnumber cynics and there *are* very substantial numbers of
people who gratefully and sincerely support radical initiatives. The
almost-desperate-sounding rhetoric of the orthodox monetarist governments in the OECD in particular is, at base, only accepted through
fear and the lack of adequately-articulated alternatives. A real negotiation for making peoples' endeavours more socially useful starts with this
enthusiasm, with the energetic promotion of ideas which are grounded
in practicality. Once we have achieved that level of interest and
understanding, have broken the chains of the grim and narrow TINA
(there is no other alternative) ideology then a new common sense can
emerge whose force will be sufficient to compel real negotiation with the
current holders of power, those who wield money-power.

NOTES

1. Much of the following has been taken from the Seminar Papers produced by
   Martin Stears and Nick Clark, direct quotes from the papers have not been
   used.
2. M.J.E. Cooley, *Architect or Bee?: Human/Technology Relationship*
   (Slough: Langley Technical Services, *c*. 1980).
3. W.W. David and N. Millward, *Workplace Industrial Relations in Britain*
   (Heinemann, 1983).

8 The State and Institutional Frameworks

From all the easy speeches
that comfort cruel men . . .
         G.K. Chesterton

INTRODUCTION

Whilst democracy only means something when it's an activity, the role of institutions will remain crucial to its operation. So any movement towards the primacy of the 'socially useful' in political economy must deal with existing institutions and map out new institutions.

At its simplest level an institution is put in place to provide a number of key structures and practices which create, maintain and regulate an area of human activity. Institutions however are usually something 'more' than agency or organisation, they provide a form of legitimacy, a cornerstone and a norm.

It is somewhat fruitless to indulge here in detailed analysis of institutions as an organisational form, or to carry out theoretical work on the differences between an institution and an agency. Basically we mean by institutions those bodies which make up hegemonic entities or major parts of entities which dominate in economic, political and social life.

However we make a distinction between organisations we commonly describe as institutions, such as the Department of Employment, and *ideas* that organise accepted social behaviour. Ideas as an institutional force are a component of what Antonio Gramsci called 'Hegemony'.[1]

International finance institutionalises inter-country financial relations (and inequalities), and sets in place a framework for transnational capital's operations. Transnational bodies such as the World Bank and the International Monetary Fund are examples of institutions in this sphere, whilst international commodity markets (e.g. the oil market in

Rotterdam) and transnational corporations are key institutions for transnational capital. They legitimate a certain way of dealing globally with economic relations in order to maximise capital accumulation.

Monarchy, 'the family', household units are similarly institutions, though with very different organisational forms. Here, as in many other spheres of life the actual institution is reified, an abstraction created and recreated consciously, though seldom by those actually supposed to comprise the institution. The same must increasingly be the case for 'the poor', with government ministers in particular referring to these people in terms reminiscent of kings in history books who had to deal with 'the mob' or 'the rabble' from time to time – an institutional management of millions of people through a demeaning so-called social security 'system'.

Institutions are therefore the successful culmination of historical forces which, by and large, are no longer thought to be open in any meaningful way to serious questioning. To be an institution is to 'have it made' – just as we sometimes refer to outstanding individuals as 'an institution'.

INSTITUTIONAL CHANGE

To put in place a socially useful economy necessarily means institutional change, firstly it needs ways and means of removing or changing certain existing institutions, or at the least, changing the ways they are managed.

At the most fundamental level we (and many others) have to try to remove the institution of prejudice against people of a different colour, race or creed, for, not only does it harm oppressed and oppressor, it feeds an abstract, militant nationalism – whose awful features are most usually perceived when we look at another nation. This bundle of prejudices make up an ideology which stunts consciousness. In any multiracial society such as Britain not only must we create equal opportunity but also be open to the enormous opportunities that being cosmopolitan can bring. Fear and anger breed isolation and conservatism. The similar institution of prejudice on sexual grounds may have even more far-reaching consequences. There is an important approach to economic strategy proposed by Anna Coote[2], Sheila Rowbotham and others.[3] This approach places childcare, servicing of households and other 'conventional' womens' work firmly on the agenda of any socially useful economy – the institution of prejudice not only makes second class citizens out of women, it also correspondingly ignores non-waged work despite it having profound economic importance. Major amounts of disposable expenditure need to be correlated with the 'hidden' costs of care of children, elderly people, those with disabilities and the like. Oppressed and oppressor alike suffer, though not in equal proportions. The suppression of women is as large a phenomenon worldwide as is class oppression, although the two cohere in reality to a very large degree. So the common constitution of an individual's rights and worth is already institutionalised by accident of birth. This is an anathema for the very precepts of a socially useful economy, for it imposes structured norms which distort the potential contribution and fulfilment of a majority of the British population – or rather, the population of those in Britain. So here our task is massive, ranging from independent disciplinary procedures to root out racial prejudice amongst employers, the police etc., to the enactment of new legislation on equal pay and opportunity for women, to longer term measures which effectively place a real and recognised value on non-waged work. Virulent prejudice against sexual relations between those of the same sex has also to be firmly and quickly demolished, not least because it is part of the institution of 'manhood' or 'womanhood' which divides person from person quite unnecessarily, and creates damaging fears and guilt which lead to conservative oppression.

Nationhood, manhood – beware of the hoods for they are false idols, demi-gods of institutions which turn our attention away from a host of real (not imagined) grievances.

Institutions in society which fundamentally affect peoples' rights, worth and experiences have many roots – very few of them bear up to examination. Black people 'had' to be inferior because the British ruling class made a lot of money and gained a lot of power through slavery and exploitation of a near-slavery kind. Women had to be 'kept in their place' through fear and narrow self-interest on the part of males. Poor and disabled had to remain disenfranchised in order that they remained 'outside' of society – that way they could be dismissed from the mind. Those with a homosexual orientation didn't conform to the 'hoods', were (and still are) seen as a threat to sets of morals which themselves are of dubious validity. Much more could be written, and has been elsewhere, but it is worth reminding ourselves about the truly offensive nature of some of the most basic institutions which govern daily life. It is worth remembering that not very long ago people openly talked about 'society' as that upper crust of titled and/or rich people. That so-called 'society' still exists, though its open pronouncements are now more coded than before. *This* is the 'society' that by and large created and recreated many of these basic institutions.

The housewife, motherhood, the 'sacred' duty of procreation, the family of 2 adults and 2 children, the household – these and many other institutionalised ideals and practices conform neatly to the needs of other institutions – the institutions of money power. Mass marketing directed towards these markets (for that is what 'the housewife' is in this light) is itself an institution on an increasingly global scale. The presentation of commodities *to* commodities (i.e. people) is an institutionalised process – promising utility, prestige, excitement, progress, value-for-money ('look how clever you'll be, getting this cheaper'), and all the other messages that cohere into ideology of the 'consumer society'.

MARKET INSTITUTIONS

The consumer society idea is of course just about meaningless at root, but as an ideology, created and recreated by money power it is truly powerful. It offers choice, individuality-through-consumption, higher status, feelings of worth, and so on. Exchange value rules of course, where art is auctioned to the highest bidder, where house prices reflect prestigious locations, or where baked beans packaged under one label cost more than the same packaged under another label. Here the institution of trade, an old and infinitely variable human practice has been fashioned into a globally comprehensive and dominating *meaning*. It is no longer a basic means of exchange between people, nor even the creation of a market for capital accumulation (though it remains that of course), but a relatively seamless institution of measurement, against abstract ideals directly associated with meaning attached to commodities.

Thus the marketplace as an institution makes commodities of us all. The choice we have is in reality heavily circumscribed, our consumption-led strivings can never succeed in bringing us most of what we want or indeed need in many cases. This institution needs to be dismembered, for otherwise we will tend to remain bedazzled by its high powered projections, its promises which lie at the end of the rainbow.

For a start well over 7 million people depend on supplementary benefit in Britain, so their disposable income is barely enough to even get a foot in the door of 'the market place'. Add on millions subsisting on other benefits, e.g. unemployment, retirement pension. Then add a few more millions who didn't claim benefit but who are on low pay (around £100 per week or less), and you get perhaps a quarter of the total population with little or no opportunity to 'benefit' from the market. The next quartile *can* start to get 'the goods', though always at the cheaper end of things – choice in any real sense is still severely limited. It's only within the top quarter of the population that 'choice' as popularly promoted comes to have any real meaning, e.g. between a luxurious car and a sporty one.

So while the market may provide certain basic types of commodity to many, only relatively few can actually 'enjoy' the things that are projected as 'meaning success'. Then of course we have to look at all those areas where the market causes distress. There's housing, fuels, transport for instance, where pricing and availability creates actual inequalities and difficulties which significantly magnify differences in people's income. The market provides dangerous goods; it also fails signally to deliver goods or services for a host of unmet needs, our old people die of hypothermia, wheelchair design proceeds at a rate which would compare favourably with chariot design in Roman times, Coca Cola is easier to obtain than food in many Third World countries.

So, like any good ruse, 'the market' thrives by pretending to deliver what for most is in reality unattainable. This global supermarket must be criticised, both for what it does, and for what it doesn't do. And in its place we need to put markets which maximise Use Value. Our institution would break the monopoly of ideas fostered by the present marketplace. It's starting point must of necessity be the fulfilment of unmet social needs – and these don't have to be 'worthy but dreary'. Why shouldn't decent housing at a realistic price be exciting and much in demand? People *do* like to support tangible aids for people with disabilities – why shouldn't 'space-age' radar for blind people be interesting? The work required to develop and supply items and services for unmet needs would put paid to mass unemployment too. Then of course our market institution would provide so-called consumer goods with designs which would enhance the ability to repair, renovate, and understand them. It would remove unnecessary duplication associated with false choices, and it would open up possibilities for new products – which at the moment are suppressed or ignored because of the dominance of Exchange Values in the market.

In order to create our new institution of the market further we first have to consider that most basic institution, that of paid work and all that it implies.

For most people work is important and not solely for the money that it brings. Work provides all sorts of satisfactions; it helps give people a sense of worth, of 'being in society'. Historically it has provided the majority of people with some sort of challenge, for instance through use of craft skills or technical skills, or through subtle measures to undermine managerial controls over work. And here we must make it quite clear that we're not just referring to the conventionally skilled person – under current pay, grading and occupational divisions, which deny vast swathes of skills and knowledge that exist among so-called unskilled people.

USE VALUES AND INSTITUTIONS

Use values of products and services have a real existence in the work process. Yet the institution of the enterprise and of managerialism by and large deny these use values to working people and put in place abstractions such as careerism, phoney status symbols, and token pay differentials. The institutions which shape work practices, norms and expectations obviously legitimate and pursue capital accumulation, and have little or no contact with the actual needs, wants, aspirations and experiences of the toiling millions.

Yet over the years there has been a large (and largely unwritten) body of opinion and experience of working people who sought to change work practices, controls over jobs, the relations between employed and employer, even the very product of their labours. Even today, when managerialism is thought to be *the* process for the control and direction of work of all sorts, people actively pursue fundamental change. People who work in the arms industries seek to use their knowledge and skills for peaceful ends. Hospital cleaners and ancillary workers prepare and fight for contracts which enhance safety and health for patients. Computer staffs leave the big corporations in droves in order to unshackle themselves from narrow constraints. The surreptitious manufacture of 'foreigners' (unscheduled items, as it were) continues in engineering shops throughout the country. Public transport staffs are fighting job losses through public awareness campaigns about reductions in the quality of service provided to users. At least one of the DHSS trade unions actually warns claimants of their rights if they're visited by the DHSS 'fraud squads'. Working people in many transnational corporations are forging new international links with their counterparts across the world in order to bring forward more accountability. Local authority staffs are creating a multitude of new experiments for the creation of new forms of working and work relations. There is now perhaps the highest ever activity amongs working people to 'get to grips' with many aspects of corporate strategy and policy.

Obviously these democratically-oriented initiatives are crucial for the development of the socially useful economy, for what is produced, by whom, in what way is a key element in the equation. The institution of 'the firm' – be it in the private or public sector has to be changed.

The institution of 'private interests' expressed in private sector enterprises is a gross distortion of reality – for legitimate interests in enterprises can be claimed by all consumers, all employees, people whose environment is directly or indirectly affected by enterprise operations, sometimes whole communities of people whose employment, training and local government services are affected by enterprise closures or cutbacks. Ownership of private enterprises is often held in the majority by large numbers of people whose pension contributions (i.e. deferred wages) provide equity based capital resources. Taxpayers may also have a stake through private enterprises' income derived from the public purse – a major source of income for many commercial sectors. Moreover the constitution of 'public' companies clearly implies responsibilities which are far from being private.

Private interests in this regard denote secrecy, non-accountability, and the unhampered pursuit of capital accumulation, culminating in a major form of money-power. Yet as we know the large corporations in particular exert a dominating influence over markets, artifacts and services, work, the environment and so on. 'Interference' from outsiders is fiercely resisted, unless it be from enterprise's banks, City investors or pension fund agencies. But, nevertheless, what may 'make sense' for one set of private interests can create enormous economic and social dysbenefits for others with a legitimate (though public) interest. The 'private' interests of course maintain that their interests *must* reflect the interests of the community at large, for economic success, competitiveness, exploitation of markets, etc. can provide the only efficient way of providing work and goods, and more money for redistribution.

Up to a certain point this may be true (it is after all an historically uncontested issue); yet the British economy and the welfare of its society continues to give much cause for concern. Recent public arguments over the coal industry's 'economics', the financial practices of the oil giants and major pharmaceutical corporations point clearly to deep structural inadequacies in the notion that private interests serve the public good. Surely it is not in the public interest to create unemployment, obsolescent goods or make whole towns 'surplus to requirements' – it might serve so-called private interests and money power though . . .

A first step in the remedy would be to give means of expression to all those legitimate interests which connect with the 'private interests' of corporations. Where the public purse pays private interests must be genuinely accountable – 'no subvention without accountability'. Where local amenities and services are affected by private interests, local government interests may have to be served through carrot and stick methods. Democracy in the application of pension fund monies is a crucial financial means of affecting private interests. Industrial or worker democracy is central, as is 'consumer democracy'.

NEW INSTITUTIONAL FRAMEWORKS

Real private interests, such as in a small family firm would remain private, to do otherwise would impose non-legitimate interests. But in mainstream industrial and commercial operations our institution of the enterprise would reflect the truly 'mixed' nature of real interests. So, in firms which receive in net receipts 50% or more of income from the public purse, a public agency would have formal, legitimate influence, proportional to its net contribution to the firm's coffers. Part of this formal influence would be devolved to local governments, where the firm employed, say, 5% or more of the populace. Consumer democracy would be legitimated outside of the market, the exact nature of the agency to be employed depending on the sector or service involved. In the NHS medical/patient associations would be created to instruct and directly advise on equipment design for example, while requirements for domestic goods may be developed through voluntary associations with *formal* powers of instruction or advice. Pension fund power would be passed to representatives of those whose money it is, with independent advice being provided on investment options. It should be noted that an 'ethical' pensions investment organisation recently showed a greater capacity to provide for their pensioners' money needs than that of most conventional pension fund investment firms.

Employees' interests would of course feature large in our institution of the firm, and their expression would fundamentally change the institution of work. First, information disclosure would become a major *activity* in the firm, formal negotiating rights would be established for many new areas of operation, and new arrangements made for employees to meet together to plan and implement new enterprise policies. Two fundamental issues would thus be tackled, that of use value of products or services provided, and use value of the labour process itself, i.e. *what* is the firm's function and *how* should it function?

First, use values in work are at present largely overlaid by exchange values and the so-called cash nexus of waged labour relations. Use values in work involve job content, job control, job satisfaction, and possibilities for personal or group initiative. Given the opportunity, labour history shows us that significant numbers of people *do* obtain much more out of work than cash. The 'artisan' idea is more than romantic idealism; it has a past and present that is real, though continually undermined by the current institution of work which makes a commodity out of labour. If just 5% of the working population decided to take up our option and actively changed the scope of work we would have over a million experiments. The use values of the products or services thus produced would similarly be changed. Here it is not fanciful to envisage the creation of new products, dramatically changed services, alterations in investment policy, new attitudes towards the procurement and application of technologies. At first we would envisage employee-based changes which would enhance employment opportunities and security. This might mean the adoption of longer term timescales, for development for instance, and the removal of short-term rationalisation programmes. In packaging for example we might see whole new activities arise from novel uses of returned (returnable) containers, or novel uses of existing laminating technologies. In the petrochemicals industry new strategies may be developed, which cohere with a long-term energy policy for Britain's exploitation and use of oil. Meanwhile, given the opportunity, the new information and communication technologies could be used for purposes of adult education and other measures which would help to create a more 'transparent society'.

The lines from 'modest' job-protection policies to the creation of wholly new use values through novel applications and developments of technologies and skills are not linear, and experimentation must be accepted as a legitimate norm. The extent of this process at any one time would have to be regulated to some degree, but it *would* nevertheless comprise a legitimate institution for new practices in work. In essence exactly the same processes can be applied to public sector operations, though here we might have to formally ensure agreement over key objectives, such as the maintenance of a pure water supply, a weekly refuse disposal service, or a specified public housing maintenance standard.

Of course critics will say 'how do we afford it?', and our reply is laid out in some detail in the following chapter. However, a few key facts should be brought forward here, which show the nature of our thinking.

Firstly, mass unemployment is expensive, direct and indirect cost of over 3 million unemployed range from £15 to £20 billion a year. The cost of the lost product of unemployment – assuming a national average per capital rate of value-added is in the region of £30 billion a year. So for a start real job creation, if looked at from a properly comprehensive viewpoint may be actually cheaper at the moment than the economic dysbenefits of unemployment. Secondly, our notion of the firm stresses a reflection of the mixture of true interests that exist in and against private interests, so the creation of supernormal profits, the abstraction of money from resource use, would tend to cease. The re-introduction of exchange controls, and the effective removal of money power from money as such is also important. The asset-base of Britain is severely denuded by current financial operations; resources – people, machines and premises – lie idle, and productive resources are used to create weapons of war which have little or no real value. A socially useful economy, with new aims for full employment, new approaches to employment and the provision of goods, does away with the enormous wastage of resources and money that currently takes place. This provides a massive basis for endeavours which may not provide conventional profit. Some 40% of all pension fund investment brings returns which are completely inadequate for the financial needs of pension schemes – that's in the order of £30–40 billion in Britain. So 'socially useful' pension fund investment of this order of magnitude is in principle available, with no other changes wrought.

But perhaps the most basic issue for the development of a new institution for the firm lies in the financial field, of returns on assets, the major directions in investment, trading patterns, and Britain's cumulative financial relations with others. The socially useful economy is not a siege economy, rather the reverse.

New institutions are required to regulate profit, and change its meaning. Use values are given primacy and legitimacy through a *process* of enterprise development, employee rights are given equal status and power to that of consumers, public agencies, and outside investors. Planning based on optimisation of resource use is built into the development process, and this planning procedure involves employees and the other associations as of right. Enterprise aims are redefined, certainly key money and resource issues will have to be sufficiently defined and met in order to maintain basically viable operations, but whole new sets of aims will be put in place too – those which maximise use value. And we should again remember that use values *have* a positive economic impact. The production of say new house insulation materials by a laminates packaging plant (which may still continue to produce packagings), with extra labour, will contribute beneficially to energy policy and depletion, and provide extra resources for spending elsewhere in the economy by the householder, whose fuel bills will decline as a result. Meanwhile extra paid work will provide additional sources of demand.

Our view is based on a version of underconsumption which holds that economic activity (in our terms the application of available resources) is very much lower than it needs to be. It is lower because private interests, whose policies are directed towards money power, extract their returns through the 'cheapest' means of employing resources – which may, paradoxically, mean also a profligate use of resources, whereas a socially useful economy stresses the optimal use of resources. It is worth returning to the notion expounded in Dalton's 1946 Budget Speech, which proposed the creation and maintenance of a low-interest economic sector, within which a range of infrastructural and long-term investment activities can take place. In effect this is a socialised version of Japanese financial and commercial practices.

So, new financial institutions will be put in place which encourage and regulate new areas of social/work activity, and new accounting practices developed to support them. Meanwhile enterprise activities which are relatively non-problematic will continue – we will after all still require industrial products and a vast range of fairly conventional consumer goods. What has to be regulated here rests upon relatively straightforward supply and demand equations; so short term investment and application of resources would continue. Obviously the distribution of surpluses is now a matter not determined by private interests, nor is capital formation.

Capital markets, speculation on firms' financial outturns, commodities and currencies will have to be redefined, abolished in some instances. In the real world convertibility of the pound sterling would have to be maintained, but tough exchange controls and regulation are needed. City institutions as a whole would be scrutinised to determine what use values are created; for instance some flexibility would be desirable in matters such as mass commodity procurement. So a form of commodity exchange must be maintained. But profits obtained through banking, 'brokerage' and related financial operations would have to cease, and be replaced by our low-interest strategic investment. We see a cumulative encroachment on money-power by institutions which give use value primacy, and which continually and incrementally legitimate interests of so-called ordinary people.

At this point the reader may well ask exactly *what* new institutions would be put in place to develop and nuture a socially useful economy, and deal effectively with non-legitimate private interests. What follows is an attempt to illustrate the nature of our new institutions, but it must be borne in mind that what matters is *the processes* which are put in train, as much as structures for legitimation and regulation.

THE 'MECHANICS'

In order to start to 'allow' the socially useful economy to develop overall economic aims and measurements must be changed. The current dominance of money supply measurements such as M3, M2 and M0, must be shown up as the narrow exchange value criteria that they are. Their relations with rates of monetary and consumer inflation are problematic at the least. How we measure money is less important than how we measure utilisation of resources, and actual distribution of human and material benefits which thus arise. Similarly, balance of (money) payments, whilst remaining *one* measure of *one* aspect of the pound sterling's rate of exchange internationally, and *one* measure of imports and exports, is less important than measurement of the state of resource utilisation in Britain, compared to that of other countries. Such measurement also provides a framework for informing decisions about desirable patterns of trade. Inflation as we commonly know it cannot of course be ignored, but again it is only *one* measure of a monetary institution which proceeds largely on its own course, with little reference to what we as 'ordinary people' do. Tighter exchange controls and the development of the low-interest fund will tend over time to reduce external influences on inflation. The great institution of our time, the Public Sector Borrowing Requirement (PSBR), similarly diminishes as use values predominate, for its political importance changes dramatically in the light of our new version of the 'mixed' economy. High public spending on investment and jobs, for instance, is directly advantageous if related to utilisation of resources. This powerful bundle of institutions which supposedly provide *the* main set of macroeconomic measures of what we do and how we do it, has to be effectively challenged, both by formal ownership changes and by the development of different economic *practices*. As a start we must reintroduce exchange control instruments which re-appropriate over £20 billion that has been taken out of the country by multinational and financial institutions over the last 5 years. In line with this we need to re-create mutual societies and other forms of common ownership which can take over ownership and control functions from private interests. We have to put in place democratic institutions which legitimate and directly express interests other than those for whom managements at present act. Examples of monetary re-appropriation include pension funds, life assurance monies and related savings, and donations by companies to political parties.

Then we must develop our new 'account' practices, based on new or revised criteria. It would seem necessary here to create a specific development programme of applied research, and to make political appointments so that staffs will have a clear duty to apply the 'account-ing' principles and practices that a socially useful economy requires. So-called 'social accounting' procedures require development so as to produce accurate opportunity-cost equations. For example what exact-ly is the difference between a £10 billion 'investment' in Trident and a similar resource allocation to engineering, the Health Service, or certain infrastructural rebuilding programmes? The results would be taken at local, regional and national levels, and include jobs, net social–economic benefit/dysbenefit, and use values for producers and consum-ers. Use values themselves will of course require some elaboration to bring them out of the 'social welfare' ghetto and into mainstream political economy. A high use value to producers – in terms of working conditions, control over work, etc. – would be given a certain value, as would that of use value to consumers (e.g. warmer houses), and use value in terms of costs of resources utilised – including long-term raw material/resources depletion policies.

Redefinition of productivity and efficiency is an integral part of new accounting practices. This would also be undertaken through the applied research programme. A new Department of Economic Affairs will have to be constituted (but not under George Brown this time!), together with a Development Agency (which administers the low-interest fund). This new economic institution, whilst having the national legitimacy of being an economic institution and a government agency, has to be structured to encourage and receive investment and other resource allocation proposals from producers, local government agen-cies and consumer associations. The institution's deliberations would be open to examination and cross-examination through an appeals procedure. A new Planning Institution is required to operate alongside it. The planning institution's task would have to be one of medium to long-term resource planning, based on area and sector inputs, again from producers, etc. The 'DEA', the 'DA' and 'PI' constitute an institutional framework at the 'top end' to express and help administer use value in a socially useful economy. In tandem we would of course have to change the Treasury's structure, power and responsibilities. Its proper job would be to advise on ways of maintaining non-damaging currency relationships, and the accurate measurement of public and private money flows – for our other institutions. A new Finance Act would be required to set this up, which would also provide the institutions with powers to protect the pound against the wrath of international private money power. A specific, and large scale educational budget would be put aside for the applied research programme – which could be drawn upon by active local government, local community and trade union units, trade unions and others, as well as by conventional academic bodies. The low-interest fund should initially be able to benefit from the £20 billion repatriation monies.

A new Companies Act is required, which would re-arrange the order of legitimate interests in firms' activities which have a public liability. It would also make plain firms' legal requirements vis a vis the DEA, the DA and PI. With regard to transnational corporations we would have to make a start by withdrawing objections to the EEC's 'Vredeling' Directive – which gives producers new rights for information and control. At the same time we need to recognise that EEC regulations and practices are heavily attuned to exchange-value criteria by which we cannot permit a socially useful economy to be tied. Beyond that we would need the Companies Act to provide powers to prevent any wholesale removal of resources from Britain. A new democratic planning procedure has to be set up, of course, to provide the means for effective expression of producer, consumer, local government, and other interests. An enabling law is required in the first instance and this would include provision for paid time for producers' stategy meetings and the like.

A new Company Act is needed to modify ownership rights vested in 'persons' in order to remove obstacles to the use of resources and give scope to social rights and 'legitimate interests' of social groups. The concept of 'legitimate interest' provides a cornerstone to a style of thought that moves us away from the sterility of conventional approaches to ownership – i.e. private ownership or common ownership (primarily coops) or common ownership through nationalisation.

A socially useful economy is based on democratising *activity*, whereas 'ownership' is the principle and practice of withholding from others – be it corporate secrecy, professionals' cartels or patenting/licensing of technical innovation. Ownership *is* necessary in some circumstances to define rights of access to means of economic activity, e.g. ownership rights to work land for self-sufficiency, but in reality it will play little or no *positive* part in developing a socially useful economy. Also who really does own coal or oil reserves, plant and equipment bought through now dead labour, pension fund money or bank overdrafts? And who 'owns' the creativeness of people?

Economic enfranchisement of peoples' legitimate interests seems a more commonsense and fruitful approach. For instance I 'own' part of a house; the Building Society actually owns 90% of it and yet my minimal actual ownership gives me freedom to paint it or whatever. Formal ownership gives me certain rights, but if those rights (e.g. to decent housing that you can paint purple if you like) are *directly* expressed, then most of the ideological meanings of ownership are redundant.

This approach also has the value of legitimating rights directly and putting them into practice through actual activity. (What matters is rights that open ways to activity in practice rather than 'rights' enshrined in abstract constitutions such as those of the USSR and other countries.)

Change of ownership in itself may be pretty meaningless. What we are addressing are rights (and duties and responsibilities) to determine who gets what out of resources used. To try to make some of these ideas a little more specific imagine that the Company 'owning' a plant in our neighbourhood or for which we work decides – because it is losing markets, or to suit the strategy of a transnational corporation by which it is 'owned' or for whatever reason – to close or to declare a lot of the workforce redundant. For argument's sake suppose this company is in the packaging business. 'Legitimate interests' are, of course, not at all the same as the formal owners and would include trade unions representing the workforce, the local authority, consumers and others. These social goups would have the right to call on research resources to help them explore the situation in depth. This done, plans would be drawn up for alternative use of resources and a generally favoured plan would be put to the DEA for endorsement. The DEA, after scrutiny and coordination with other interested parties, would formally recognise the proposal as a socially suitable use of resources, after, possibly, requiring some alterations to be made in the original submission. Suppose the plan is mainly to produce laminates for house insulation: control of the new operations, on which the about-to-become-redundant resources are to be used, would now pass to a Mutual Association with a managing committee of representatives from the various democratic interests involved, e.g. the shop stewards' committee, councillors, tenants associations and so on. Funding equivalent to the social cost of the unemployment prevented would be available as of right under the new Company Act and, with DEA approval, special low interest loans would also help the Mutual Association to launch the new activities envisaged in the proposals endorsed by the DEA. Guarantees for the purchase of a certain volume of products (at approved costs and subject to quality tests) would be given by the DEA, Councils and other user or marketing institutions. In this instance Councils would eventually become the main purchasers of output in the normal way to meet housing requirements. Furthermore the DEA and others would be empowered to back research into new products, involving user–tenant research into their own needs and their expression in production specifications. Also when scientific research by universities, polytechnics or other research bodies was wanted by the Mutual Association or the 'legitimate interests' involved, facilities would be made available.

Here and now before an institutional framework for a socially useful economy exists, it would be politically and educationally valuable if grassroot organisations, of trade unionists, community workers and others, collectively thought out how they might plan use of resources with which they are directly associated. Such specific exercises in collective thought that is concrete and practically oriented would deepen understanding of alternatives to market economics, indicate means of filling the wastes that result from overdependence on markets and define possibilities for monitoring and controlling market-regulated operations. It would also help to define needs for external support and advice or supplies from outside. At the same time it would add to political strength because it would define realisable objectives clearly and marshall an alliance of interests desirous of their achievement.

When suggesting above the need for DEA, DA and a PI, we are not laying down a blueprint for a New Order but simply trying to help discussion of alternatives in practical terms, to get the feel of the feasibility of managing use of resources democratically along different lines. One essential difference about the socially useful economy we are envisaging is that its development and dynamism comes from democratic involvement at the grassroots. 'By definition' it is a mode of economic cooperation that should not and cannot be described in too much detail in advance, from outside, as it were, by the imposed ideas of 'experts'. This difference – the practical incorporation of democratic decision-making – in itself presents a problem since for thousands of years the mass of people have been excluded from decision-making by ruling elites eager to keep social and economic control firmly in their own hands. What democratic pressures so far have achieved does not go much beyond forcing undemocratic structures to accommodate popular demands. Elitist rulers and undemocratic decision-makers have been forced to listen but the very structures of which they are part inhibit ability, even when the wish is there, to respond to demands that a democratic economic structure would make feasible. Nonetheless we still tend to expect others to explain to us exactly how any favoured new system will work – forgetting that in so far as any new system is truly democratic it will be such as we ourselves cause it to be. We need to acclimatise ourselves better to the democratic dimension of the economic changes that are now becoming essential. Yes, some provisional blueprinting of the future is useful – but we should keep reminding ourselves that we ourselves, the grassroot collectivities through which we act and live, are now the draughtsmen and draughtswomen responsible for new-style blueprints of the future.

A new Trade Union Development Act is needed, to provide new powers and rights to enable producers to carry out their new responsibilities, as a legitimate right, indeed a duty. Similarly a Consumers' Act is required to provide paid means to express their requirements. A Pensions Act would immediately place all pension monies under the control and direction of representatives of contributors, though initially actual administration might have to be carried out jointly with the DEA. Local Governments obviously requires a new set of powers, duties and responsibilities, which enhance their democratic role in economic life.

Obviously through measures such as these the economy will become properly 'mixed' – reflecting the real and legitimate interests of society. However a fairly conventional 'public sector' will remain in existence, most usefully covering major resource providers, such as coal and oil, and common services such as health, water supply, social welfare and the like. The exact size of the public sector is now not a contentious issue. However, new institutions must be put in place here too. Cost–benefit and Opportunity–cost equations have to be elaborated through the development programme; obviously a long-term price and depletion policy is required for the energy industries, the broad economic benefits to the community of Health Service investments have to be established, benefits of different types of infrastructural re-creation must be determined. Here again democratic processes are to be employed, involving producer, consumer and other legitimate interests. We may also find that public policy formulations thus developed may come to impinge on firms in other sectors, e.g. medical equipment development and sourcing. Here, as in other examples new institutional agencies are needed to finally determine outcomes in problem areas – of which there may be many. Such agencies should be based in existing institutions such as the NHS – not least in order to help create more change 'from within'.

Far-reaching changes must be wrought in the 'social services' field, which impose new rights and duties, and which help to re-enfranchise millions of people who are currently marginalised. For a start the oppression of degrading means-testing must be removed forthwith, for instance by providing a comprehensive disability income to all who suffer any significant disability. Broad indicators are needed for people's rights – to housing of a certain standard, to fuels, to transport, to help with childcare or the care of elderly relatives or others. Some rights would have to include a clear money income, others involve resource allocation – such as day nurseries. Obviously some kind of distinction must be made between those who have ample personal money or resources, and those who don't. Some form of 'points' system is needed, but it can be kept simple – and would apply to those in *and* out of conventional waged work. A national minimum wage has to be instituted too, again in order to help ensure equal opportunity to engage in mainstream economic and social life. Pay bargaining becomes a quite different process in a socially useful economy, for pay is now openly only *one* element of resource allocation to people. Firstly, a much more progressive income tax structure would be applied. Secondly, an overall differential range would be agreed and implemented at the level of personal disposable income. Thirdly, price controls would be re-introduced – based heavily on social and political decisions, e.g. special low telephone rates for elderly people. And in time we would also look to producer forums to gradually develop mutually agreed job/pay differentials. Women who work *and* have prime responsibility for child care or relative care would of course have a fiscal advantage (as would men in this position); and we suspect that a powerful sex and race discrimination agency would be required for some time.

Thus the DHSS would have to be significantly changed, as would the functions of a new Department of Employment. Pay, resource provision, tax and welfare benefit arrangements would have to be encapsulated within a new institution, which effectively crosses over from DHSS to DE and back again. The role of powerful new institutions of this sort is not confined to the overt function, but includes the spread of counter-vailing practices which come to shape other currently-conventional practices. At times it may be necessary to create specific agencies with a clear remit, to operate for a limited time only – for instance a body to investigate and propose regulations on private ownership of houses or flats, and private rent arrangements. We must be clear in our minds about the difference between setting up an institution, and creating an agency whose task is to investigate and illuminate a particular problem area.

Finally, we have to address what all these measure mean for the State. First we propose a charter of civil/human rights (see last chapter), which will enshrine people's powers in key areas *vis-à-vis* private interests and those of national bodies, local government, etc. Thus general limits are placed against the State's powers *vis-à-vis* the citizen. Many State agency functions are to be redefined in principle and practice through the various measures outlined previously. Laws are to be changed, and whilst the current separation between the legislature and judiciary functions must be maintained, the latter is in dire need of fundamental reforms. All professions associated with legal practice will need a thoroughgoing overhaul in order to bring them rather more in line with the spirit and practice of our new arrangements. Policing functions have similarly to be reformed, with democratic accountability being the first priority. Our national 'defence' system and structures will have to change (see Chapter 10). The nature of the changes proposed will significantly reduce the somewhat arbitrary and secretive practices of the State. At every turn the citizen will be given the right to obtain sufficient information about how any particular part of the State operates; s/he will be put into an effective position to ensure that State functions *support* rights of citizenship. A Freedom of Information Act is of course a necessary part of the process, and it is worth considering the creation of a teletext-based information system for easy and free access to the tax, social welfare and many other relevant aspects of law and regulation and rights associated with citizenship.

The institutions which have to be removed, changed, and created in order to properly allow the development of a socially useful economy will intentionally lead to a significant increase in 'extra-parliamentary' democracy. Government of the economy and consequential aspects of society will pass more into the hands of the citizenry. However, it should be clear that the nature of the changes proposed *could* exist within a parliamentary democracy, albeit profoundly affecting the nature of much parliamentary business. And in our view the processes for developing a socially useful economy can and should be electorally advantageous, which would render our new institutions strong in society. Enormous pressures would be brought to bear on government and society by powerful private national and international interests; the 'money power' deployed against a socially useful economy would be immense. However, the exercise of money power against quite modest reforms – as in Mitterand's government in France – *can* be expected and planned for in advance. To continually avoid dealing with these pressures has been our historical heritage, leading to a political economy in which very few people obtain returns commensurate with their efforts and real abilities. Strongly-rooted institutions which clearly legitimate and encourage a popular and active agenda of social and economic change are a necessary expression of power which will signal an intent of sufficient strength to overcome wrecking behaviour by money power. Countervailing power will be strongest where there is popular understanding and support for the idea of the socially useful economy.

A few examples may clarify what we mean when we speak of enfranchisement of activity as more significant than ownership (see p. 173).

Example
Company Y is a major firm in a designated 'key' sector for Britain, say, computing. It is understood and agreed that certain hardware and software operations must continue with little change – as they are needed to stop IMB or Fujitsu from swamping the market and gaining unassailable technical leads. However substantial intervention is needed to circumvent IBM's product/market domination, and to create a lot of new use values in the information technology area.

Company Y, following straightforward investigation by the DEA, is 'owned' by 50% pension funds, 20% by employees, 20% by banks, and 10% by individuals. The bank stake is disregarded unless the banks can show that their disenfranchisement means clear-cut problems for their non-institutional depositors – assume that the case cannot be made.

Legitimate interests in Y are its employees, union reps of the 10 major pension funds investing in it, 3 local authorities where principal plants are located, individual equity investors, and a special DEA 'task force' on the IT applications. Company Y becomes Mutual Association Y, which comprises representatives of these interest in the proportions: 40%, 20%, 10%, 10% and 20%. These proportions are based on defined regulations in the Companies Act. Individual equity investors *can* take out their funds, but based on the original £1.00 share issue value – and subject to income tax at a consolidated rate a little above standard rate.

Association Y agrees and defines 1, 2 and 3 year programmes for enterprise activities re. IBM, which are regarded as necessary for viability of the enterprise as a whole. Existing managers may or may not be kept in these operational areas, any 'mass evacuation' will result in fiscal penalties levied on all managers' incomes.

Association Y has to define short and long term development plans, necessary time and resourcing coming from the DEA 'task force' and the DA. Short term plans to be defined within an agreed timescale, otherwise DEA and DA support is withdrawn, the same applies to long term development plans. Many proposals for development come out as having possible consumer implications, e.g. a 'teletexed' information system on social security/welfare rights for all. Here the Consumers Act provisions are invoked by the DEA, and a consumers' association created – through legally-required 'advertisement' in all media. Association Y then has Project A, whose management committee or agency has a 30% interest from the consumers' association – all other interests being reduced in direct proportion.

This major project is properly costed in terms of *both* cost and benefit. So Association Y operates in 2 ways, one being definitely oriented towards development plans – which are funded significantly by the low interest fund, but operating surpluses are still sought and obtained (though 'profit' no longer applies).

The Socially Useful Economy would initially develop through plebiscite-based definitions of perhaps half a dozen key sectors or areas which are popularly regarded as particularly problematic by people, or which have strategic general importance, such as IT. It is also based on intervention, for example, where unemployment is occurring or soon to occur. The former, political, decisions would become part of a rolling programme, with other priorities tackled in Year 2, Year 3 etc.

Example

In Year 3 of a socially useful economy, an issue of general concern raised through several organisations is that of the effects of low-frequency noise generated by lorries of 20 tons and over. Research programme monies put into this reveal that the single most important culprits are, say for example, Ford's 'Cargo' range of trucks. The original organisations which raised the problem are invited to ask for specific research funding to propose practical solutions, and existing organisations, such as the Road Research Laboratory are given this as a priority research area.

Practical solutions are put to an agency comprising 'technical experts' from outside Ford (50 per cent represenation), and from the truck producers (white & blue collar staffs). One is chosen as the most effective, which also requires relatively small changes to design and manufacture. This solution is put to the Company, which turns it down, for its own reasons. The production plant then comes under the control of a mutual association for a specific period – that which is required to comprehensively investigate, develop and sell the redesigned trucks. The Association is given direct resource assistance for this period, e.g. 2 years, and results monitored jointly by the Association and the DEA's 'task force' for this area. If successful in terms of sales (i.e. a superior product) the whole site, including other production lines are continued under the Association. However a type of consumers' association has been agreed to monitor the actual performance in terms of low-frequency noise and vibration – organised through the original complainant organisations. This Association has the right to come back to the site Association if it is not satisfied, and to force a project meeting (project EGM as it were), with a 50 per cent representation. As before, non-problematic truck manufacture on site would continue as before, but under the Association, and short and long term development plans would be created, again as before.

NOTES

1. Christine Buci-Glucksmann in Anne S. Sanssoon (ed.) *Approaches to 'Gramsci* (p. 18) defines 'Hegemony' as 'a political principle and a form of strategic leadership'.
2. See Anna Coote and Beatrix Campbell, *Sweet Freedom* (Picador, 1982).
3. See GLC's Popular Planning Unit's papers on childcare and related topics.

9 Financing the Socially Useful Economy

> Money is like muck, not good except to be spread.
> Francis Bacon, *Seditions and Troubles*

INTRODUCTION

The myth of finance is the illusion that principles to protect money-capital and interest payments make for economic efficiency in the sense that they at the same time ensure socially good use of resources. But from the fact that currently prevailing financial principles are not 'socially useful', it would be wrong to deduce that 'socially useful finance' is a contradiction in terms and that all concern about alternative financial policies is pointless. It is indeed true that a commodity economy subordinates use-value to exchange-value and that money expresses exchange-value in its most universal form; but the commodity system, by which our social life has long been organised, has established a financial apparatus so tightly interwoven with the fabric of contemporary existence that it is utterly unrealistic to contemplate such a complete untangling of present economic relationships as to make money and finance altogether superfluous as a mechanism for allocating resources. If this is so, the question to be pursued is whether and how existing financial mechanisms can be adapted to purposeful democratic control, escaping the blind compulsions of self-expanding capital and the irresponsible power of those who own or manage it.

When people dubiously or accusingly ask 'How can socially useful projects be paid for?', they in part express illusions about money but in part also some matter of fact realism. Social cooperation, as it is today, is coordinated and articulated by money. Money gives you and me a share in what the work of others creates. Money defines what you or I do as employees in a complex social system. People interact with other people via money relationships. If we reject the way the financial system arranges these relationships, some other way must be found, a new system is needed to structure our social cooperation in economic matters. This is why primacy must be given to understanding the financial system we at present have and hence what changes are necessary to serve the deeper social, political and moral purposes that demand attention urgently and in a practical way.

THE BACKGROUND TO THE SYSTEM WE INHERIT

Socially useful production is not self-subsistence; each producing unit is part of a far-reaching social complex. Instruments of coordination are essential. Finance is such an instrument: *but it would be utterly wrong to think that financial systems are no more than systems of instrumental mechanisms*. Finance is at the same time the living soul of the capitalist social order. Conflict over financial policy, whilst often phrased in the language of technicalities, usually involves the deepest confrontation of interests when capitalist argues with capitalist and, when the financing of social policies is at issue, it touches underlying class interests and the most basic principles of economic structure and motivation.

In earlier discussions and papers examples have been given of seemingly technical concepts (such as PSBR and M3) clothing and, in a practical sense, guiding political or class strategies. Underlying these strategies is the basic principle of keeping capital free to invest, move and engage in economic activity without let or hindrance other than constraints imposed by competition and market profitability. In essence the political meaning of strategies to minimise restrictions on the turnover and reproduction of capital, is protection of a social order which is economically underpinned by commodity-exchange and the cash-nexus, in a word, by 'money-power'. Money-power is today the primary and dominant form of social power. However, whilst not losing sight of the fact that the financial system today in Britain and the world constitutes the essential mode of existence for capitalist power, one needs to examine the same system also from another standpoint, namely *as a social mechanism* for allocation of resources. The organising principle guiding economic activity in Britain has long been and remains that of commodity exchange. Money motivates work in that people sell their skills and energies for wages and salaries or use capital to make money. Buying and selling on the market allocates resources to consumption and investment. Money is the universally exchangeable commodity that embodies generalised exchange-values and, as such, governs most forms of economic activity.

Money as precious metal had a life of its own as a commodity like other commodities but it was at the same time a special commodity, rising above the rest because it was universally exchangeable into any of the other commodities. It had a sort of universal use-value because it could become anything whereas the other commodities had only their own particular use-values. Today however the financial system has so evolved as virtually to have ousted precious metals from their money-functions, substituting bank-created credit as the essential form of money within each national economy – and now even internationally through the very extensively used Euro-dollar system.

Originally euro-dollars are created when the owner of a deposit with an American bank transfers the title to that deposit to a bank based, say, in London. He then has a dollar claim on the London bank, and the London bank has a dollar claim on a New York bank. At this stage, a euro-dollar is simply an indirect way of holding a deposit with an American bank. When the London bank starts lending its euro-dollar assets, however, the situation changes. If the dollars lent by the London bank are redeposited in London, the euro-dollar liabilities in London will no longer be fully matched by claims in New York. By making loans and taking deposits, banks in London can create euro-dollars in excess of the extent to which they hold deposits in New York[1].

The credit policies pursued by banks must, of course, significantly influence the allocation of resources. Governments, whose economic strategies rely primarily upon the smooth continuation of capitalist production and reproduction, will use their powers to control the credit system so as to substitute as best they can for the automatisms of a gold standard (i.e. a gold-based money system) and to ensure that profit-regulated allocation of resources is sustained. However, whilst still looking to capitalist commodity-exchange mechanisms to articulate economic activities generally, they can use financial policies to stimulate or restrain capital-turnover. Keynesian economics is in its essentials concerned with the way Governments regulate credit in pursuance of social policies. It is a body of theory particularly relevant to an era in which credit-money has taken away from precious metals most of their money functions and become the primary money form for the economic system as a whole. Keynesian policies relate to broad-brush injections of purchasing power which originate typically as public expenditure. Of old the state authorised the units of precious metal used as money; today it is the custodian on behalf of society of the financial system by which credit-money is generated. However the powers that public authorities now exercise over the conduct of the financial system need not be limited to banking procedures and public expenditure at national level; they may also be used specifically, 'qualitatively', in support of specific modes of allocating resources. Financial controls during the Second World War demonstrated this possibility and some points will be made below about how resources were then allocated, by principles quite other than those of the market and commodity exchange. The political circumstances of an anti-Fascist war generated a social dynamism which made possible remarkable departures from capitalist and commercial norms – but even so it never ceased to be reiterated that what was being done was an exceptional wartime expedient 'for the duration only'. The Keynesian management of the Welfare State in the two decades following the Second World War depended upon credit policies (i.e. creation and allocation of money as purchasing power) which served as instruments of social policy. Conservative and capitalist strategy generally during this period had in it something of what Antonio Gramsci called 'passive revolution', that is, social changes which had to be conceded to the 'subordinate classes' were managed from above, forestalling the danger of grassroot organisations taking control into their own hands and effecting an 'active' democratic revolution.

Financial systems in the capitalist world have developed in such a way that the ultimate regulation of money values can no longer be determined by the commodity value of precious metals. Now money values are profoundly dependent upon credit-creating policies and in addition the credit-creating policies profoundly influence the allocation of resources. Since times long past state authority has determined what is and what is not legal tender; to this now is added control over banks as agencies of credit-creation. In theory, 'ideally', financial policy is administered so that the 'bank-created money' behaves as 'commodity-money' (that is, precious metals defining, through their own market values, units in which the values of all other commodities are measured). But of course financial counsels even of Governments loyal to the ideals of capital suffer many temptations to administer not according to the ideal but according to political expediency – and to this fact the whole world today is witness. But, from the fact that finance may escape the automatisms of commodity economics, we as protagonists of the socially useful economy should take heart. *Technically* it is possible – indeed quite easy – to use financial mechanisms to allocate resources according to principles quite other than those of the market. The problems and difficulties are not technical but the problems of the class interests of money-power confronting wider community interests, the problems to which contention between opposed social and economic philosophies gives rise when each is struggling to determine how decisions are made about the use (or non-use) of resources. The big and stubborn problems are those of consciousness and organisation to implement the purposes that a new economic outlook gives to democratic movements for change.

THE TECHNICAL PROBLEMS OF FINANCING SOCIALLY USEFUL PROJECTS

Technically, it may be argued, financing socially useful production does not present any serious problems. Mostly it involves common sense measures that in one context or another have been used before. The first necessity is reintroduction of the exchange controls that the Thatcher Government abolished within months of taking office. It is essential to be able to control the movement of money capital and to be able to discriminate as to what goods are imported and exported to or from which destinations. If not liable to such controls, money-power will be deployed in ways that seriously conflict with strategies for putting resources to work for socially useful ends. Uncontrolled capital movements may, for example, start harmful inflationary tendencies or lure resources away from socially useful programmes. Effective use of exchange controls will certainly be attacked by a barrage of 'expert criticism'. One such criticism that is common is that controls to support use of home resources imply going over to a 'siege economy'; another is that they invoke damaging retaliation. To the first there is a simple answer: finance that brings unemployed resources into use will enlarge demand for components, raw materials and consumer goods and even if the imported share of this demand falls, the absolute amount is likely to increase, and, on the supply side, increased use of capacity decreases unit costs and will make export sales that much easier. Trade policy using controls today in UK stands a much better chance of increasing trade than does a free-exchange, free-market policy. To the second line of attack the answer is that, yes, there will be retaliation and stubborn opposition to a national policy guided by resource-use and to restrictions on the freedom of money-power. Retaliation and opposition there will certainly be *from some quarters* but from other quarters there will be support that we at present lack. There are plenty of movements abroad that would be eager to see international exchanges less dominated by financial interests and would encourage some planning of mutually-useful foreign trade. Indeed in most countries there will be two sides to the tussles about foreign trade and such tussles are a necessary part of the learning process out of which economic change is born.

Another objection that is often raised is that foreign trade no longer can be controlled because so much of it is not foreign trade as previously conceived, but within-company transactions by 'Transnational Companies' (TNCs). This is indeed so; however coping with this situation is not a technical problem but a problem of power. If we cannot negotiate with TNCs about what they do and do not produce and buy in Britain, we cannot change the overall direction of British economic life. As the Lucas experience shows, involvement of workers in conscious monitoring of the use of resources, makes it possible to define what TNCs are required to do and to check that they in fact stick to what is agreed. This 'difficulty' is useful to think about because it helps one to see that effective use of resources at home and effective control of foreign exchanges would require an awakening to consciousness of 'the collective worker'. Commodity-economics expects workers to sell their abilities to management and not concern themselves with their use within the collective operation for which they are hired. Similarly consumers are required only to be conscious of their needs as individuals. But if resource-use criteria are to make good the inadequacies of money and profit criteria, the collective knowledge of the units that group people in production and in the community will need to be called upon to recommend production possibilities and to control projects that it has been agreed to undertake. In short, men and women through shop stewards' committees, through community organisations and in other ways will need, if socially useful economics is to function practically, to make explicit their collective consciousness of needs and productive potentialities.

Protected by exchange controls, the financial apparatus can facilitate public expenditure and link credit-creation to the social usefulness of projects (instead of just to 'financial soundness' measured in terms of profitability and ability to repay). In so far as funds created by banks stimulate useful economic activity, they are not inflationary since they cause *pari passu* with enlargement of purchasing power creation of goods and services on which money can be spent.

During the Second World War it became necessary to devote available resources directly to needs dictated by the war. Financial practice was quite simply adapted.

Whilst the administrative arrangements for financial control were formally preserved, there was brought into them a flexibility and a discretionary element which would never have been contemplated in peace-time (see Ashworth in *History of Second World War*).[2]

The Treasury. . . was often not prescribing policy but translating into financial terms decisions reached elsewhere . . .[3] (ibid. p. 32)

Working capital was provided by i) bank borrowing ii) loans iii) advance payement and iv) progress payments and special liaison (Scheme C) was established with the banks to see that Government contractors got the finance they needed and to clear difficulties (see ibid., p. 186). In practice a greater volume of production was financed with a smaller demand for bank advances and average interest rates were held between 4.7% and 4.3% (see ibid., pp. 234–6). Speaking in the House of Commons, as Finance Minister, Pethwick-Lawrence said: 'The financial prosecution of this war has taught us one striking fact which is that nothing which is economically possible ought to be financially impossible'. (17 June 1943)

Using somewhat similar techniques socially useful production could be steered by some simple basic principles. Once a collectivity of workers in industry or a group of people in the community had worked out a specific project for using available resources for purposes that seemed to them appropriate or were suggested to them from outside, the project could be submitted (at local, regional, national or even international level as required by the scale and impact of the project) to receive formal authorisation by, for example, local councils, by Parliament or by specially elected bodies, (as outlined in the previous chapter). Once a project had received this formal authorisation necessary funds would be guaranteed by the financial system and any other help required would be seen to administratively (e.g. technical advice, priority deliveries to clear bottlenecks, research help and so forth).

Hugh Dalton's postwar budget speech in 1946 utilised war-time economic experience by composing ways of creating a low-interest portion of the economy (e.g. for housing) which added to the nature of the guarantee – just as the post-war Japanese economy has provided low-interest loans to whole industries that were thought to be important for recovery.

Such provisions would facilitate 'production', that is, the setting in motion of processes to use resources. Financial provision would also be needed to underpin disposal of what is produced. For some goods ordinary market sales would be adequate – for example, finance stimulating production of furniture, together with finance for other projects, would flow in part into incomes that would be spent on furniture. In other cases the 'market' would be 'local authorities', nationalised industries or Government departments; public expenditure itself would look after the allocation of such products to their appropriate uses. Where, however, there was uncertainty whether markets would take up products, it would be desirable or even essential for public authorities, locally or regionally or nationally, to guarantee to purchase at 'floor prices' any authorised output which could not be otherwise disposed of. (Such provisions are not unusual in agricultural support policies, for example.) In parallel with undertakings of this kind public authorities could run marketing agencies which, as well as meeting home needs, could support economic and political purposes abroad.

The essential difference in principle between commodity economics and socially-useful economics is that the guiding criterion for the former is exchange-value and, for the latter, *resource-use*. Economic practice involves continuous decision-making about the use of means of production: commodity economics assesses output in terms of the exchange-value it generates, that is, in terms of money-power, whereas one could instead directly assess the social usefulness of production possibilities and the extent to which they are subject to democratic control. In either case finance may serve as an instrument in the allocation of resources, but markedly different criteria determine how finance is used.

FINANCING AND ADMINISTERING THE ECONOMY AS A WHOLE

Socially useful production as a mode of production distinct from and in contrast to commodity production implies *conscious collective activity*. Groups of people in industry and in the community need to take qualitative decisions about how resources are to be used and what needs they are to serve. The same point may be put in another way, that is, without democracy in the fullest sense (industrial democracy and social democratisation, workers' control over work and people's control in the community) a 'socially useful economy' cannot be developed. Central government can facilitate but it cannot impose 'socially useful economics' since it implies self-managing initiatives at the base. From this it follows that in the country as a whole the socially useful economy must necessarily exist patchily alongside the commodity regulated economy

and other economic structures (such as bureaucratically planned
undertakings) which do not involve grass root cooperation. From this
coexistence of economic forms two important points follow:

(1) It is essential to campaign vigourously for widespread understanding and support for socially useful economics, along with critical
awareness of the defects of commodity economics, so that there will
be plenty of people with a clear understanding of how to apply
criteria of social usefulness to financial and administrative problems in practical situations.
(2) The management of the economy as a a whole must be capable of
coping with interactions and interfaces between 'socially useful
projects' and other modes of production. *In this context* 'Left
Keynesian' theory and practice might be applicable; but there is
need for more academic research and discussion about public
expenditure policies, fiscal policies and the more general aspects of
financial policy required to support an economic strategy that gives
first priority to resource-use based on grassroot initiatives but has to
sustain the functioning of the economy as a whole as effectively as
possible. (Keynesian economics, as conceived by Keynes himself at
least, seeks quite frankly 'to make capitalism work'. If that aim is
made the end of the matter, socialist economics as negation of
commodity economics is quite blocked out. However once economic zones giving democratic control over resources have been
firmly established, is not the overall situation radically different and
may not Keynesian techniques be of value to control the zones in
which market forces are left free to operate?)

The power of the existing economic order and the power of concentrated control over money-capital is very great indeed. Against this a
long formidable campaign is required to win understanding of the
resource-use alternative. Realisation of such an alternative will not be
possible until people generally have acquired a sense of what they can do
and see for themselves that resource-economics under grassroot control
is feasible. In short, it is essential to see economics as struggle between
contending modes of production and to see this struggle as one between
contending ideas as well as between economic and political structures.
This struggle should not, however, be conceived as one between
alternatives that cannot coexist. On the contrary the two modes of
production inevitably must coexist nationally or on the world scale for a
very long time. So the essential perspectives of struggle are first to win

understanding that there is an alternative to commodity economics by beginning, even in very limited ways, to try to apply in practice the criteria of resource-economics. One way in which to make a start is forthright defence of public expenditure for social use. Also where non-market principles already guide social practice, we need to defend them more lucidly and more stoutly on economic as well as humanitarian grounds. From bridgeheads so estabished a way opens up towards economic bases that offer an alternative to market-economics on which we have become overly dependent for our 'social-life-support-system'.

Social power is sustained by economic power; but grassroot control over resources not only provides a democratic power base, it provides an economic logic that is an alternative to the logic of commodity exchange. The socially useful economy seeks conscious allocation of resources to useful ends and socially useful finance uses financial mechanisms as means to those ends!

ASSESSING REALITIES

The line of argument presented so far simplifies a complex reality to point to the feasibility of an alternative approach to finance from a point of departure well rooted in existing economic structures and practices. But the very exercise of *selecting* positive possibilities is liable to make an undertaking that must, politically and economically, be extremely tough going, seem too clear cut, too easy. In the seminar discussions emphasis was laid on the importance of seeing the difficulties within the possibilities.

As Vella Pillay stated in his 'discussant' paper:

'The above line of argument correctly sees what is there called 'money power' as the commanding form of social power and that the financial system is today considerably more than a mere mechanism of coordination and discipline in the advanced capitalist economies such as Britain. The transformation of the forms of money as a result of the effective abolition of the gold or precious metals standard, the parallel emergence of bank credit as the dominant measure of value and the most liquid of 'liquid assets' (as bourgeois economists would put it) is one of the most striking outcomes of the international monetary crisis. This immediately raises an issue of some importance, which possibly forms the basis of much of the assumptions above about the technical feasibility of financing socially-useful products in the mixture of modes of production that is envisaged. The issue is that while bank credit can be used in the exchange process, it contains little or no exchange value. Given the acceptability of this inconvertible bank credit in the exchange process, its creation becomes a matter of conscious policy and hence the means for financing a growing economic sector of socially-useful production and exchange. If policy can be changed in this direction, that is if the social and class situation is moved in the direction of what is above called 'an active democratic revolution', then all is well and the financing problem is rapidly solved.

Evidence for such possibilities is adduced from Britain's wartime siege economy and to a lesser extent from the early post-war Keynesian programme of deficit budgeting with a system of controls over the direction of credit creation favourable to the Government's borrowing requirements at relatively low interest rates. If only some of these controls can be reproduced, and above special emphasis is given to exchange control, then through a kind of supply-side expansion of investment in and production of some set of predetermined socially–useful products, a parallel expansion of demand and employment is induced with the added outcome of a virtuous non-inflationary growth of the overall economy.

In itself and within the framework assumed for the above analysis these conclusions are undoubtedly valid. In the socialist countries of the USSR, China and Eastern Europe the state controlled banks issue credit to enterprises according to their planned needs for working capital, the volume and structure of which govern the dynamics of the output–capital ratio and the rate of the turnover of working capital and aggregate output. These state banks monitor the expenditure of the wage fund, and their provision of credit and transaction services are closely linked with indicators of the effectiveness of what hopefully is socially-useful production. Whether or not these practices and policies on credit creation in the socialist countries are successful is a matter of argument, especially in the light of the reservations expressed above about the bureaucratic systems of planning in the socialist countries in which grassroots power is patently absent. However, it is reasonable to believe these experiences in the socialist countries do provide us with a model of a kind on how and to what degree credit formation can serve a transformed capitalist economy where socially-useful production occupies an increasingly commanding place in economic activity.

But, note well, the banking and financial system in the socialist countries is nationalised, if not socialised, and this I believe raises a critical dimension to the problem as presented above. There the argument is that Government controls over the banking system need to be expanded beyond mere monitoring and supervision of the growth of the money supply, and towards qualitative intervention in support of 'specific modes' of allocating credit as working capital. In Britain as in other advanced capitalist countries bank credit has assumed complex and heterogeneous forms – a group of assets with a so-called high degree of 'moneyness'. The mere provision of bank advances forms only one element in that group. Equally significant is a range of other liquid assets which are actively traded in highly sophisticated secondary markets and several of which are increasingly divorced from the real economy. Indeed some Western economists go so far as to claim that the production or supply of these liquid assets by banks and other financial institutions is similar in character to the production of commodities. Given the enormity of the scale of world-wide integration of financial markets and trading in these liquid assets, the profitability of banks is now crucially governed by the degree of their participation in such markets. Exchange control may not be enough, nor, it is reasonable to think, would an increase in government controls and supervision be sufficient to redirect the flow of credit in Britain to the proposed specific modes of socially–useful production. The banks are today too deeply immersed in their international and other liquid asset generating business to allow what seems to be prescribed above (that is a simple resteering of financial mechanisms) to succeed. What may well be necessary is a mechanism for a more far-reaching degree of bank nationalisation calling for a high level of social control. An alternative, and as no more than a half-way measure, would be for the government to set up its own structure of financial and credit-creating institutions in active competition with the banks for deposits and employing its financial strength to build up the socially-useful production sector.

To depend, as precedents, on the exceptional circumstances of wartime Britain or even on the Keynesian welfare system of the early post-war years as a basis for directing credit towards the socially–useful sector, is of dubious validity. Those circumstances had then provided the *raison d'être* for a specific seige economy, in which credit and foreign exchange were rationed according to the government's needs and priorities, and supported by a comprehensive system of labour, raw material and capital control and mobilisation. The above presentation of a socially – useful financing may also underestimate the role of the transnational corporations in determining the flow of capital or the role of foreign trade and Britain's integration in international production. Nor does it consider the considerable size of Britain's foreign investments which serve British capital and the parallel overseas expansion by British banks in the recent period. How these structural characteristics of Britain's imperialist economy can be changed in an alternative economic strategy having among its aims the issues raised above is a larger question and obviously cannot be fully explored here.'

Clearly – and over this there was no division of opinion – the power of money–capital is very great indeed. It has to be taken seriously into the reckoning when seeking finance and credit for policies favourable to the socially useful economy. It would be dangerous to dodge questions of property and ownership and the necessity, at some stage, of nationalising major financial institutions. But it would be equally very dangerous to think that socially useful financing could be realised purely by legal formalities, such as nationalisation, without widely distributed and active consciousness of new economic criteria and new forms of democratic control.

Vella Pillay continued:
'A socially-useful economy must inevitably coexist with a continuing commodity regulated economy for some protracted period of transition assuming success in any campaign and struggle to achieve the industrial and social democratisation of the productive process. The key to this is politics: the build-up of mass awareness of socially-useful economics and the fashioning of policies for the management of an increasingly influential socially-useful sector which is both credible and convincing to working people of the country.'

SOME IMPLICATIONS

A great struggle is being fought out all across the world. The fact of this struggle is obvious – oppressed, unhappy, distressed, wronged, starving, impoverished, outraged people seek change, people with new visions of how people might relate to one another seek change, people thirsty for a robust compassionate morality without the sentimental deceits that today blur human action, or people eager to give the substance of deeds here on earth to the good words of older moralities, declaring against privilege and for freedom, all these and many more are seeking change. But the multiplicity of their struggles is confused and contradictory; some better compass bearings are needed to give unity of purpose. Contradictory aims in economic matters most easily cancel out the potential strength of numbers; but from the discussions at these seminars some clarity seemed to begin to emerge about how to integrate struggles originating from differing positions. Banks, money and the motivations of money obviously are not going to be immediately assigned to the dustbin and change hinges on a strengthening, alongside and against the old, of new criteria to govern financial decisions and to help make flourish social activities aimed directly and consciously at socially useful purposes. This implies new organisational forms in finance and in social activity, but with new ways of doing, essential also are new ways of thinking, the practical guidance of new economic theories. New concepts help activity on the ground, but they are also essential rallying standards around which to muster political strength. Many areas of social life already in fact are shaped by criteria other than market profitability; but considerable as these areas are, money-power is left ruling the roost and free to attack finance for social needs and to cripple organisations ostensibly organised on principles other than those of the commodity system. (It is for example, well known that merchant banks have chosen much of the top management in nationalised industries.) The seminar discussions brought out (see Chapter 3) the potency, as instruments of political action, of theoretical concepts for which, however, justification on theoretical grounds was extremely weak. The 'strength' of such concepts was pragmatic, that is, the practice resulting from their application accorded well with the aims of those who managed the major conglomerations of capital in finance and industry. By contrast potentially robust concepts of economic cooperation to serve social needs directly, remained 'underdeveloped' and so lacked social currency and political force. Indeed participants in the seminars, long critical of capitalist economics, surprised even themselves at the lack of substance they found in accepted economic categories and levels of achievement, once these were looked at critically 'from outside' that is, from the standpoint of human values as against money and exchange values.

Theory, concepts, ideas are just one aspect of struggle for change – an indispensable aspect of activity, but divorced from activity nothing at all or something quite different. Moreover it is grassroot activity that alone gives substance to the democratic element that is necessary to the purposes of change. This also is the soil from which new practices and new understandings grow. This in itself dictates the importance of questioning the reasoning behind all financial decisions. On this ground alone it is proper for trade unions to ask questions about the way their pension funds are invested. It is instructive, taking this as an example, to see where such questioning has lead. Status quo practice and the law, they were told, requires trustees to invest wherever it is most profitable;

political bans (e.g. on investments in South Africa) are, therefore, said to be unacceptable. However experience in USA shows funds with such bans to be getting better returns than others without them. In fact trustees with such bans still have a very wide choice of investments and possibly because of the scrutiny to which they are subject are more on their toes. What motivations predominate for managers of funds that do not have trade union representatives, for example, looking over their shoulders? They presumably will follow the normal investment practice of insurance companies and other such financial institutions, which is to make safe investments in big companies and follow the ethos of the major institutions. In their own way they too are making political choices favourable to the status quo and the good health of money-power rather than choices to maximise employment or weaken racist or fascist regimes. The funds collected from the population at large as payments towards pension schemes, insurance policies and so forth are, one finds, a huge part of the capital deployed as 'the private capital' of the giant companies that operate all across the world. The incomes of the masses of the people are in fact the springs from which flows the capital of the alien institutions by which their economic existence is ruled. An elite few at the top use personal wealth combined with links to major financial institutions to exert a leverage of power that lifts, shifts and displaces the wealth of whole peoples. What questioning has revealed to trade union representatives about how pension deductions from wages are used, leads them quite naturally to go on to demand a say about how these funds are used. Attempts so to do have however been overruled by the Courts (*cf* judgement against the NUM in July 1984). The Courts require trustees to be guided solely by commercial profitability; they jib at accepting criteria of social purpose or social usefulness, since it is not only the economic structure but also the legal structure that is geared to regulation by exchange-values. So questioning of financial decisions, as each answer leads to new questions, throws a lot of light on the social structures by which they are shaped.

A limited, specific question about pension funds opened up much wider issues and with them a deeper understanding of the economy as a whole. This demonstrates by specific example why good intention is not an acceptable criterion of good investment in a structure dominated by exchange-values and returns on money capital; but it also demonstrates that there may be room for limited improvements and modifications that go against the logic of the dominant structure.

For many decades now there have been cases of the nation state using its financial and other powers to influence investment policies and their social effects. This is yet one more ground for democratic organisations to question the reasoning behind financial decisions. Governmental polices can break away from the automatisms of capital turnover motivated by profitable expansion. However, the special position of the nation state as controller of legal tender and monetary procedures, whilst carrying within it possibilities of support for structures amenable to other than capitalist criteria, also implies a degree of nationalistic isolation. It in fact obstructs the internationalism of money-power that likes to move freely across frontiers; but though it breaks links that free market exchanges and free monetary transactions establish, it can and needs to establish politically negotiated links in support of new democratically based economic policies as well as for diplomatic reasons. Curbs on 'market internationalism' will need to be stoutly defended by a determined and conscious alternative internationalism of a new kind, supporting economic projects useful to those who suffer from international money-power and countering tendencies toward nationalistic isolationism.

If the well-understood criteria of a market economy – such as money cost, saleability, competitive success, profitability and so forth – are to be rejected where they fail to be socially useful, more explicit criteria of social usefulness than at present exist will be required. The framing of new criteria raises a host of problems to which participants in the seminars were throughout alive. However it is perfectly possible to move away from exchange-value criteria and tentatively develop alternative criteria out of quite crude and simple assumptions at the outset, which are in reality no different to the types of assumptions used by money power – such as the assumption that employment on what people themselves think useful is socially more useful than unemployment. There is a theoretical aspect to the problem of criteria; for example, what are needs and when is their satisfaction to be judged socially useful, how far does exchange-value already measure social usefulness in that the buyer by buying expresses his or her judgement of social usefulness and in what respects is this 'voting through the purse' defective? There is also a practical aspect; there already exist many forms of economic cooperation which are not disciplined by money criteria; it is possible to learn from the adequacies and inadequacies of existing practice, but also – and this is likely to be more significant and fruitful – democratic consciousness and attempts to exert control over economic undertakings in which people are collectively involved will lead to judgements of social usefulness being explicitly made over and over again in practice. Critical assesment of such experience will be of crucial importance and will provide a basis for more precise formulation of criteria. The defects of the criteria deduced from the economic theories of the market and commodity-exchange are so evident that we should not hesitate to use alternative criteria, however crude, where market regulated economics is patently giving bad results. Political considerations invariably underlie economic decisions: again and again it has to be asked 'Who then decides what is or is not socially useful?' and this question itself shows that the issue is much more one of political power than of techniques of economic management. If people are able themselves to control the use of resources, it is not unreasonable to define the socially useful as that which people choose for themselves. But such ultimate arbitrament by democratic power is valuable only as a distant compass point by which to steer a general direction. Tangible economic achievement in practice implies economic cooperation at many levels from the immediate community to international exchanges. Where there is cooperation, domains of independent and dependent responsibility have to be recognised; the reality of democratic power can not be abstracted from the structure by which it is articulated. To escape articulation by money, it is necessary to reject money *as the universal measure* of economic achievement; but this does not mean rejection of all measures. Indeed many new measures relevant to judgement of social usefulness may prove to be needed. What such measures are and how they can be used, can only be worked out by practical experience and generalised as theory only from such experience.

The status quo is well charted territory; the new is uncharted and those who move towards it are understandably nervous. So the world-wide struggle between the status quo of wealth, on one side, and democratic dreams for change, on the other, has no simple clearly defined demarcation lines. But in this struggle financial policy is certainly a battlefield – possibly the most important one of all. On it battle rages over a melee of jumbled policies such as those that purport to tackle inflation before unemployment or vice versa; but the real struggle is whether financial policy keeps money-power in the driving seat or puts instruments in the hands of democratic forces to use resources as they would choose.

NOTES

1. Andrew Crockett, *International Money* (Thomas Nelson, 1977) pp.172–3.
2. William Ashworth, 'Contracts and Finance', in War Production series of *History of Second World War* (HMSO and Longman Green, 1953) p.20.
3. Ibid., p.32.

Part IV
Two Case Studies

While we have referred wherever possible to real examples, actual things that happen in society, case studies are useful to show in some depth what we mean with our arguments for a Socially Useful Economy.

Militarism is a topical and key example of how current economic thinking is damaging to society as a whole. Chapter 10 exposes the many myths perpetrated about the value of high military spending, and shows how this vast and expensive enterprise is not subordinate to any *real* economic scrutiny, not being subject to market criteria nor to criteria of social usefulness.

The second case study takes the polar opposite and examines the assumptions and inadequacies of the economics of health. Chapter 11 shows in microcosm what the essence of a Socially Useful Economy means – especially how it differs from current economic thinking. It points also to the corrosive effect when a conflicting economic ethos dominates society generally.

10 The Political Economy of Militarism

'In 1984 Britain's annual defence expenditure reached the staggering sum of £17 billion pounds. This is the largest expenditure of all the European members of NATO, both in absolute terms, and also in money per head of the population. It means that an average family of 4 persons, would be spending £24 per week on defence, £12 per week on research and development and production of weapons, and £12 per week on the pay of armed forces and civilian employees of the Ministry of Defence.' (Figures from Donald McKenzie's seminar paper).

INTRODUCTION

Militarism is obviously a major obstacle to developing the socially useful economy. Between a twentieth and a tenth of the world's resources are devoted to war, and the preparation of the means of war. That may not sound a lot, but it forms a large proportion of those resources that are surplus to people's immediate needs for survival. The resources of time and material goods with which we can more fully express and articulate our humanity, the resources out of which we build and make the future of our species, resources we invest to create the circumstances of future existence, to express ourselves artistically, to effect social change and develop the potentials of our scientific and technological knowledge. Clearly the huge military expenditure to which we commit ourselves is *not* decided by the dictates of market forces, but by political and social will superimposed on the structure of commodity relations that the market forces govern. This expenditure is an expression of the current ascendancy of certain economic and social values.

Much of the time we as human beings spend on work of one kind or another is spoken for by need for food, shelter and warmth that cannot be denied; the further activities, to which we devote the surpluses of time and goods available, give expression to new and additional

203

creativity, they express the soul of our human society as we look towards the future. However, the proportion of research and development activity devoted worldwide to military ends has been estimated at between 25% and 40%. Over a half of central government expenditure in Britain on research and development is military. It has been estimated that 55% of research and development physicists in the United States work on projects of 'direct military value'. That so huge a part of the economic activity that most essentially represents our moral and cultural calibre should be dedicated to the culture of militarism, should cause deep questioning about the mechanisms of economic and social decision-making. How comes it that our most uniquely human activities have become so perverted?

The scale of this military budget has enormous economic and social consequences. Valuable resources are allocated to the production of weapons, in preference to the building of the quality of life. Orthodox economic theory is remarkably silent in providing any justification for this huge misallocation of resources.

'WAR CULTURE' AND ECONOMICS

Militarism accentuates the problem because it perpetuates and legitimises a false need of being prepared for war in ever more destructive ways. The cold war mentality and concepts of 'deterrence' have provided a 'magic formula' for ensuring that arms spending takes precedence over other spending. This severely undermines the capacity of the planet to solve its more fundamental problems. Creating the condition of peace, a process to liberate us from an obsession with defence, to use resources to solve the real problems, is a crucial element in developing the socially useful economy. Although state military expenditure defies all the rules of market economics, it provides an important measure of protection for private industry. This means that the 'viability' of our leading private companies such as Lucas Aerospace, Ferranti, Plessey, Marconi, British Aerospace operating in the areas of electronics, aerospace and shipbuilding are heavily dependent on government military funding. For example, some 70% of the sales of Lucas Aerospace is obtained from Ministry of Defence contracts.

Military expenditure and military culture so viewed announce to us an important economic truth – namely, that economic philosophy and social philosophy are inseparably intertwined. If socially useful economy is to be built, it is not enough just to see that new ideas and new democratic procedures guide *economic* practice; it is essential to develop new attitudes, new philosophies *for social activity as a whole*, if the way resources are used is properly to express our cultural and moral values, our feelings about human how life should be lived.

Though it is rare to hear monetarists attack militarism, the military economy completely contradicts the monetarist arguments for reductions in government spending. While essential public services are being slashed in pursuance of monetarist theories, real spending on armaments is increasing by 3% per year. This clearly illustrates the argument of Chapter 3, that the allocation of resources is not in fact based on the approach of 'orthodox economics'. The real justification of military expenditure arises from the analysis in Chapter 1, which emphasised the nature of the capitalist framework, *money-power*, and the legitimisation of transactional activities based on a harnessing of technology that is heavily subsidised by government funding. Military expenditure protects and supports the interests of capital, both nationally and internationally, in the face of external and internal threats. Furthermore the firms with military orders, engage in profitable activities which cushion them from some of the vicissitudes of the market to which the production of civilian commodities is exposed.

It is also important to note that the established order of society has long been wedded to some of the social aspects of the military philosophy, such as official secrecy, authoritarian discipline and anti-democratic legal powers – all of which are justified on grounds of military expediency. Departure from the philosophy that national defence requires greater and more sophisticated power in the military's weaponry, would significantly change the existing social order – or at least is perceived as being likely so to do in the dominant thinking of the existing order. So perfection of weaponry goes on and on as if governed by a momentum of its own, without regard to social consequences or overall social rationality. But the socially useful economy cannot develop unless the social usefulness of defence policies are subject, just like everything else, to a new democratic rationality in decision-making. Raymond Williams[1] has rightly said that to build peace it is necessary to build more than peace. For us this same proposition, turned around, is also true: to build a socially useful economy it is necessary to change more then just economic theory and practice.

Within this framework, often referred to as the 'Military – Industrial Complex', decisions are taken as if no choice or alternatives existed. These decisions, concerning 'credible' defence strategies, and the technological advances required to retain military prowess, only serve to legitimise the existing structures of power and authority, without proper public accountability (as was discussed in Chapter 5). This is especially the case with nuclear weapons where decisions are shrouded in great secrecy and little effective consultation takes place. For example the Attlee government made the decision to produce the A bomb, but it was kept secret from British Parliament and public. The legitimacy of these decisions is often justified in terms of defence needs, but the real choices are never presented for public debate. This is why the nuclear disarmament movement has been a crucial element in bringing the real choices into the forefront of public debate, to unite people in recognising the need to eliminate weapons of destruction, and to shift away from our obsession with defence to more socially useful activities.

Military spending is also 'justified' on the grounds that it helps to raise the standard of living, by increasing demand for goods, creating employment and accelerating technological progress. But as a Trade Union paper[2] on military spending argues, these assertions are false. There is now substantial evidence that the heavy burden placed on the economy by years of high military spending has boosted inflation, drained scarce resources, inhibited advances in civilian technology, lowered our standard of living and generally undermined the economy. In short, military spending actually damages the economy and costs us jobs!

The *opportunity costs* of military spending have never been properly evaluated, but they must be considerable. Much-needed socially useful investment, to restore our infrastructure, public services and industrial base, is being sacrificed in order to satisfy the insatiable appetite of the arms industry. The arguments concerning the technological 'spin off' of military spending in promoting certain products are becoming less convincing. The Japanese and West German post-war experience illustrates that military production is not necessary for the development of civilian products. In fact because military production is now so specialised, it has less relevance to civilian 'spin off' effects. Because of the increasing capital intensity of military production, the argument that defence spending creates jobs is contradicted by the evidence of increasing redundancies in the arms industries, in spite of the increase in government expenditure. According to research[3] carried out in the US, the shift of spending from defence to other forms of expenditure such as transportation, housing, health care and education would create many more jobs.

Thus the struggle for disarmament and reduction in arms spending should not be viewed as a threat to employment, but as an essential precondition for the protection of jobs, providing greater stability and prospects through the transfer of resources and research to civilian production to enable urgent social needs to be met. Converting 'swords into ploughshares', could become the central focus which links together many of the social movements concerned with the development of the socially useful economy.

We should remember that the military – industrial complex is a key element of transnational money–power. It distorts international relationship between peoples. It reinforces international cartels of money – and political power and influence – which are profoundly anti-democratic. It cripples trade unionism by making whole areas of investment planning 'secret'. It takes away vast resources from applications which could meet urgent short and long term social needs. As a central part of the orthodox political economy, militarism exhibits clearly so many of the features that militate fundamentally against a more socially relevant and useful economy.

Readers will be able to find a substantial amount of published material on all aspects of this subject. In this short chapter we have only outlined the key features of the political economy of militarism.

NOTES

1. Raymond Williams *'Exterminism & The Cold War'* (Verso, 1982) p. 85.
2. Transport and General Workers Union, Strategy for Arms Conversion (TGWU, 1983).
3. Marta Daniels, *Job Security, Arms in Connecticut Mid Peninsula Conversion project* (Ploughshare Press, 1976).

11 Political Economy of Health

INTRODUCTION

Health in itself is a classic use value – when you have it, it *allows and encourages* you to do a great many things; when you've 'lost' it, its value is almost infinite – being more important than money itself, in however large quantities. 'Lost' health cripples, degrades and undermines people, and focuses attention on the pain, fear and discomfort of it, largely to the exclusion of other, life-enhancing things.

At present large parts of the globe have endemic ill-health, or rather a lack of good health – through malnutrition, poor sanitation, in a word, through *poverty*. In the so-called 'Developed' world the old scourges of smallpox, diptheria, etc. have gone – but to be replaced by a bewildering variety of physical and mental stress illnesses, cancer, and cardio-vascular disease; problems commonly attributed to 'affluence'. But is this so? On the surface one would think that affluence would provide people with that marvellous 'condition' – *choice*, choice in jobs, choice in food, choice in recreation, and therefore the *ability* to stay healthy. Patently this isn't so – the conventional market mechanisms by *no means* guarantee, or even encourage good health.

Put crudely, there are two 'sides' to health, one concerns the personal, social and environmental conditions that create illness or lack of good health; the other concerns the ways in which a health-giving service (including removing or dealing with disease) operates in a society. This short chapter shows how both 'sides' can be enormously enhanced by the socially useful economy, and how they are put under attack by conventional economics.

One final word before we start this analysis. We are concerning ourselves with Britain today in the main; there is not space to delve into the important historical issues of this matter, nor to deal in any way adequately with other countries, particularly those suffering from

208

extreme poverty. We must ask our readers to accept the limitations, though we hope you will be able, like us, to draw further conclusions from our analysis.

WHAT MAKES US ILL: WORK

Work can make us ill, even in recent years many more days have been lost from work through illness than through strikes. Stress is often a key factor – and unlike the stories put about in the Press, epidemiological evidence shows that stress is *not* a problem confined to top-level executives; indeed stress is much *more* prevalent amongst semi-skilled and unskilled workers; Department of Employment, and Local Authority studies show that women workers in particular suffer from stress.

It doesn't take too much imagination to understand why stress should be so prevalent. Sheer pace of work (e.g. in assembly line work), the constant underlying fear of 'retribution' if one doesn't manage to fill one's quota of work, the fear of possible unemployment; and the grind of *having to* work – with little or no chance of changing working conditions significantly – in order to pay the bills, are perhaps the most obvious causes. But new technologies and new working conditions impose further hazards. There is a growing body of research which shows that wordprocessing, constant computer-aided design work, and other computer-paced work puts a severe additional strain on people. Even bus-driving has become appreciably more stressful in recent years – as increasing traffic congestion, and more 'efficient' timetables have put greater pressure on drivers (with the much-vaunted one-person-operator buses making the pressures even worse.)

And the pressures grow worse in many areas. Rapid technological change which is designed simply to increase capital accumulation and/or reduce labour costs and workers' control, is tending to make people's skills and knowledge redundant at a faster and faster pace. Some management consultancy organisations have devised 'profiles' of ideal workers – based heavily on age. For example the 'optimal' (in terms of output/return on capital/person employed) age of a pure mathematician is about 23 years, that of a computer systems analyst, about 28 years; motor car firms themselves occasionally acknowledge that line-workers are 'burnt-out' by the age of 40. The rat-race to keep abreast of new information, new skills is *itself* an important new dimension of stress.

And what happens to the increasing numbers of people who, by this line of conventional economic argument, are 'over the hill'? We must all have seen examples of this – frustration and despair – a fine combination of conditions to enhance health!

Work continues to make us ill through the medium of occupational disease, from varieties of pneumoconiosis in coalmining, textiles, etc., to the use of new (often untested) chemical agents – increasingly seen as potentially carcinogenic – and the effects of low-level radiation via VDUs, on pregnant women. The amount of research into illness caused by work is small by comparison to the deleterious effects it has on the populace. More importantly, the resources put into the implementation of proper safeguards (before as well as after application) are criminally inadequate; otherwise we would have seen some marked diminution of occupational illnesses and disease over the last twenty years or so. The Health and Safety Executive reported a few years ago that the cost of occupational 'accidents' and prescribed diseases (which certainly doesn't cover the range of the real problems) was in the region of £800–£1500 million a year – these are *direct* costs only. It is thought that upwards of 600 000 people a year are involved in a prescribed 'accident' or occupational disease. Add to that all those 'non-prescribed' health problems and we must be talking of over a million people a year. *And* to add insult to injury resources are being cut back, with for instance the recent cuts in factory health and safety inspectors.

Increasing pressures for 'efficiency' at work are also forcing more people onto shiftwork. A recent NEDO study found that at least 20% of people who are put onto shifts suffer from appreciable sleep deprivation, and/or gastro-intestinal upsets. As people are less and less able to opt out from shiftwork – 'take this job or you won't have a job' – it follows that increasing numbers of people are suffering ill health as a result of new working patterns imposed by employers.

There is a host of evidence which points to ill-health being caused by particular work conditions and working arrangements – any reader wanting to pursue this further will find no lack of available material. But is is important to remind ourselves of the key fact that work-induced illness is *not* seen as a responsibility of employers. Like environmental pollution, it is an 'externality'. Providing that the work process does not induce symptoms too rapidly or too obviously the employer *does* use methods to increase control over, and productivity of, employees. Resulting illness is seen as an individual's problem, or that of the State's health-care service.

WHAT MAKES US ILL: NO WORK

We know less today about the social and individual effects of unemployment than we did in the 1930s – whose studies were an important input into Wartime welfarism, and the post-War social reconstruction, including the creation of the National Health Service. Only in recent years has there been a re-kindling of interest in the subject; paradoxically perhaps arising out of the work of Dr Harvey Brenner and his colleagues at John Hopkins University in the USA. Brenner's work showed that a 1% increase in the unemployment rate over a 6-year period correlates with an increase in numbers of 'premature' deaths totalling 36 887, and other significant increases in diseases.

Similar research in Britain suggests that an increase in unemployment of one million people leads to an additional 50 000 admissions into mental hospitals over a subsequent 5-year period, with an additional 50 000 deaths; at current prices the public costs of these effects are around £1 billion. Physical diseases associated with this increased morbidity rate are primarily stress-related. Less direct health costs/damages include increased incidence of child battering, more children put into care, higher rates of alcoholism, a substantial increase in suicide attempts.

Where do the health-related effects of unemployment fall? On those enterprises that create it, on a government whose policies may be said to have helped create it? Obviously not, much of the misery occurs and is dealt with at the privatised, individual level, family members have to deal with it, overworked and underbriefed GPs are at the receiving end too. Meanwhile massive numbers of hospitals are closed, with total NHS expenditure failing to keep up with the increased demands from unemployment, and the vastly increasing numbers of elderly people – including the large increase in numbers who have taken (or been forced to take . . .) early retirement.

Furthermore, resources devoted to dealing effectively with depression, frustration and despair that arise from unemployment (itself well documented now) are inadequate and/or inappropriate; the 'best' we can do is often the application of tranquillisers or anti-depressant drugs. Not unusually, an advertisement for 'Serenid D', one of these drugs, shows a picture of a mother with children, obviously living in poverty, captioned with the words 'She can't change her environment, but she can take Serenid D'; the implication of this and similar advertisements in medical journals and magazines needs no elaboration . . .

WHAT MAKES US ILL: COMMODITIES

Cancer in particular is associated with cigarettes, but also refined foods, and certain petroleum-based products. Breathing difficulties and disease are associated with badly heated and ventilated housing. Enormous carnage is created through physical and chemical dangers of commercial and private motoring. Military products by definition are bad for health. Certain drugs have dangerous so-called side-effects. Some toys can be dangerous. The use of non-toughened glass in homes and other features of domestic design and technology cause enormous numbers of otherwise-preventable accidents.

We have of course no generally-applicable design criteria for products which would render them safe. Products are designed as commodities – a means of creating surplus value, money, and money-power. The sugar industry isn't interested in the vast disease-inducing effects of the heavy promotion of sugar-based products, nor are oil and petrochemical companies interested in removing lead from petrol – that is regarded as a *diversion* from their normal business strategies. All we have are under-resourced 'safety-net' agencies – which seek to avoid the worst and most obvious safety problems in products, and a rag-bag of organisations that 'blow the whistle' when they can about health problems. Indeed when Lucas Aerospace workers tried to change their firm's product policy, to put more emphasis on medical and health-related products, the company's General Manager publicly proclaimed that this was a diversion away from Lucas's 'proper' business concerns (expensive military aerospace hardware).

All in all, health as a use value is not only *denied* by market mechanisms – as they exert their controls over work processes, the size of the employed labour force, and the nature of the commodities produced – but is often acted *against* by those mechanisms. A socially useful economy which put as a priority the optimization of health, would by definition *not* support military investment, would very significantly change the agri-business/food processing industry, would drastically change design in vast swathes of consumer goods. It would also create a different 'agenda' for worthwhile jobs, and for work practices and processes. Because of the lack of adequately resourced research it is currently impossible to measure the economic dysbenefits arising out of conventional economic practices; but we think the case is adequate to put a cost against the problems outlined previously which runs into several £billions. At a deeper level the social costs are immense, and one should seriously question whether a so-called civilised society can sustain such widespread imposition of ill health on its populace . . .

HEALTH SERVICES AND TECHNOLOGIES

Just as we do not have an 'economic philosophy' for areas of life that make people ill, so too we have problems with our ostensible approach to health-giving services. Whilst in so many respects the National Health Service is a powerful affirmation of social usefulness – equating a 'right to not suffer and die unnecessarily' with a substantial institutional provider, it suffers from a lack of underpinning economic philosophy.

Even the monetarists hesitate somewhat to deny that a National Health Service is a societal asset, they can seldom attack it head-on. Even so, the NHS *has* been subjected to conventional managerialist thinking, which measures for instance hospital 'productivity' by numbers of patients using 'a bed' per year, i.e. patient through-put; cost-effectiveness in drug prescribing is another key managerial control mechanism. In neither instance is efficiency of *health care* considered primarily, or even secondarily. Why though has the imposition of cash limits, crude and narrow 'cost-effectiveness', been able to have been imposed – by Labour governments as well as Conservative?

As Lesley Doyal pointed out clearly in her Paper,[1] the NHS is very much a 'mixed economy' operation, containing financial and non-financial private interests (the drug companies, the 'semi-private' top physicians), alongside truly public provision. This ambiguity extends to the broadest technical level, with people – rather 'patients' – being treated somewhat as if they were bits of machinery, and with high-technology acute interventionist medicine having high status; and on the other hand encompassing a strong tradition of caring, witness the almost unfailing praise of nurses – with their human skills to the fore.

The contradictions reflect unresolved historical pressures. Whilst being a 'carer' has a generally unsullied motivation, the *organisation* of 'care' has lead to the creation of conventional professionalism – where care is 'doled out' from the top to the bottom; there's little or no democratic thinking within the organisation of care. The development of new technologies and techniques for treatment have on the one hand had an egalitarian effect, allowing more treatment to go to more people, but private interests so often determine the parameters of invention and application. A recent example has arisen through CAITS and other bodies, where enormous social and medical needs for breathing aids were not being met by a major manufacturer, until community-based organisations started to invent better equipment, whereupon the firm responded rapidly with better designs – this would not have happened otherwise. The very organisation of resources for health care is not democratically based, though purporting to 'serve all the people'. . .

Thus the health service, whilst being popularly defended against privatisation, and the more general application of private interest economics, has a number of foundations which actually contradict its social aims. This has made it harder for people to simply equate defence of the NHS with the promotion of a key bit of a socially useful economy.

The only way out of this impasse is to develop a more coherent economic philosophy for health care, and to develop it democratically, taking into account all the legitimate interests that exist in the field; for we cannot simply assume that there are unproblematic and common interests. Workers in the health service, those in nursing, technician and 'ancillary' jobs in particular, can and do often have interests which lie broadly along the lines of 'patients' interests. Even here though we need to create structures in which differences can be dealt with – at the moment none exists. However the key physicians and senior administrators often seem to have interests which hardly intersect with the needs of those they're caring for and these top 'professionals' tend to dominate important health care decisions, though often under pressure (not always accepted unwillingly) from companies with huge vested interests. It is therefore crucial to democratise the development of medical knowledge and means of application which are so dominated by these elites. Key areas such as research directions, technological applications, diagnostic and therapeutic techniques must be placed in the public eye, and means found to democratise their assessment and implementation.

People's experience of heath care is *the* basic ingredient of a health service system which can overcome the historical contradictions that make the NHS so unpleasant, so awesome, or inappropriate for people. Health education must mean more than exhortatory 'self-help' leaflets. It means workplace facilities to help people identify and deal with health problems arising from the world of work. It means health centres being transformed into open education and directional agencies. It means the opening up of NHS decision-making to wider user/worker participation as a major political priority.

Allied to this we require to start putting a measure on the economic dysbenefits of the actions of private interests and commodity produc-

tion – those actions which cause ill health; and we need fiscal or other
checks applied to those who create disease or other illness. Good health
requires economic recognition – as an economic *benefit*, based on its
clear use value.

Exchange values have no place in decision-making over health, their
undoubted presence at the moment is a significant cause of ill health.
Use value is all in this area, our task must be to put sufficient collective/
democratic input into it to make the use values public property, encoded
adequately for us to make the best decisions based on *health care
efficiency*.

Once we have armed ourselves with the idea that economic activity
could be governed by criteria of social usefulness which override
exchange-value, reflection on the economics of health carries us into
strikingly new territories. Market economics radically transformed
human societies, in many ways for the better, and certainly opened up
extraordinary new human potentials; but as the economics of exchange-
value spreads so as to pervade every nook and cranny of the social fabric,
what was once acceptable new scope for social capacity turns into
unacceptable domination by money values, in fact into social disease.
And are there not a thousand signs that our society is now sick? So must
we not now give health – social and individual – an economic priority
that overrides exchange-value? And how else can we do this but by
building up the power of people – at work and in the community – to say
for themselves how they are to work and live? This would mean people
vetoing decisions dictated by criteria of exchange-value when they
perceive them as being harmful to their well-being. In short, the seed
from which social health will grow must be involvement of producers
and consumers collectively so as to control for themselves the manner in
which resources are used. Social health is central to the aims of the
socially useful economy and is inseparable from the democratisation of
decision-making.

NOTE

1. Lesley Doyal prepared a paper for our seminar on this subject, but was
   unable to address the meeting. This chapter is drawn in part from her paper,
   from the paper of a previous CAITS Workshop on the subject, other related
   CAITS material, and issues raised by seminar participants.

Part V
Building the New from the Old

Part V draws together a great many of the ideas and concrete proposals raised in the seminars upon which this book is based. Chapters 12–14 show the bridges that can be made from the old to the new.

Chapter 12 revisits trade unionism, explores its roots and current practices. Through a critical analysis, and referring to concrete examples it shows that a reformed trade unionism in Britain is a key element in any move towards a Socially Useful Economy. Without ducking some of the great problems that exist in the trade union and labour movement the argument explains how this important social force in society can be architect for economic change.

We then consider in a little less depth the constraints and possibilities that are around us today. We put particular emphasis on three main routes for the achievement of a Socially Useful Economy, the union movement, local government, and a new type of consumerism.

We conclude with a short Chapter 14 which encapsulates many of the ideas and proposals contained within the book, by putting forward a 'charter' for change. This 'shorthand' form of argument for a Socially Useful Economy is offered to the reader as a summary, and the authors are only too pleased to receive your comments.

active role
/
historic por⁻ - v. large
prop⁻ not explored.
voluntary org⁻ -

12 New Functions for Trade Unions

INTRODUCTION

Much of the previous argument in the book may lead the reader to wonder what role our trade union organisations may have in developing a socially useful economy. Our contention is that these organisations have a *central* role. Around a half of Britain's workforce are in the trade unions, very little of that proportion coming about through 'enforced' closed shop arrangements. This despite a seven year aggressive campaign against most aspects of trade unionism, of a virulence and continuity seldom seen before this century. The fact that so many people join and stay in trade unions – which in the main are voluntary organisations – *is* important in itself; compared to membership of any other voluntary organisation trade union membership is both bigger and more extensive than anything else seen in the country; nor, unlike, say, membership of an insurance scheme or the Automobile Association, does membership *automatically* confer specific financial or material benefits.

Obviously people join unions in the *expectation* that they will provide a means for protection and advancement of pay and conditions at work, but a deeper motivation often still persists. Many industrial sociology surveys in the 1960s and early 1970s concluded that very substantial proportions of all sorts of workforces could not be described as simply 'instrumental', that is, that many people seek more than wages from work; why then would these people join unions so readily? A basic sympathy for, and understanding of the need to combine collectively in the face of 'force majeur' is self-evidently present. This phenomenon cannot be crudely reduced in size or significance by reference to low Branch Meeting attendances – as Right Wing critics so readily do. In 1984 over 100 000 mineworkers went on strike for a very prolonged period, their families formed support groups all over the country, literally millions of people gave active or financial help. Yet a detailed

survey of Branch Meeting attendance figures would certainly suggest
that only a tenth or a quarter 'should' have got involved in this dispute.
And we should remember that the dispute was not about wages, but
about jobs, and about subtle and deep feelings towards the social and
economic life of numerous communities.

It is not denied that some people are trade unionists, as a kind of
'insurance policy' – though much depends on unions' own policies and
activities as to how prevalent this attitude is (more of which, later). But,
in 'Building the new from the old' we must address just what it *is* in 'the
old' that can be built upon. Desperation and anger about working
conditions in the last century and this found early expression in
collective worker organisation, there was and is usually no effective
alternative. Out of this came, historically, the Labour Representation
Committee and then the Labour Party. Out of this came legislation, on
child labour, health and safety, wages and much else. Out of this came
syndicalism, Guild Socialism, nationalisation, a Welfare State, even, to
some extent, political enfranchisement. And out of this came countless
experiments, ideas and ideals about different ways of running a political
economy.

ROOTS OF TRADE UNIONISM

The experience of work is a central social and political force in modern
history, through trade unionism it also developed an economic force.
And as we've tried to show, economic force is not simply measured by
crude calculation of aggregated wages-take in the economy, or implied
from increases in labour costs as a proportion of Gross Domestic
Product. For contrary to all current efforts to marginalise unions, the
collective experience of trade unionism remains a deep and wilful
element in society. Out of desperation and anger came a multitude of
strong forces for education and enlightenment, indeed for a great many
years the trade union movement was people's *only* vehicle for education
– even today amongst young and old trade unionism *is* regarded as a key
means of understanding many aspects of the world, through courses,
and through the activity of *being* an 'active' member or representative.
Out of this strong educational tradition came notions of social and
economic justice, and all the political change briefly mentioned above.

So, *protection* in many human and organisational guises was and
remains a central element of the phenomenon known as trade unionism.
That this may appear to be reactive, even a negative force in society
cannot be denied historically, but equally defence against employers'

force majeure must frequently appear to be so. Trade unionism cannot normally command a fraction of the opinion-forming resources that are available to money-power. Further, it has been argued that trade unionism has frequently been forced to adopt a seemingly negative stance, even if its members and organisations wish otherwise. Professor David Noble of the Smithsonian Institution, Washington, has pointed out powerfully that the Luddites 'had bad press'; Luddites, known as backward-looking machine-wreckers, semi-criminals, had *no other* practical option when they saw mass unemployment and disruption looming through new textile machinery. The Luddites had no political or economic leverage, what were they to do? Writing letters to their Members of Parliament (had they been allowed so to do) would have done nothing, 'social accounting' hadn't been developed. Their 'crime' was to stand in the way of those with money power who saw a way of extracting more money from labour, i.e. they stood in the way of 'progress'.

Equally so today, trade unionists are usually given no option but to accept labour-saving machinery, or refuse to accept it – and probably lose their jobs. So, the only course that seems available is to try to negotiate to mitigate the worst effects of its introduction, even in that endeavour they are frequently labelled as obstinate or obstructive. Nevertheless protection, despite all the problems associated with it, remains part of the core of trade unionism. In the 1980s such a collective function *is* still of enormous importance to people. Being 'negative', saying 'No' is after all supposed to be a human prerogative in a 'free' society. In all areas of high unemployment, factory closures and mass job losses are quite understandably met with a negative response; where the new technology de-skills people there is a human right to resist, just as there is a right to object to new processes which might create health and safety hazards.

Terms such as 'it's a sell-out', or 'they've sold us down the river' are very common in the trade union movement. It means that protection has been exchanged for uncertainty, or for something worse, it also means that someone has 'sold' something – such as a job – that shouldn't be in the market *to* to be sold. So, what is being protected obviously has a deep, and often quite subtle meaning to people. It has to do with dignity, pride, a sense of self-worth, a sense of position in society, the importance of an active community, and much else besides. These are not trivial matters, they often have little or nothing to do with 'markets', for, unlike the monetarist or neoclassical economists, people seldom *actually* look at themselves and their worth in general market terms, except perhaps through comparing their wages with those in a few other local firms. Labour market information is usually scarce, inadequate or inappropriate – as any serious-minded wage bargainer will concur.

Protection isn't necessarily the same as wanting everything in the world to stay the same. Many people after all hope for some material advancement, better security than they have now, or for a chance to do a more interesting, relevant or creative job. No, it's when change is imposed from outside, when change has detrimental effects, or when it looks somehow terribly unreasonable that people object. So some means of dealing effectively with change is important to people, and that's where trade unionism has had an impact. And for employers to call that attitude obstructive is to somehow remove 'workers' from the rest of human race, 'they' are expected to accept changes that no employer would reasonably accept for himself . . .

Protection is of course also a key to wages and pay bargaining. When an individual or group has no long-term secure future economically, it only makes sense to try to and maximise today's pay packet. For many years, when we *did* have an appreciable number of apprenticeships, people would work for five, six, or seven years at low rates of pay – in the expectation of a secure medium-term economic future. So, people will willingly sacrifice today's earnings for tomorrow's – but only *if* there is an economically secure tomorrow. For the majority of people at work, the effort to obtain better pay is part of an insurance policy, protecting them against worse times. Indeed many commentators ascribe high productivity in Japan to the very high bonuses that can be obtained, for in Japan relatively early retirement and poor social welfare means that average individual savings are several times higher than those in other OECD countries. It is thus just too easy, and wrong, to equate pay demands with 'greed' – we can safely leave greed to crooks of one sort or another, and to people like Sir Michael Edwardes – quoted in the press as saying he expects an income of £1 m a year.

As for the other adage, that people are 'not earning their way', that is, that they demand wage increases at a rate which is higher than the increase in value of their productivity, things are again somewhat more complicated in practice. First, few people are given adequate information about how their work actually relates to their employer's income. Second, if they are given such information, it is usually in such an aggregated form that it's impossible to relate it back to their efforts. Third, over the years there has been so much inadequate, inappropriate information, sometimes to the point of being misinformation, that they feel they cannot trust their employers when they tell them what their work is 'worth'. Fourthly, there has been so much movement within and between productivity schemes, value-added schemes, measured day-work, group bonuses, factory bonuses and the like that any normal person is likely to be simply confused about what in reality their productivity is. Fifthly, there are great disparities between, say one production department and another in terms of value-added, market conditions, efficiency of plant and machinery etc., which means that 'productivity' in one may be vastly different to that in another – the difference having absolutely nothing to do with what the employee does at work, how hard s/he works, etc. Lastly, and by no means the least important, the implication of 'earning one's way' is that workers here must increasingly accept pay and conditions packages that apply in other countries – for that is what they are supposedly being measured against. Who here would want to work under conditions which apply to those unfortunate people that labour in the Phillipines or South Korea?

Once again protection is paramount, how can someone easily accept a change in the pay/productivity equation when one or more of the six problems outlined above exist? So trade unionism seeks to understand, exert control, and sometimes object to new pay/work deals proposed by employers. Essentially the same argument applies to conditions bargaining. People want protection against new shift arrangements – believing them to be introduced for someone else's benefit, not theirs. Working hours and holidays (the working year) should be minimised, so that, should 'hard times' come along, they've got more leeway in possibly bargaining away rights; it should be remembered that this *does* happen, in 'concessions bargaining' in the USA for instance.

In the absence of formal constitutional rights, people quite rightly create their own societies and organisations for protection against those who would seek to diminish their worth or influence. Trade unions are perhaps the most important of these organisations. So here we have a kernel of consciousness of a collective kind, fought for throughout the last 150 years. At best it represents the practice of communality, of self-sacrifice for others, of social justice. It contains politics of justice, of opposition to demeaning or degrading processes in society, of equality and the common good. These are significant building blocks for any socially useful economy.

THE PROBLEMS IN TRADES UNIONS?

But, like any organisation in society trade unionism is not without its faults, and we should be clear about these for they may obstruct the very real contribution that trade unions can make. Just like the professions, and many other strata of people who wield money-power, trade unions have created cartels. Trade unionism's history has mainly taken place against a backdrop of mass unemployment, underemployment, and conditions of the most demeaning kind – such as casual employment, sweatshops, etc. In such circumstances organisations of workers have tried to protect themselves through creating barriers to accession, i.e. the so-called Labour Aristocracy idea. Yet these people have perhaps a much more understandable reason for creating cartels than highly-paid 'professionals' – whose self-seeking behaviour has not been impinged upon by mass unemployment and pay cuts. So a certain degree of chauvinism amongst grades of workers who have managed to climb out of 'the hole' a little is to be expected. The effects of labour cartels has not simply been to diminish others' opportunities however, for these more 'successful' groupings have also been used by others to more strongly highlight their own plight, and to thereby strengthen their own position. The sheer power and dynamism of the 'new' General Unions that grew up during and after the first World War attests to this.

Nevertheless labour cartels have had a divisive effect, and many current industrial relations pressures – such as that to create 'multi-skilled/flexible' crafts – exert influences which tend to maintain efforts to create and support labour cartels. However over the past 10–15 years in particular new groupings have emerged – often from within cartels – which substantially break down these divisions (more of which later). But after all this is taken into account, 'labour aristocracies' of one sort or another *have* frequently pointed the way to political, social and economic change – simply through having managed to 'elevate' themselves into a position where some general leverage has been attained. Obviously we have the recent miners' dispute in mind – where the socio-economic aspects of energy policy and coalmining planning were vividly raised. Highly-skilled aerospace workers tried to practice a new syndicalist approach in pre-Second War and post-war eras. Even today computer staffs seriously engage in public discussions about whether their skills should be used on weapons of war.

There is much to be gained from a proper appreciation of such so-called 'aristocracies', for when they are at their best they raise funda-mental questions about the social value of their work. So far we have considered the powerful trade union practices of human protection and political ambition, and both have something to contribute. But building on both traditions workers' groupings have in more recent years moved beyond the constraints that these traditions have imposed. In the 1950s and 1960s a *de facto* democratisation of trade unionism took place, albeit around conventional pay and conditions bargaining; the role and function of lay representatives – 'amateurs' if you like – became much stronger and more clearly defined. Here we had a revitalisation of a more democratic process, where individual trade union members had an increasingly effective involvement in decision-making in union activity. Distortions and problems undoutedly arose – with new echelons of elites arising in places. But despite this, one of the important charateristics of modern trade unionism is the significance of lay representatives. Pre-existing trade union structures have had to accommodate them – in both constructive and destructive ways.

Certain trade union bodies have perceived greater activity 'at the base' as a threat to existing power and authority relations, and have sought to circumscribe this activity, sometimes in quite brutal ways. Others have sought to 'regularise' their position – most notably seen in the Bullock Commission era of the late 1960s. But overall 'the base' has not been too anxious to be 'regularised' or regulated according to the interests of others. This had led to some quite deep differences between unions, with some increasingly involving lay representatives in an expansion of trade union activity, whilst others have made great efforts to re-establish the supremacy of Executive bodies and full-time officials. In the latter case the gaps betwen members and their representatives (who are under great pressure 'from above') and between lay representatives and union officials has grown – to the detriment of all; often leading to the expenditure of great efforts in internal 'in-fighting'.

Despite these problems, and sometimes because of them, we have seen in the last fifteen-years a range of outward-looking union activities, often emanating from 'the base' and involving large numbers of members and lay representatives. Taken together they cannot realistically be said to constitute a new 'movement', but nor can the events be taken as unique or isolated. We have seen the factory occupation, the work-in, the sit-in, alternative workers' plans for new production, whole scenarios for new social uses for industries, quite complex antiprivatisation campaigns, joint worker-user campaigns, collaborative ventures with environmentalists, with womens' groups, and so on. Clearly we have witnessed struggles to break out of the constraints that have been imposed by protectionism – though at the same time they owe a great deal to protection – of jobs, conditions, services.

These strands of new union activity have if anything increased in significance during the past few years, as Government and employers have sought to marginalise trade unionism. It has become clear to many union organisations that they cannot simply carry on as before and wait for the election of a more amenable national government. The imposition of legislation to force unions to ballot their members on the existence of a political fund has for instance concentrated the collective mind enormously; why should unions have political funds, what should they be used for – answers to these basic questions are being sought urgently. The role of 'the base' has, paradoxically, been strengthened by anti-union legislation!

Basic beliefs in trade unionism as a necessary collective grouping and activity for 'ordinary' working people continue to be expressed in concrete ways; there are many signs that greater diversity of activity is developing, and from a more democratically organised base. There remains however a constellation of political problems, involving the understanding of broader objectives of trade unionism. Some maintain that trade unions can and should do no more than obtain protection and limited enhancement of pay and conditions for members, accepting a relatively unchanging capitalist framework, e.g. Business Unionism in the USA. Barrie Sherman illustrated this problem in his paper, 'Economics and The Labour Movement':

'In almost all respects the Labour movement exhibits a more touching faith in the efficacy of capitalism than does the Conservative Party. This manifests itself at the macro-economic and micro-economic levels by both unions and the Labour Party itself.

At the level of the economy as a whole the Labour Party fought the last election on a manifesto that was widely thought to be very socialist!. In fact its main economic planks were to protect and then cajole companies in the UK and it was assumed that they would respond to this treatment by becoming more productive.

At the level of the firm trade unions have consistently bargained with management on the assumption that there were given parameters, the most important of these being the total right and desirability of management to take all the decisions regarding the product mix and the methods of manufacture, distribution etc.

Neither of these factors, nor others which tend to work against the longer term interests of working people and families and dependants, are new. When Lloyd George offered the country to the trade unions and they refused and the TUC/Labour Party Committee was subsequently formed the movement had clearly chosen the path as outlined by the establishment. The game might well be fought honourably and very hard but the rules and the referee meant that gains would be limited as both were supplied by those defending the status quo.

The Labour movement's view of the economy and its chosen method of curing ills and maintaining itself is basically Keynesian with a very small dash of supply side intervention. This means that demand is managed and as so often happens when something goes wrong the traditional remedies of incomes policies and other deflationary policies are trotted out. The Social Contract showed that a good deal of goodwill existed for these tactics within the activists in the trade union movement but that it evaporated in a matter of three to four years.

Whilst it is tempting to argue that all incomes policies are bad and that working people have been damaged by them it is clear that in the period since 1945, one when there have been 18 separate phases of incomes policies, the material standard of living of workers has risen dramatically. Whether it would have increased more is quite another matter if a free settlement of wages and conditions had prevailed.

This view still prevails in the policy making echelons of the movement as the 1983 manifesto implicitly included an incomes policy which would have been both severe and designed to transmute incomes foregone into profits. These tactics are theoretically at odds with what the trade unions demand in collective bargaining although in practice there is a compatibility.

Whilst unions do use the argument that higher profits should mean higher wages and it is always easier to persuade members of the rightness of their claim in such circumstances, the end point is always a trade off between the continued existence of the enterprise and thus employment and wage levels bargained. Given that the survival arguments are mounted by management who have the market and competitor positions it is difficult to challenge them so that settlements are basically on management terms.

Whilst the members of unions take an interest in the bargaining on their behalf and can indeed determine the outcome in theory, there is no such interest in the remote business of policy making. Even if there were it is done at so many stages removed from the rank and file membership that it is well nigh impossible to influence it. The TUC is remote from union national officials, remoter from local officials and as accessible to the ordinary members as the House of Commons. The internal mechanisms of unions are not geared to the collecting and checking of policy options at a TUC level and cannot be deployed speedily enough.

This would be a serious disadvantage if it were confined merely to the TUC Congress but practical policy has been made over the past eight years at Liaison Committee level. The chances of amending, correcting, or initiating policy at this level is well nigh zero. This disenfranchises most union members and even if the representative democracy system is working well (and by and large it does not) most of the activists too.

In short the Labour movements' economic policies have been to create growth in GDP in any way possible and often at the expense of working people. This is not to argue that other alleviatory measures have not been taken nor that there is a lack of basic sympathy. It is however to argue that the policy making mechanisms cannot adequately reflect the union activist at a national level and in the national arena. Even the longer term policies have converted to short term expedients whilst in a parliamentary democracy there can be no guarantee of a long term anyhow.

The microeconomic framework within the labour movement has worked is, if anything, rather more rigid in its philosophy. Much of this is a function of the centralist view that the Labour Party takes (regional policy or sector intervention are devolved mechanisms in this context) combined with the development of collective bargaining and union mechanisms.

Unions and the full time professional and lay officials who run them are basically concerned with day to day practicalities. Constraints on time exist and disciplines have to be maintained that other parts of the movement do not have to cope with. The long term, forward planning, dreams or visions tend not to intrude on what is basically a reactive movement.

Bargaining thus has a time horizon based on the yearly cycle, or less in some instances, the only exceptions to this, in formal procedural terms, have been some technology or information agreements. Any bargaining on product mix or capital changes would exceed this horizon.

Bargaining has traditionally been based on managerial prerogatives and a view that the market place is both given and paramount. When for example Lucas Aerospace stewards challenged both of these notions the union(s) were unable as well as unwilling to follow the matter through.

There must be some caution exercised in this matter. It is too easy to complain about a union's bureaucracy and blame all evils or omissions upon it. The brutal fact is that to bargain effectively management must believe that the members of a union would, in one way or another, disrupt the running of the enterprise if the claims are not met. In all cases this means convincing union members that such action is in their interests sufficiently for them to appear militant. The longer term the demand, for example switching out of defence industry work into 'socially useful products', the more difficult successful persuasion becomes. This gap between theory and practise accounts for the relative failure to advance at the micro levels.'

DEVELOPING NEW FUNCTIONS

How then are we to transcend these difficulties, are they indeed amenable to change in any meaningful way? The Lucas Aerospace Combine Shop Stewards Committee mounted a very substantial campaign in the late 1970s, to try to introduce 'socially useful products' into their company, largely to help create greater job security for their members. Their campaign led them into negotiation with the (Labour) Government, the Company, and indeed with a confederation of national unions (Confederation of Shipbuilding and Engineering Unions). By and large the response they received reflected many of the problems outlined in Barrie Sherman's paper. Yet whilst their specific challenge to managerial prerogative and policy was defeated by the combined forces of the three powerful bodies involved, their example has been taken up in various forms elsewhere. In the Scandinavian countries, in Australasia, West Germany, and in Britain there is a continuing experimentation with ways of overcoming the 'locked-in' practices of the trade union and labour movement. No one will own to having a simple solution, nor perhaps is that necessary or desirable.

In Britain at least (and it is not alone in this) the growth model of corporate development – be it public or private – of the 1950s, '60s and part of the '70s has been substantially replaced with rationalisation models. Continuing world recession and Britain's own Depression have encouraged enterprises to maximise the extraction of surplus value from labour, rather than to seek to maximise incomes; at the least the balance between the two has shifted towards the former. In this context trade unionism has been forced to confront a number of new and difficult challenges from employers. Technological change for instance no longer necessarily means job security – as 'investment' was once thought to provide. Business reorganisation is no longer something that 'they, the managers' do for esoteric business reasons – reorganisation is now often intimately tied into schemes to change work practices, work organisation, job design, bargaining arrangements, all of which may have detrimental effects on trade union members, sometimes on a union as a whole. International development of a corporation now increasingly means multinationalism, where British capacity comes into direct competition with the firm's overseas plants, and frequently leads to cutbacks here as a result. And, as explored elsewhere, public sector operations are increasingly being run in new ways, which borrow much from their private sector counterparts.

Old practices and old structures in the trade union and labour movement are failing to adequately meet these challenges. The choices are stark, either to essentially accept most of the consequences of this more aggressive private and public sector business activity, or to develop an effective means of opposition. This pressure increases with time.

Obvious problems for unions, such as falling membership (essentially a result of rising unemployment), members who will less and less go on strike or whatever, simply because the union 'says' they should, these problems are *connected* with the wider problems of unions' structures, ways of acting, even their fundamental approach to their own functions. Trade unions *are* being marginalised by aggressive employer and government policies because trade unionism now has an inadequate response, at the formal level at least. Yet side by side with this is the *fact* that being a member of a union is still almost as 'popular' as it was ten or fifteen years ago. The 'old verities' referred to earlier remain in force, and these continue to find new expressions; for instance much of the 'old' industrial syndicalism has been replaced with new syndicalisms in public sector services – with the National Communications Union for example campaigning for member action over jobs through new information technology policies.

In short, this is a period of great change in trade unionism, a very mixed scenario with defeat and opportunity both encapsulated within the same challenges. That trade unionism is basic for the development of a socially useful economy cannot be gainsaid. What employers do, and what employees do and want, is a central conflict and negotiation of economics, social interests, politics. The collective social force of trade unionism has proved to be liberatory, judicious, and at base, 'human-centred'. Elsewhere in this book we have outlined possible mechanisms for trade union involvement in a socially useful economy. However we must conclude here with some observations on the ways in which trade unionism can and should itself develop, in order to fulfil its role in a new economic order.

Union structures, which in so many ways embody the institution of trade unions, still largely reflect employer organisational structures which are long gone. In particular they do not meet the very structures of many modern challenges – the multi-site, multi-union employer, the multinational enterprise, the multi-occupation/multi-union impact of technological change or corporate rationalisation and reorganisation. Then again, there are problems at so-called sectoral levels, where for example *political* decision-making is profoundly important – such as the health services, or public transport, North Sea Oil and its dependents, defence/arms manufacture, fifth generation computing, and so on. Here the current impact of trade unionism may be found only in the tripartite consultative Economic Development Committees or Sector Working Parties of the National Economic Development Council. Then we have again inadequacies in union structures when we come to certain regions and localities – which may be heavily dependent on just one industry or employer.

So, union structural reform is a necessity to deal with the very nature of modern employer challenges, with sectoral and regional problems. Structures in unions have, by and large, been set up to provide local and national member protection, advice, education and bargaining representation. And, despite populist Right Wing rhetoric, these structures are based heavily on democratic traditions – albeit now excessively *within* individual unions, with union autonomy being quite fiercely guarded from time to time. Yet unions have changed their structures and procedures over the years – our argument being that insufficient weight has been given to innovation.

It is quite possible to contrive new structures which relate to the nature of the problems being faced. Lay representatives' bodies covering all of a large firm, or split into groups reflecting the main business divisional operations, can co-exist with policy formed through more conventional union structures. International representatives' bodies can meet (as they are increasingly doing) to discuss and decide on policies required to be taken up by all the appropriate national union organisations. Inter-company union organisations at both official and lay representative levels can (and occasionally do) come together to debate industrial sector policies – *and* trade union strategies and tactics. Basically, to see lay representatives as a source of crucial information and part of the very substance of union activity simply reflects much of the reality of modern trade unionism. To consider new groupings which consist largely of shop stewards as a threat is simply negative.

In line with new structures are new union activities, where the traditional anti-intellectualism of British trade unionism is firmly put in its place – as *one* aspect of effective bargaining. Compared with employers' paid 'thinkwork', trade unions have almost nil resources – with very small research capabilities that frequently have to span an inordinate number of subjects. Yet the experience of an increasing number of representatives' committees shows that so-called 'ordinary' members and representatives can engage in profoundly useful and relevant applied research. What is so often dismissed as 'industrial subculture' by sociologists, actually contains a wealth of relevant information about the employer's practices and policies. Organisations such as CAITS have amply demonstrated that research capabilities of unions can be enormously enhanced by harnessing and involving members and their representatives. Much management information does after all derive from information of all kinds processed and created by the workforce, and by judicious methods it is possible to bring that collective knowledge to bear in the creation and implementation of important new trade union activities. Similarly, such processes form entirely new kinds of trade union education – shop stewards will after all be much more inclined to seriously strive to understand their *own* employer's finances, rather than to learn more abstracted general principles about finance.

So, the creation of new structures, new methods for research and education are central in any scheme to encourage workforces to be actively involved in the creation of a socially useful economy. *They* know where profound mistakes occur, they know how short-term accounting-led business policy has deprived them of capacity and jobs, they know just how badly much 'new technology' works. But furthermore they can and do make serious-minded judgements about broader issues of business and economic policy in their firm, sector or service. What *needs* to be done is to properly encourage this activity as a bona fide, integral part of a new trade unionism – that re-asserts its 'old' values in a modern and appropriate way.

All this does not and cannot deny unionism's function to bargain to obtain decent remuneration and reasonable conditions of service. But the experience of recent years has shown that pay alone, or 'staff status', is becoming ever more inadequate as a representation of employees' true rights, concerns, and social value. Bargaining packages – briefly popular a few years ago – need to be brought forward, at local, individual union, company, sector and service levels – reflecting the 'legitimate interest' concept referred to in Chapter 8. The trade union movement's rights to real economic enfranchisement go *far* beyond the wage-cash nexus.

Once we have put wages and conditions properly in place the contribution of trade unionism to a socially useful economy is immense. It should be noted that Low Pay and 'sweatshop' conditions are both integral for trade union development – these are not being ignored. A legally-backed Minimum Wage is necessary, thereafter inter-union cooperation, backed by a statutory framework for intervention, can ensure that new ghettoes of Low Pay should not appear. It is after all in *no* union's interest to accede to Low Pay. Similarly a Statutorily based framework of employment rights can and should be introduced, again followed through with inter-union cooperation. Indeed, the 'Social Wage' notion *must be* developed in a Socially Useful Economy – which means not only certain minimum pay and conditions, but the wider application of employers' responsibilities to their workforces and communities. Thus whilst low pay and poor conditions need to be tackled intensively as issues in their own right, it is argued that they will become part of a much wider social and economic enfranchisement – which in itself is intended to prevent the recurrence or re-emergence of 'Third World' labour practices.

If just 10% of working people applied some time to thinking and acting on the real substance of their employment, we would have literally millions of people involved in redefining what they want from their work – in all senses. This extraordinary liberation *can* take place. The arguments for it need to be promoted now, the structures changed to facilitate it, and activities developed from already-existing processes firmly encouraged. Even in a conventional electoral sense such a programme would provide an immense popular boost for a more human-centred approach to economic life; for unions it provides 'in passing' a superb mechanism for ensuring that political funds are supported.

In representing almost half of the working population, trade unionism is clearly a substantial force and representative body. By opening ways of acting in the general long term interest of people, rather than money-power, unionism's status in all important respects can only be enhanced. Furthermore its impact on the Labour Party would be deepened. In the authors' view the lack of innovation in broad political terms within trade unionism has historically crippled both the vision and practice of the Labour movement – up to and including the Parliamentary Labour party. As Barrie Sherman has so ably shown, this historical inadequacy has led to an extraordinarily damaging lack of vision for a new economic and social order. By drawing the boundaries of trade unionism's protectionist function so narrowly we have missed out time and time again in properly expressing an agenda of social, political and economic justice.

It is our considered judgement, drawn from experience of thousands of trade unionists, that it *is* not only possible, desirable, but also

intensely *necessary* for trade unionism to come to represent a core
element for social and economic change. The 'collective worker', which
is increasingly represented by women, by unskilled workers, by the
work experience of ethnic minorities, *already exists*. S/he already *knows*
of a million ways to make work more useful, more creative, more
sensible. For a properly grounded development of a socially useful
economy the collective worker's conscience and knowledge is centrally
important. For true protection people have to be enfranchised, and
trade unionism is a key form of organisation for bringing this about. For
people who join unions simply as a kind of 'insurance' policy, this much
more central role for trade unionism in bringing about economic and
social change must surely be a bonus too.

And as for Labour Aristocracies, the new 'aristocrats' must surely be
the hospital cleaners who campaign against privatisation – in order to
ensure that hospitals are safer places. It is the public transport trade
unionists who connect their own jobs with a deep understanding of
service to other people. It is people who want to use their skills and
knowledge for peaceful purposes rather than for arms manufacture. It is
those in the new international workers' networks who seek actively to
bring multinational corporations to account; for example recent conferences, and new international workers' secretariats, being set up in
Ford, General Motors, Kodak, Philips, and others, attest to this –
crossing barriers between 'communist' unions and other unions that
were set up immediately after the Second World War. It is computing
staffs who try to grapple with the formulation of a democratic and
socially relevant information technology in Britain and elsewhere. It is
regional and local trade union bodies that assert their right to protect the
populace from the ravages of rationalisation within the major enterprises in their areas. There are many other examples; but these people
don't see themselves as somehow 'special', certainly not as a latter-day
labour aristocracy – but as people who see their salvation as lying *beyond*
the stale and inhuman constraints of narrow monetarist calculations.

13　Practising the Socially Useful Economy

MYTHS AND MYSTERIES

Experiences shape us, chronic lack of money diminishes us, those with some money fear losing it, those with a lot of money use it. Problems of starvation affecting between a quarter and a fifth of the world's population are portrayed and seen and understood as primarily social and humanitarian issues, whilst charities collect pennies from people in the streets. The commonly-perceived standard of living in Britain seems to inexorably decline against that of many other countries, and the cause of this is supposedly recalcitrant trade unions, all of *us* being too greedy, or pricing ourselves out of jobs. The 'poor' are portrayed as either irrational, egotistical people who demand more money than they have 'a right' to get, or are portrayed as a social problem, 'those people' who are feckless, who cannot stop their children from taking drugs and so forth. We are all exhorted to be more 'open to change', to learn new skills, to get on our bikes and find work, to be mobile, flexible and agreeable – yet are given little indication of how we are supposed to do this. The supreme difference between what G.K. Chesterton described as 'cash and lolly', i.e. the money that we have each week and what we do with it, compared with 'the economy' has become a mystery of almost metaphysical proportions.

Everyday representations of reality lead us into frustration, aggression and fear which stunts our conciousness and quite intentionally turns us away from asking simple but profound questions about where we fit into the scheme of things. The other side of fear is conservatism, and we have an ever-increasing panoply of spectacle and money-based 'diversions' into leisure pursuits and the like, which in part provide us with a *sense* of adventure and ways of finding individual solutions. So does capitalism insert its mechanisms into the very fabric of human existence, where even personal health, including mental health obtained from the latest American 'self exploration' techniques is a business activity. The

237

present government's emphasis on job creation through the development of greater service and leisure industries, designer tracksuits, and video games is a clear indication of the mentality of money power which seeks to subsume everything within its sphere of influence and control. What is free, our heritage, is shrinking in size and variety. The very idea and ideal of public service is now in a ghetto, fairly safely confined and separated away from what is regarded as the mainstream of economic activity.

So, the age-old idea and practice of social justice is diverted and channeled into the cash nexus of wages, the mechanism of the market and consumerism, and adherence to a legal system which is based on a complex of historical accidents and the conjuncture of particular political forces, rather than any substantial affirmation of citizenship or civil rights in society. These mechanisms essentially strangle commonsense and profound ideas about democracy in society. Put this simply: current constraints are indeed formidable, and the pressures against trying to obviate them or throw them off are powerful. The money system cannot be beaten with money.

But people still *are* more than consumers, more than wage-slaves, they still have ideas and they still do things that do not conform to the so-called reality which is purveyed so assiduously by those with the money power. Stubbornness, obstinacy and sometimes sheer bloody-mindedness is still, thankfully, a wide-spread part of human experience. Quite separate in many respects from the actual outcome of the miners' dispute, their struggle, or the profound undermining of local government and local democratic organisation, and from a multitude of trade union and community struggles, we have seen a dialectic in operation over the past five years or so. The 'rightness' of campaigns against oppresive immigration laws, of struggles to preserve viable communities and so on are etched deeply into the consciousness of thousands and hundreds of thousands of people and their unselfish and difficult struggles against what is seen to be socially and economically unjust remain a force to be reckoned with. Evaluation of these experiences is of great importance in developing the socially useful economy in many ways; for example it is valuable to see how much in practical terms can be achieved, what it is that obstructs achievement, how far attempting to do things for real is an effective form of democratic/political education, how far such attempts enlarge understanding; and by harnessing the wisdom and commitment of people at the so-called grass roots, how far this begins to develop a new sort of economics. Discussion at the seminars drew on the experience of local government as well as from 'workers corporate plans' in industry, commerce and the public sector.

Mike Cooley, Technical Director at the Greater London Enterprise Board and formerly a member of the Lucas Aerospace Combine Stewards Committee, spoke to the subject of current constraints and the possibilities, and an edited version of his talk is given below (pp. 239–42).

CURRENT POSSIBILITES (1)

Once a problem is well defined one is often three-quarters of the way towards making its solution. For instance the attempt that some local authorities are now making to shape and control their local economies moves them sharply up against the constraints that block practical achievement. The population of several million in the areas covered by London and other metropolitan authorities leads, on the surface, to the argument that since they are as large as many states why should they not plan the use of resources, like a state.

But this approach brings one hard against a different reality; the 'local state' is not and is nothing like a small scale model of a nation state. Local government is subject to heavy limitations derived from a constitutional history that pays only grudging respect to active democracy. Even before 'rate-capping' and the Thatcher government's onslaught on local government, local authorities have no power to tax other than through rates with all the limitations built into the spending of them; legal restrictions hamper investment, trading and direct use of resources; the penalties by which these restrictions are enforced are speedily invoked through the agency of the district auditor and fall heavily on the personal assets of the councillors (who enjoy none of the protections which safeguard the personal fortunes of company directors). And, despite the never-ending rhetoric associated with local authority spending, the actual cash available in these bodies is minute compared to that available to even medium sized corporations; it is much smaller in terms of money power than that wielded by the corporations that dominate the economies of such metropolitan areas. For example, in Lucas Aerospace the Stingray Project (a very dubious technical and commercial enterprise) cost around one billion pounds sterling, yet an inadequate or inappropriate or damaging use of such a large sum was not subject to any real restrictions, such as would befall councillors who wish to spend money in a similar way – yet councillors are dealing in millions of pounds, corporations in billions of pounds. The limits of what can and cannot be done within the sphere of local government has been a very important educational exercise in reality.

. Some have pointed out that large metropolitan authorities such as the GLC have a high degree of political influence and economic power through their buying capacity. Yet experience shows that appropriate expertise and suitable occupational or ideological attitudes are in the main not present in these authorities, and strong legislative bonds and crushing penalties also attend any significant experimentation or development of alternatives in this area. For example, the elaborate tendering procedures which are called for when ordering supplies and then numerous special limitations where some municipal enterprise is permitted (as in direct labour in building) all enforce, legally and administratively, the basic principles of commodity economics. That is economic relations are governed by exchange values and market competition, and criteria of social use do not get a look in. And within this so-called market competition, fair competition is hardly such in reality, the large firms are those best equipped to win orders. So, local authorities can do nothing to marry needs policy to employment policy because a barrier between the two is thrown up by the sacred criteria of money and the market.

Nevertheless, these barriers have not been left to go unchallenged, and efforts made in recent years to tackle local employment and economic problems through the apparatus of local government have constituted a path-breaking advance for socialist theory and practice. The legal, financial and organisational obstacles in the area of local government have shown up something of the nature of the problems that are to be faced at a national level. These sorts of obstacles are to be *expected* and very clearly show up the need to tackle them in a systematic manner; coherent alternative policies must also incorporate *the means* by which they are to be realised.

Our assessment about what has been done in the GLC and other local authorities needs to take into account a *lack* of constitutional rights at the local level as well as the national level. Local government is mainly a mechanism through which central policies are locally administered; in Britain there are no constitutional rights such as those possessed by German states, and local government elsewhere. Tradition and institutional factors have tended to reinforce a passivity that awaits instructions from Whitehall. Local initiatives, in order for them to be effective, require a different political framework at a national level and a development of new practices at every level in society. Furthermore, in reflection of this historical heritage many policies have simply been *reactive*; demands for example are pressed by trade unions, by homeless people, from groups suffering from discrimination, and councils try to do something to meet these demands. This is fine and educative both for the organisations that present demands and for the politicians that try to meet them, but invariably they reveal the lack of adequate local infrastructure for meeting these needs.

A twin to this multi-faceted economic domination is the dominating approach to technology which comes from the biggest of big business, the kind of job spectrum for instance which is suggested by Sizewell, with investment per job running at about six hundred thousand pounds. Local government administrators, having in general no industrial or community experience approach training, labour power and technology in an arrogant and bureaucratic manner. The traditional 'local government type person' is in fact counter-productive in the long term, and to develop local economies democratically requires means to tap into the 'tacit knowledge' of people in industry and the community. Technology, the application of dead labour and invention to solving problems is regarded as an 'expert' endeavour, and local authorities usually aggregate their responsibilities in this area and simply accept what the larger employers tell them. Thus the GLC idea of Technology Networks has met with enormous resistance and disbelief and is disregarded by the majority of those operating in the Authority. That is, the idea of helping so-called ordinary people to explicate their needs in a technical way and for others to utilise their time and skills to meet them in a way which is largely outside the market mechanism, is regarded as a diversion, an amateur pursuit in the worst sense. In so doing, intelligent and insightful people within the community are essentially told that they have nothing to say or contribute. This attitude is nevertheless being challenged through numerous practical efforts in London, Sheffield, the West Midlands and elsewhere.

And the complex, difficult and fraught experiences of trying to promote a socially-aware and democratic alternative within the sphere of local government is rich with experience which must be transmitted in all possible ways to the trade union and labour movement throughout the whole of Britain. Yet it must be said that in London for example, County Hall is under little or no pressure from the Labour movement to advance its alternative economic strategies. There is no attempt through Labour as a political party to synchronise and coordinate the struggles of people exposed to poverty and deprivation. Instead, the high profile politics of the Labour movement is that of top-down bureaucratic organisations, and attempts to strike political postures in parliament and to the media. Indeed, some socialist cynics have jeered at the economic plans of local authorities, as being no better than trying to water a city's gardens by 'spitting from a helicopter'; such 'realism' is no help to people living in a real world, where doing comes from learning and learning comes from doing. The great virtue of those local authorities who have tried to apply democratic and socialist principles to the local economy is that they have learnt and taught economics in the only way in which, in the last analysis, democratic economics can be learnt and taught, that is by *doing*. And there have been some real achievements, in London for example two thousand jobs (costing seven thousand pounds each) have been created. Obviously such achievement is miniscule in relation to the economy of London as a whole, and to the rate at which unemployment has been growing; however, the experience of creating and maintaining jobs is crucial, and as an *exemplary* demonstration of what can be done it has been a real achievement. So, practical achievements have demonstrated that there *are* possibilities of advance even in the most hostile political and economic climate. At the same time understanding has been won of what in a different environment could be done, and imaginations have been fired. Finally, concrete attempts to implement democratic policies have indentified and made tangible the barriers that stand like a wall of glass between people and the useful activities they could be engaged in.

Mike Hales, who also works in the GLC, presented a paper which tackled another approach to the experience of the GLC.

'I'd argue that one of the most radical aspects of the current GLC approach to economic issues is the commitment to tackle them through linking 'academic' research with actual investment practice in and against the market. 'Research' is a dirty word in many parts of the Left, and many socialists use the word to mean simply grubbing for statistics. One of the more marginal Left cultures over the last couple of decades has argued that ('real, rigorous') research must become an integral part of real life. You can view current GLC practice in the industry and employment field as a serious attempt to put a practical meaning to this proposition.'

The democratic principle that control over research into needs must lie with those whose needs are studied, also involves discovery of *new research styles*.[1]

So, despite all the difficulties, despite a most hostile political climate nationally, there are still possibilities to be found by local authorities putting together projects to try out new ideas.

The development in the last five years of new radical local economic development strategies by some local authorities, as Dave Williams (of the Leeds Department of Industry and Estates, Leeds County Council) said, has highlighted the importance of community based action. Support has been centred on those groups who have been most vulnerable to the destructive effects of state and multi-national policy in cut backs, plant closures and workforce 'rationisation'; women, ethnic minorities and working class communities have been the focus of the new approach.

Local councils have undertaken this work in the face of efforts by government to limit their freedom of action, culminating in abolition and rate-capping legislation. One alternative has been exploitation of the existing funding opportunities available through the MSC, European Social Fund, Urban Programme and other schemes. In the initial development of local economic strategies, the training emphasis of the first two sources has enabled the build-up of training programmes aimed at developing skills and opportunities for employment amongst the most disadvantaged groups, for whom the normal educational channels provided no opportunities. (This policy has however failed to cater for certain groups, such as adult workers, who fall outside the standard programmes of training.)

In Leeds, training is being linked to wider community-based developments, with a possibility of moving on into start up companies and cooperatives. This approach raises in a very specific way the important possibility of locally promoted undertakings being firmly geared to supplying specific needs of the public sector and being strongly supported by appropriate expertise in the public sector.

To quote Dave Williams again 'The role of local authorities can be twofold. Firstly, to act as an agent of technology transfer, by implementation of local or national programmes to encourage the development of employment from the capital and human resources of the public sector, and secondly to encourage the development of community owned enterprises.'

It is clear that a wide-ranging assessment of these new local authority initiatives, experiments and experiences is absolutely crucial for the Labour movement.

CURRENT POSSIBILITIES (2)

Much of these new local authorities' initiatives in the industry and employment field had their roots in a variety of trade union and community struggles waged during the 1970s. Certain key struggles in particular provided tremendous impetus to these local government initiatives. The Upper Clyde Shipbuilders in 1971 occupied their plant, and against closure and job loss threats, both physically and ideologically laid claim to their legitimate interests in the workplace; and as a leading spokesman of UCS repeatedly stated to the Media, they were *not occupying*, because they were not a foreign force or foreign power, occupying something that was not theirs; and he put the emphasis on the action being a 'work-in'. In the following years a number of community development projects were set up in inner city areas in the country where unemployment 'black-spots' were beginning to be uncomfortably visible. These CDP's started to carry out economic and social audits of their environs and in many cases clearly laid the blame for deprivation and desolation on the actions of major employers in their areas. The beginnings of a relatively democratic and independent critique of the effects of private corporate decisions on public interest thus became established. This process was given a big push in the mid 1970s when the Lucas Aerospace Shop Stewards Committee pioneered a worker-led initiative against unemployment and job loss in their company.

As Mike George pointed out in his paper to Seminar Two, the basic ingredients of Lucas Aerospace were:

(1) job threats arising out of corporate restructuring, in a relatively booming market;
(2) an inability to address job threats through existing trade union and political insitutions;
(3) a campaign, at the base, to create more effective means of combating closures and redundancies;
(4) a recognition that existing corporate policies were damaging to the employees;
(5) a growing recognition that Lucas obtained most of its income from public sources, yet had little public accountability, and created costs to the public purse through the jobs shake-out; and
(6) an attempt to define work which could be undertaken in Lucas, which would save jobs, and address certain obvious needs in the medical, energy, transport, and other fields.

One aspect of Britain's 'mixed economy' was therefore challenged – that of private companies that receive significant amounts of public funding but create substantial public costs. Lucas was by no means alone in paying almost no tax to the Inland Revenue. Most major manufacturers like Lucas receive Government grants, help from the Export Credit Guarantee scheme, local help from Councils who provide rent/rate holidays, and cheap factories. And, although estimates vary, a majority of manufacturers receive income through sales to agencies that buy through public procurement – Lucas received over 70% of sales income in this way. Yet Lucas, and many other firms create thousands of redundancies, and decimate the economic basis of whole communities.

Looked at in this way the company's policies were clearly *not* viable; at a national level the company 'cost' Britain more than it contributed.

The 'viability' of Lucas Aerospace's product could only be measured in terms of surplus value creation – which has been pretty meagre anyway. Its major products – military aerospace equipment – actually become economically useless as soon as they're consumed, if not before. Product viability in Lucas's case was an intensely *political* issue not an economic one.

At about the same time a multi union steward's committee covering several firms in the power engineering industry were beginning to campaign for changes in product and investment policies, on the basis of a longer term and less volatile power engineering industry order book – thus trying to ensure some continuity in employment and avoiding devastation of a number of areas which were heavily dependent on this technology. In the following years, from 1976 through to 1980 the idea of alternative corporate plans developed by workers, which became known as 'workers' plans', started to take shape in many other companies and industries. Shop Stewards and convenors in the automotive and vehicle industries started to push for alternative strategies in the interests of the workforce and the relevant communities. At the same time there was an increase in the numbers of 'audits' and alternative plans laid down by workers and community activists in several areas of the country.

Many of these efforts concentrated on trying to encourage and cajole and pressure the then Labour government into putting into practice its policies on enterprise planning (planning agreements) and intervention in the interests of labour and communities through the National Enterprise Board. Without exception their initiatives were hindered and in most instances suppressed (administered out of existence as it were) by the government, the civil service, threats by employers to go on an investment strike in the UK, and even some unions – that viewed such developments as being outside the scope of normal union activity procedures.

Nevertheless the pressure did not disappear, new organisations and relationships have continued to grow, even though the level of activity has taken a severe knock through the anti-union legislation and practices of the Thatcher Government in the 1980s. With the continuing large-scale labour shake-out which accompanies the current 'model' of corporate development (rationalisation, reorganisation), an increasing number of trade unionists are seeing the *need* to move beyond the conventional activities and procedures of trade unionism, as the only way of being able to effectively defend jobs and retain some measure of influence over employers' decision making. The previous chapter explained this phenomenon in more detail, and providing that the organs of the trade union movement and the Labour party are at least to some extent able and willing to support these initiatives, this is indeed an important possibility for the development of future action to bring about a socially useful economy; a combination of this with the experiences of those in local authorities can form a significant type of alternative thinking and action – the real challenge lies with those who may or may not cling to outmoded organisational forms and aspirations in the broader trade union and Labour movement.

CURRENT POSSIBILITIES (3)

Michael Foster and Frank Mort, in their Paper 'Planning, Pleasure and Popular Consumption – What Is 'Socially Useful' Production?', argued that we have to take *consumption* more seriously.

'Along with the Welfare State and a commitment to full employment, Keynesian based consumption 'for people' formed a central part of the post-1945 political settlement. The telly, the fridge, the new car, the washing machine, Spanish holidays, the boutique, the glossy magazine were major ingredients in the cultural re-shaping of British society from the 1950's onwards – the cultural dimensions of the economic boom. Despite the recession this consumerist culture has not disappeared – video games, home computers, music centres are the latest in a very long line of goodies. These cultural forms have been crucial in the re-making of working class culture since the 1950s and are now deeply written into popular aspirations and consciousness. The problem is that the left has never really come to terms with this development, let alone realised that it has any progressive political mileage. And we don't think it's any accident that the various 'socially useful' plans have steered well clear of this area. The right from Macmillan through to Thatcher has been much more successful at articulating consumerism and the culture industries to its own political ideologies: identifying people's positive aspirations here with the power of the free-market, private enterprise and the restoration of the capitalist ethic. The left has tended to see that alliance between conservation, leisure and consumption as a natural rather than a constructed one; contributing to *embourgeoisement*, that most slippery of concepts – the belief that the working class has been politically 'bought-off' by the fruits of consumer capitalism. We reject that simplistic notion and would argue that while popular consumption has had important political and cultural effects on the working class they are not ones that are naturally or inevitably Conservative. Indeed, as we say, part of the problem here is the left's failure to come to terms, complexly, with this phenomenon.

The consumption embourgeoisement couplet often implicitly rests on a yearning (by middle class socialists) for the working class in its pure form, untainted by capitalism. This approach tends to be extremely moralistic and puritanical, denying or dismissing popular aspirations for a better standard of living through popular consumption, preferring 'safer' images of working class culture – the working men's club or trade union banner as opposed to the package on the Costa Brava or Tesco's and C&A's.'

Foster and Mort also said:

'Popular cultures of consumption are not a pure expression of new forms of political awareness, of course they are deeply contradictory and continually recouped and shaped by the capitalist leisure industries. But to fail to recognise their *potential*, to ignore that they have something to say to socialists about where popular consciousness is at is to bury one's head in the sand.

There is a further point here which socialists ignore at their peril. These forms of consumption do not just meet socially constructed needs, they produce forms of pleasure and *desire* which are not all morally bad or purely manipulative. Fashion, home decor, children's toys, videos obviously produce forms of pleasure which tie in with the social, political and economic organisation of modern industrial societies – pleasure is individualised, pleasure is normative. Many feminists have pointed to the way in which the pleasure/consumption couplet is a powerful regulator of women's behaviour. But pleasures *are* contradictory, and at times contain a progressive potential – there are pleasures that 'slip through the cracks' and prefigure new forms of social organisation. Take fashion – for women the pleasure extracted from dressing up has much to do with conforming to norms of feminity, and getting pleasure because 'your man' approves, but it also may be a pleasure of 'looking good' for yourself, of feeling confident and self-assertive.

There is a terrible danger that as socialists we will become defined as pleasure denying and moralistic, because of our valid objections to the current organisation of pleasures and desires. Concepts of pleasure sit uneasily with post-1880s versions of socialism and with our own current political agenda. (As one gay male trade unionist put it recently about his experience of working in NUPE – " 'right's and needs' I can just about get away with, pleasures no way.") The complex and often contradictory ways in which popular culture and consumption produces pleasures for 'the people', and dare we say it for ourselves, should force us to think through this issue in the context of popular planning. Planning for needs also means taking contemporary definitions of pleasure seriously, rather than dismissing them as capitalist 'hype', or taking the line that we only discuss them in workshops on film or sexuality.'

And they conclude that what is needed includes the following:

'To start with, the fields of expertise – design, marketing, research, etc – have the potential to be challenged by workers, dissident experts and consumers. Matching skills and needs isn't all common sense – the different relations between planning and consumption need to be rethought. Secondly, in developing new tactics, instead of setting definitions (as in market research 'types' of consumer, 'up-to-the-minute' design or technology, *and* popular planning criteria of 'community needs') we must recognise that popular consumption has its own sense, needs, pleasures and politics. Finally, for popular planning to enter this arena it needs to shift its sights and its mode of address – what's good for a radical policy on transport and health isn't necessarily the answer when it comes to home furnishings or hairdressing. Shops, glossy magazines, advertising, promotions, need to exist alongside community centres and the benign offices of the local state.

Consumption has been the unsung lyric in the construction of popular consent for post-war hegemony. It is a central element in the life experience, the consciousness of many of the groups which socialists look to for challenging Thatcherism – youths, blacks, women, gays, white collar workers and the skilled working class – and putting together an alternative hegemonic block. If socialism is to say anything to these groups it must engage politically with their language and expectations, drawing on the progressive elements within their discourse – and that includes popular consumption.'

This important area of possibility is currently pursued in somewhat narrow and unfortunately sectarian ways. The challenge here to what is conventionally thought of as 'political' is even more demanding perhaps than those previously described. But it remains crucially important in order to avoid the double standards that politicians of the Left (indeed politicians of all hues) maintain; that is of a type of 'hard' politics which supposedly covers all the important areas of human existence, whilst in reality the things like pleasure, enjoyment and excitment are subsumed within totally individualised life existence.

SOME CONCLUSIONS

Organised labour and industry has to be helped, not hindered, to recognise the economic potential its collective work represents. Similarly new frameworks and better resourcing is needed to help community organisations collectively assess social needs and relate these to resources available for meeting them, and to articulate demands for extra or different resources. We have to harness the collective wisdom of organised labour, those operating in local authorities and elsewhere to pin down the legal, financial, administrative, economic and cultural obstacles to change and to pool knowledge about how to overcome them. The information and technology revolution has to be grounded much more clearly in the need to exchange ideas between so called grass-roots organisation to create solidarity and unity of purpose, and to foreshadow economic and social complementarity that a socially useful economy requires. We need to have space to help define a framework of national policy capable of sustaining democratic control over resources; in particular we need to identify ways of providing immediate financing of feasible projects that have been democratically arrived at. Campaingning for the widest popular support and understanding of the practical feasibility of alternatives to market and money motivated economics is fundamentally crucial, and requires truly subversive messages and means of ensuring that they come about.

History is not that 'freeway to the future' with the absurd signposts seen in the USA saying 'if you lived here you'd be home by now'. It is fashioned by human beings, by social movements, by political pressures and by economic necessities and desirabilities. As our net contribution from North Sea Oil declines in the latter part of this decade the untruths of conventional economics and the 'hire purchase' mentality of politics will be ever more exposed. Current constraints *must* therefore be used as the very basis for us to develop current and future possibilities for action of a truly democratic nature

NOTE

1. See Action-Research Project in Brighton, described by Suzy Croft and John Beresford in *Social Work Today*, 17 Sept 1984.

Central theme

OPE is a
closed system
the alt is SUC

14   A CHARTER FOR THE SOCIALLY USEFUL ECONOMY

The whole argument of this book, the discussions, thoughts and struggles that helped bring it about comes back again and again to a central theme; that 'OPE' (Orthodox Political Economy) is essentially a closed system, and that we need 'SUE' (Socially Useful Economy) to open up the system so that we may all have rights, powers, facilities and satisfactions that are currently denied us.

Whether one believes that 'Thatcherism' is qualitatively different to other epochs, or that this political phenomenon is in reality an extension only of pre-existing tendencies, it is true that since 1979 key economic, social and political issues have become highlighted in a way not seen since the post Second World War settlement, perhaps even before. Social authoritarianism is being re-asserted from 'the top', from Government, financiers and the so-called 'captains' of industry. Exhortations to make sacrifices for the common good are daily occurrences. And these messages contain a single 'truth', that we must all leave the big decisions in the hands of those that 'know', and accept that *we're* to blame for the country's economic and social ills. This leads us on to the associated message that democracy in this country is best served through market-led economic democracy, i.e. that we can all be equal in the eyes of the market.

This clever formulation gives the illusion that we live in a pluralist society – one that contains, and should contain a multiplicity of views and interests – after all we have clubs for everything, we can purchase specialist items. Yet it *is* an illusion, transnational corporations wield more power than most nations on earth, the international market 'successfully' persuades people in poor countries to spend on arms and carbonated soft drinks. Whole swathes of decisions about who invests what, where, and for what reason, are taken by those who cannot reflect popular needs, who will not accept that others have legitimate interests and therefore rights to determine these decisions.

Discontent with this state of affairs is successfully bought off by the myriad spectacles of the market; it is bludgeoned into silence through sheer brutality; it is controlled and limited with a plethora of 'administrative-looking' rules and conventions; it is muted through the continual and powerful declamation of the ideology of TINA – 'There Is No Alternative'.

When the explosion of 'the market' opened up an escape route for people, away from feudalism, hopes were raised that this type of economic democracy would usher in equality, new freedoms. Did not possession of money override privilege and all make equal? The reality is somewhat different. New elites, the oligarchies of money-power have overridden and perverted the partial and limited democracy of the market. The democratic rights for which Chartists struggled a century and a half ago, gave only democratic control over political representation; they did not give democratic control over economic resources. Unconstrained by economic democracy, money-power rides roughshod over the so-called powers of representational democracy. Without economic power, political power must always be uncertain and insecure.

All is not gloom however, and we hope to have at least outlined some ways in which democratically-based alternatives exist and those which are developing. An important and useful way of encapsulating 'SUE' is to suggest a charter for The Socially Useful Economy – one which lays out the backbone of rights which make 'economics' something powerful for us all to control and use in our best interests; not as privatised individuals involved in self-seeking activity, but as social groups with natural affinities. We have to make collective ownership, control and values *mean* something . . .

The following are initial thoughts; if this book has had any use-value, as it were, we trust readers will develop these ideas further.

Elementary Rights

(1) Right of assembly for workers and community organisations to discuss and plan policies and actions to better their collective interests; basic rights to be conferred to 'units at the base', within neighbourhoods, at the place of work, etc.

(2) Right of access to information about decisions made by others, not in 'the base unit', which impinge on any areas of these people's lives.

(3) Right of access to any relevant research and educational facilities

which will further these people's collective aims.
(4) Right to express legitimate interests in all relevant economic affairs.
(5) Right to pursue relevant legitimate interests in an open political forum at all levels in society.
(6) Right of access to mass media and other related resources in order to properly express legitimate interests and concerns.
(7) Right to challenge 'managerial' decisions, and if necessary to remove and replace those whose decisions are detrimental to collective interests.
(8) Right to form democratic organisations to pursue any legitimate interest which is clearly for the collective good.
(9) Right to operate internationally in economic affairs in order to develop and implement mutually beneficial arrangements for the collective good.

Basic Economic Rights

(1) Right to work on socially useful products and services, using socially beneficial technologies.
(2) Right to develop work opportunities whose economic base is grounded in the fulfilment of social needs.
(3) Right to obtain paid work, at an hourly rate no less than 80% of average hourly earnings, and which exhibits employment conditions which are safe and democratically-based.
(4) Right to work in a full or part time capacity on labour which is directed towards childcare, or care of other dependents, with pay and conditions as described above.
(5) Right to obtain income support, as above, in the case of unemployment, disability, sickness, old age; especially to have the right of access to resources, etc. as described in the first section of the Charter.

Some Specific Rights

(1) Right to redesign technologies in ways which meet collective social needs.
(2) Right to convenient and comfortable meeting places and facilities and to cheap transport provision within the country, so that no legitimate assembly is hampered by lack of funds or provision.

(3) Right of access to communications, especially telecommunications, at costs which do not significantly affect individuals' or groups' resources.
(4) Right to determine forms of health care which best meet social needs.
(5) Right to develop, propose and implement production or service facilities in replacement of military uses.

Postcript

The Charter obviously incorporates the Labour Party Constitution, Clause IV(4): '. . . the best obtainable system of popular administration and control of each industry or service'.

Appendix

SEMINAR SERIES PROGRAMME

1. THE POLITICS OF ECONOMICS
Why are 'conventional' economic categories and principles so political-
ly powerful?
*Professor Tony Hopwood (London Business School) and Professor
Laurence Harris (Open University).*

2. ECONOMICS AND THE LABOUR MOVEMENT
Why has the Labour Movement accepted a form of economics which, by
and large, operates against it?
Barrie Sherman (ASTMS)

3. RECONSTRUCTING POLITICAL ECONOMY
What is needed for a radical reconstruction of economic principles to
emphasise Use Value rather than Exchange Value?
Ian Gough (University of Manchester)

4. NEGOTIATING CHANGE AT THE BASE
Bargaining at 'the base' for economic change and redefining the
boundaries of collective bargaining and Trade Union action.
*Nick Clark and other shop stewards from Metal Box and Lucas
Aerospace Combine Committees.*

5. NEGOTIATING CHANGE AT NATIONAL LEVEL
What changes can be made through national-level institutions to
democratise economic policy formulation and implementation?
John Ball

6. VIABILITY AND SOCIALLY USEFUL PRODUCTION
Is a 'socially useful' product viable, by definition as it were? If so, how is
it defined and how will it realistically express people's wishes?
Mike George and Dot Lewis (CAITS)

7. THE HIGH-TECH HYPE?
Technological determinism or choice in the design of production systems?
Robin Williams (Technology Policy Unit, University of Aston)

8. NEW TECHNOLOGY: ECONOMICS AND IMPACTS
To what extent are existing relations of production, exchange, distribution and consumption embedded in the design of contemporary technology?
Martin Stears (ICL Shop Stewards' Combine Committee)

9. POLITICAL ECONOMY OF MILITARISM
What are the functions of the complex of military/industrial forces, particularly in relation to the politics and economics of R & D, production and the allocation of society's resources?
Donald McKenzie (Science Studies Unit, University of Edinburgh)

10. POLITICAL ECONOMY OF HEALTH
The elements of a 'socially useful' approach to the provision of health and medical care.
Lesley Doyal (Polytechnic of North London)

11. CURRENT CONSTRAINTS AND POSSIBILITIES
A critical review of current 'alternative' approaches to key issues of political economy, investigating the limits of 'pressure politics', Local Authority action etc.
Mike Cooley (Director of Technology. GLEB)

12. FINANCING THE SOCIALLY USEFUL ECONOMY
Financial control and public expenditure for social use.
Stephen Bodington (CAITS)

MAIN SEMINAR PAPERS

THE POLITICS OF ECONOMICS: THE IMPACT OF ECONOMIC IDEAS
Professor Laurence Harris, Open University

ECONOMICS AND THE REGIME OF THE CALCULATIVE
Professor Tony Hopwood, London Business School

ECONOMICS AND THE LABOUR MOVEMENT
Barrie Sherman, ex-Head, Research, ASTMS

RECONSTRUCTING POLITICAL ECONOMY: USE VALUE AND EXCHANGE VALUE
Ian Gough, University of Manchester

DISCUSSION NOTES: SOME PRACTICAL THOUGHTS ON THEORY
Mike Hales, Industry & Employment Branch, GLC

NEGOTIATING FOR CHANGE AT THE BASE
Nick Clark, LRD, ex-Metal Box Combine Committee

NEGOTIATING CHANGE AT THE BASE: DISCUSSION PAPER
Martin Stears, ICL Joint Union Combine

TRADE UNION BARGAINING AND INFORMATION TECHNOLOGY
John Ball

NEGOTIATING CHANGE AT NATIONAL LEVEL (COMMENTS ON JOHN BALL'S PAPER)
Stephen Bodington, Economist

VIABILITY AND SOCIALLY USEFUL PRODUCTION
Mike George, CAITS

PLANNING, PLEASURE AND POPULAR CONSUMPTION – WHAT IS 'SOCIALLY USEFUL' PRODUCTION?
Michael Foster, Norwich CDA, & Frank Mort, Bristol Polytechnic

THE HIGH-TECH HYPE?: TECHNOLOGICAL DETERMINISM OR CHOICE IN THE DESIGN OF NEW TECHNOLOGY AT WORK
Robin Williams, Technology Policy Unit, Aston University

NEW TECHNOLOGY: ECONOMICS AND IMPACTS
Martin Stears, Systems Researcher, ICL Joint Union Combine

THE POLITICAL ECONOMY OF MILITARISM
Donald MacKenzie, Science Studies Unit, Edinburgh University

THE POLITICS OF HEALTH
Lesley Doyal, Polytechnic of North London

THE ROLE OF LOCAL AUTHORITIES IN COMMUNITY BASED ECONOMIC
DEVELOPMENT
Dave Williams, Leeds City Council

FINANCING THE SOCIALLY USEFUL ECONOMY
Stephen Bodington

COMMENTS ON S. BODINGTON'S PAPER
Vella Pillay, Economic Adviser, Bank of China

CAITS stands for, Centre for Alternative Industrial & Technological
Systems, an independent trade union-based research and resource unit.
It was founded in 1978 by the Lucas Aerospace Combine Shop Stewards
Committee, to further the economic, technical, social and political aims
of their Alternative Corporate Plan for the company. Since then the
Centre has worked with a great many union organisations in campaign-
ing, research and education. Anyone interested in the work of CAITS
should contact the Centre at: Polytechnic of North London, Holloway
Rd., London N7 8DB.

Index

Numbers in italic refer to subheadings of Chapters. (Subheadings of sections are normally in capitals, those in bold are from Seminar papers which are quoted in the text.)

concession bargaining, 225
Confederation of British Industries, 126
consciousness and collective purpose, 32ff., 74, 76–7, 79, 189ff.
consumerism, democratic responses to, 246ff.
Cooley, Michael, J. E., 100, 110, 147, 154, 239, 256
cooperation, different economic modes of, 29, 31
Coote, Anna, 161
credit creation, 184ff.
crisis of jobs, *42*
critical consumerism, *246*
Critique of Economic Theory (Hunt and Schwartz, eds), 127, 144
Croft, Suzy, 242, 250

Dalton, Hugh, 170, 188
debt crisis, 25
democratic control, 21, 50, 54, 74, 101, 113, 182, 189ff.; research, 242
democratic morality, 75
democratic theory, 34, 59, 251
Department of Economic Affairs, 172
Department of Health and Social Security (DHSS), 165
deskilling, 125; and job design, *99*
Development Agency, 172
discipline of money, 13, 18, 28
divine right of kings, 108
division of labour, *123*
Doyal, Len, 142
Doyal, Leslie, 213, 215, 256, 258

Eastern Bloc, 3
economic democracy, 50
economic efficiency, 19, 62, 72
economics, 69ff.; as science, *121*; and political goals, *62*
Edwardes, Sir Michael, 224
efficiency, 19
Elliott, Dave, 36
environment, *46*, 127, 156, 159
Eurodollars, 184

European Economic Community (EEC), 173
exchange control, 171, 186ff.
exchange-values, 15, 135ff., 164
experts, 107ff.

finance, 12ff., 24ff., 182ff.
financial system, its origin, *183*
financing the socially useful economy, 182ff.; technical problems, *186*
financing the economy as a whole, *189*
food, 91, 137
foreign investment, 193–4
Foster, Michael, 246ff., 257
freedom, 49–50, 103, 122
freedom of information, 99, 101, 153
Freeman, Chris, 124, 140ff.
Fromm, Eric, 42, 53, 56

Galbraith, J. K., 120, 125
gigantism, economic and social, 10, 12, 16, 25, 72
Glyn, Andrew, 44
gold, 184
Goldsmith, Oliver, 108
good, in market theory not same as socially useful, *126*
Goodman, R., 141
Gough, Ian, 142, 255, 257
Gramsci, Antonio, 160, 185
Greater London Council, 114, 128, 154, 157, 240ff.
Greater London Enterprise Board (GLEB), 139, 157, 239
gross national product (GNP & GDP), 73, 222, 230
guaranteed purchase, 189

Hales, Mike, 113–14, 158, 242, 257
Harris, Prof. Laurence, 64, 77, 255, 256
health, 208ff.
hegemony, of money power etc., 19, 63, 160
Heisenberg factor, 63
History of Second World War, 198